C000132137

DATE OF
'LES

# SOUTH

# OF THE

# CLOUDS

# South of the Clouds

## TALES
## FROM
## YUNNAN

EDITED BY LUCIEN MILLER

Translated by Guo Xu, Lucien Miller, and Xu Kun

A McLellan Book

University of Washington Press    Seattle & London

This book is published with the assistance of a grant from the
McLellan Endowed Series Fund, established through the generosity
of Martha McCleary McLellan and Mary McLellan Williams.

This volume is the result of a joint project sponsored by Yunnan Normal
University, Kunming, Yunnan Province, People's Republic of China,
and the University of Massachusetts, Amherst, Massachusetts.

Copyright © 1994 by the University of Washington Press
Printed in the United States of America
Design by Audrey Meyer
Composition by Tseng Information Systems, Inc.

All rights reserved. No part of this publication may be reproduced
or transmitted in any form, or by any means, electronic or mechanical,
including photocopy, recording, or any information storage or retrieval system,
without permission in writing from the publisher.

Library of Congress Cataloging-in-Publication Data
South of the clouds : tales from Yunnan / edited by Lucien Miller ;
translated by Guo Xu, Lucien Miller, and Xu Kun
p.  cm.
Includes bibliographical references and index.
ISBN 0-295-97293-9 97348-X (pbk.)
1. Tales—China—Yunnan Province.  I. Miller, Lucien.  II. Guo,
Xu.  III. Xu, Kun.
GR336.Y86S68  1994
398.2'0951'35—dc20  93-36563
CIP

UNIVERSITY
OF SHEFFIELD
LIBRARY

The paper used in this publication meets the minimum requirements
of American National Standard for Information Sciences—Permanence of Paper
for Printed Library Materials, ANSI A39.38-1984.

Jacket/cover illustration: Yunnan landscape, reproduced courtesy of the artist, Ting
Shao Kuang. Part title motif: Yi embroidered head ornament, from Yunnan shaoshu
minzu zhixiu wenyang (Yunnan Province Nationalities Research Institute, 1987), p. 41.

# Contents

Maps

1. Yunnan Province   2
2. Prefectures and autonomous prefectures   267
3. Counties   269
4. Distribution of ethnic minorities   271

Preface   LUCIEN MILLER   ix
General Introduction   LUCIEN MILLER   3
Introduction to Yunnan National Minority Folk Literature
XU KUN   41

## Stories About Creation

Myths Concerning the Creation of the World   Drung   59
The Origin of Making Offerings to Ancestors   Jino   68
The Formation of Heaven, Earth, and Humankind   Lisu   74
Sunbird Creates the Sun and the Moon   Miao   85
Great God Gumiya   Blang   88

## Why People Do What They Do

The Origin of the Sixth Month Sacrifice   Buyi   97
The Ancestors of Dai Singers   Dai   102
The Water-Splashing Festival   Dai   104

Why Sui People Live in Two-Story Wooden Loft-Houses    Sui    107

The Torch Festival    Yi    114

## Heroes and Heroines of the People

A Blang Youth    Blang    119

Daughter of a Slave    Tibetan    122

Wild Goose Lake    Bai    130

Wine-Flavored Spring    Hani    134

Stories about Bubo    Zhuang    137

## Animal Friends and Animal Foes

Two Sisters and the Boa    Kucong    153

The Gold Pig    Mongol    158

The Arrogant Tiger    Wa    166

The Gathering of the Birds    Yao    170

Sun, Moon, and Stars    Jingpo    175

## Wonder and Magic

The Magic Shoulder Pole    Yi    181

Nabulousi, the Life-Restoring Tree    Lahu    185

The Nine Brothers    Yi    190

The Head-Baby    Lahu    194

## Wise and Foolish Folk

Mr. Crooked and Mr. Straight    Jingpo    205

Asking Permission    Hui    210

Five Tales about Ayidan    Naxi    214

The Clever Sister    Nu    223

The Guileless Man and the Trickster    Primi    228

## Lovers

The Girl with Tufted Eyebrows   *Achang*   235
The Rainbow   *De'ang*   241
The Rhinoceros Hornbill   *Dai*   244
Longsi and the Third Princess   *Yao*   248
The Cloud That Longs for a Husband   *Bai*   255
The Nanxi River   *Dai*   259


Appendix: Traditional Yunnan Ethnic Minority Cultures
LUCIEN MILLER   265
Glossary   293
Bibliography   309
Index   321

In Memoriam

Winifred C. Miller
The Reverend Caspar Caulfield, C.P.

# Preface

A phrase that appears frequently in Maxine Hong Kingston's novel-biography-autobiography *Woman Warrior* is "talk-story." A literal translation of a common Chinese phrase, *jiang gushi* (to tell a story), talk-story refers to the oral folk art of story telling, of which the mother in the book, Brave Orchid, is a master. She weaves oral stories to ward off or invoke ghosts, to terrorize her little girl into quiescent submission to her maternal authority, or liberate her from a morbid, neurotic shyness which makes her utterly helpless in America. Through talk-story, she teaches her child Chinese legends and pseudo-history that force her to fantasize and escape reality, and to create some powerful, nearly believable myths about the family's past which make the child look hard at the present, and perhaps even face the future. In the oral art of story telling found in minority folk stories from Yunnan Province, we see the roots of talk-story, and vestiges of the live performances that sweep adults and children off their feet.

This book originates in a little talk-story from Yunnan. The contents and narrator are unknown, but the telling of the story led to the gathering of tales and translation work behind this volume, and the cooperative support of universities in China and the United States. In the summer of 1984, Deidre Ling, formerly vice-chancellor at the University of Massachusetts, happened to visit Kunming, the capital of Yunnan Province, while touring Chinese institutions with which the University of Massachusetts has exchange agreements. At Yunnan Normal University a member of the Chinese faculty told her in English a Yunnan minority folktale that she found particularly moving. "We have many more stories translated from the minority languages into Chinese," the man pointed out. "If you liked that one, you'll like some of the others even better. The only problem is that few of them have been translated into English." One story led to another, and before long, Ms. Ling, armed with a magazine (*Shan cha* [Rhododendron]) full of examples and a volume or two of minority song epics and tales, returned to her university, intending to find someone interested in translating Yunnan minority folk stories. In the spring of 1985, I began translating a few sample stories with a graduate student in comparative literature, Zhao Qiguang, and the following summer went to Kunming. There I was the guest of Yunnan Normal University, and was taken by my hosts to visit several minority areas in Yunnan and to interview storytellers and singers.

During the spring of 1986, Guo Xu, professor of English in the Foreign Languages Department, and Xu Kun, associate professor of Chinese and a specialist in Yunnan minority folklore, both from Yunnan Normal University, were hosted by the University of Massachusetts. Xu Kun had spent much of the previous year reviewing massive amounts of Yunnan folk materials, including his own extensive personal collection. From some forty volumes of works published in Chinese, he selected 150 pieces, representing each of the twenty-five minorities found in Yunnan, and belonging to the folk literature genres of tale, myth, and legend. I read these and chose fifty-four for translation from Chinese to English, on the basis of their variety and what I felt would be aesthetically appealing to the informed general reader or university student interested in folk literature and China. From mid-March until the end of June 1986, Guo Xu, Xu Kun, and I met for three or more hours, two to three times a week for our translation work. I do not think we ever argued, but sometimes our sessions together were emotionally exhausting. The particular advantages we have as translators are that two of us—Guo Xu and myself—read and speak both English and Chinese, while Xu Kun is a teacher of Yunnan folklore and an expert in minority folk literature. Of special importance to the translation of Yunnan folk literature is the fact that both Guo Xu and Xu Kun are natives of Yunnan, fluent in Yunnanese dialect, and familiar with local culture, foods, geography, climate, flora, and fauna encountered in the stories. In the course of translating, Guo Xu and I would check one another's translation, whether literal or free, from the vantage point of someone who is a native speaker of one language and a scholar of the second, and Xu Kun would clarify folklore and minority questions. The whole process of translating was an experience of talk-story, producing variant tales which formed the final version. Readers interested in our efforts to translate and talk-story will find an example under "Translation Strategies" in the General Introduction.

For the reader's information, responsibility for this book was shared as follows: Xu Kun wrote the Introduction to Yunnan National Folk Literature and an essay on the minorities, information from which is included in the Appendix, which was compiled by myself. I served as editor, wrote the Preface and General Introduction, and compiled the Bibliography and Glossary.

Names of minority persons, places, and objects are transcribed in Chinese pinyin, and occasionally in a minority language.

Following each section, as much information as is available is provided regarding Chinese sources of materials, together with names of storytellers, collectors, redactors, and translators.

As the editor of this volume, I have the pleasure of recalling the host of individuals who have made this collective venture possible. My colleagues, professors Guo Xu and Xu Kun, join me in acknowledging with warm gratitude the following persons for their support, expertise, and scholarly advice, which initiated our joint-translation project and enhanced its completion:

To past president Wu Jicai of Yunnan Normal University, who so generously facilitated this joint project, Vice President Yu Yanjing, Professors Yang Chuanzhe and Liu Qin, and Mr. Tao Naikan, graduate assistant, who, along with my friends and cotranslators, graciously hosted my research visit and travels in Yunnan.

To Murray Schwartz, former dean of fine arts and humanities; Deidre Ling, former vice-chancellor; and vice-chancellor Barbara Burn of the University of Massachusetts for their sensitive administration of this project, and their personal and enthusiastic support. To Professor Shouhsin Teng for initiating negotiations, and to past university president Joseph Duffey and past provost Richard O'Brien for making possible institutional collaboration between the University of Massachusetts and Yunnan Normal University.

To Professors Cyril Burch, David Knechtges, and Francesca Sautman for their critical reading and suggestions regarding the manuscript as a whole; to Professors Alvin Cohen, Maria Tymoczko, and Jiann Hsieh, and graduate student Jennifer Fyler for thoughtful comments on the General Introduction; and to Professor Stevan Harrell for his advice on the General Introduction and his helpful reading of the Appendix.

To Professors Jerry Norman, S. Robert Ramsey, and Janet Gyatso for help in resolving questions of linguistic transcriptions, and Professors Ruth B. Bottigheimer, Norma Diamond, and Lauri Honko for guidance on questions regarding tale redaction.

To Professors Dru Gladney, Jeffrey C. Kinkley, Kristina Lindell, and Charles McKhann for suggestions regarding minority research.

To Professors Jacques Barchilon and Eva Hung for their support in the publication of individual minority tales, and to Ed Young, Mark Bender, and Jane Yolen for their encouragement.

To the International Society for the Comparative Study of Civilizations, the New England branch of the Association for Asian Studies, and the East-West Center in Hawaii for sponsoring conference panels on Yunnan minority folk literature.

To cartographer and graphic artist Marie Litterer of the University of Massachusetts Department of Geology and Geography for maps she drew for this book.

Last, but by no means least, a hearty *xiexie* (thanks) to the staff at the University of Washington Press: to Naomi B. Pascal, editor-in-chief, for her wisdom, encouragement, and sprightly humor; to Lorri Hagman for her sensitive reading, exacting eye for detail, and patient and professional grooming of the manuscript; and to Julidta Tarver for seeing the manuscript through production.

Faculty exchange for this project was assisted by financial support from Yunnan Normal University and the University of Massachusetts. Research for the book was supported by grants from the East-West Center, Honolulu, the University of Massachusetts, and the Committee on Scholarly Communication with the People's Republic of China.

Parts of the General Introduction previously appeared as "Children's Literature East and West" in *Alumni Paper Series*, no. 9 (Honolulu: East-West Center Association, 1987). "Stories about Bubo" and "The Origin of the Sixth Month Sacrifice" appeared as "Two Yunnan Tales" in *Renditions*, no. 31 (Spring 1989). "Daughter of a Slave" and "Two Sisters and the Boa" were published in *Merveilles & Contes* 2:2 (December 1988) and 3:1 (May 1989).

LUCIEN MILLER

# SOUTH
# OF THE
# CLOUDS

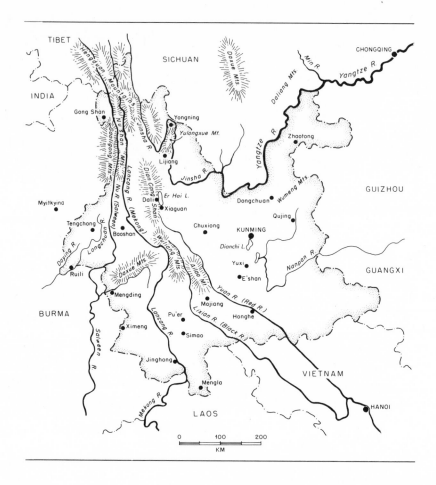

Map 1. Yunnan Province. Source: *Yunnan sheng ditu* 1990;
Stevens and Wehrfritz 1988; U.S. Central Intelligence Agency 1971;
*The Population Atlas of China* 1987; Geelan and Twitchett 1974; and Yang, 1989.

# General Introduction

## A Sketch of Yunnan

Located in the southwest corner of China, Yunnan is rich in natural re-
sources and beauty. Its name literally means "south of Yun Mountain"
(the great Jade Dragon Snow Mountain [Yulong Xueshan] in Lijiang)
and is also descriptive of the fact that Yunnan Province lies south of the
mountains and the cloud (yun) covering that separate it from Sichuan
Province to the north. The topography of the land (amply described by
Wiens 1967, chap. 1, part 5; and by Fitzgerald 1941, 1–22) is extremely
varied and complex, ranging from numerous mountain chains and river
systems to arid plains and dense jungles. To the west are a formidable
series of mountains and gorges running north to south, through which
course the headwaters of some of the major river systems in Southeast Asia: the Irrawaddy, into which the Mnai Hka and Mali Hka (Chinese: Mailikai) flow; the Salween (Chinese: Nu) River, and the Mekong
(Chinese: Lancang) River. Flowing south from Tibet into Yunnan, then
northeast towards Yibin in Sichuan Province is the Jinsha (Golden Sand)
River, which becomes the Yangtze River. The Xi (West) River in Guangdong Province is the ultimate destination of the Beipan, Nanpan and
You rivers in the eastern and southeastern sections of Yunnan, forming the province's eastern drainage system, which flows east and south.
The Yuan (Red) River (also known as the Fuliang) in southern Yun-
nan becomes the Song Hong after crossing the Chinese border into
Vietnam.

Centrally located among these mountain ranges and river systems
is the Yunnan-Guizhou plateau, ranging from 7,000 to 4,000 feet in
altitude from west to east. In the eastern part of the Yunnan plain

are the lakes region and the provincial capital, Kunming, while to the northwest is Dali, the ancient capital of the Nanzhao kingdom (A.D. 738–902). To the west, the Yunnan plain is bounded by the western gorges, while the eastern and southern parts of the plateau descend to the mountainous terrain of Guizhou Province and Guangxi Zhuang Autonomous Region to the east, and eventually give way, far to the south, to the jungles of Sipsong Panna (Chinese: Xishuangbanna), bordering Laos—an area well-known to thousands of foreign travelers who have participated in the famous Water-Splashing Festival so wonderfully celebrated by the Dai people.

Kunming, a city of flowers, is popularly known as Spring City (Chuncheng). It is situated in the high central plain, and enjoys what many consider the most temperate, pleasant climate in all of China. While industry and automobiles have brought pollution to Kunming, making the surrounding mountains less visible than in days of old, it is startling and refreshing to step from a plane in the summer, having arrived from the steamy heat of Shanghai or Canton, and to breathe the cool, clear air of Kunming, feel its California-like sunshine, and see eucalyptus trees waving in the wind, and white-washed stucco walls decorated with folk paintings of celebrated Yunnan scenery. The French loved to visit the cool environs of Kunming when they were colonialists in the torrid lowlands of Vietnam, and to live in Yunnan as well. One can still see vestiges of their presence in the shade-lined street of a former French neighborhood, in the architecture of a few buildings and homes in the city, and along the shores of Dianchi Lake nearby. The waters of this vast and beautiful lake, now sadly suffering from severe pollution, are one source of Kunming's temperate weather, and sustain a thriving fishing industry, besides being a source of local pride and a focal point of numerous folktales. Given the general loveliness of the Kunming area, it is easy to understand why the French built a railroad between Hanoi and Kunming. The Hanoi–Kunming railroad required the completion of hundreds of tunnels and bridges as it ascended and wound its tortuous way from sea level to 6,500 feet. The railroad is still one of the engineering marvels of the world, and is surpassed in China by only the Kunming–Chengdu railroad completed a few years ago.

Dali, the ancient capital of the Nanzhao kingdom of the Minjia tribes, or Bai nationality, lies about a day's journey by jeep or bus northwest of Kunming, along the old Burma Road to Mandalay, of World War II fame. The Chinese and American armies commanded by General Joseph Stillwell rebuilt the road and its extension to Ledo, Assam, in northeast India, to transport supplies from India, and over the high mountains between Mandalay and Kunming, during the campaign against the Japanese. The charm of Dali is irresistible, situated as it is at the base of the lofty Cang Mountains to the west, and located along the shores of another vast and beautiful body of water, Er Hai (Ear Lake), in a plain thirty miles long and three to four miles wide, at an elevation of 7,000 feet. Home of the Bai people, Dali and Er Hai are the center of rich folklore traditions. The ancient Nanzhao kingdom and its successor, the Dali kingdom, resisted Han Chinese conquest for six centuries (Wiens 1967, 154, 158–59, 248–63). At various times during its most flourishing era, between the eighth and ninth centuries, the Nanzhao kingdom occupied what is today Yunnan, along with parts of Hunan, Guizhou, Guangxi, Sichuan, and Burma.[1] The Dali kingdom was not overcome until the arrival of the Mongol emperor Kublai Khan in 1252. *The Travels of Marco Polo* describes the destruction left by the Mongols and seen by Polo, while he was on an inspection tour through Yunnan for Kublai Khan (Polo 13th c., 1931 ed., 187–200; Wiens 1967, 163). The deforestation visible today along the Burma Road from Kunming to Dali, and in the mountains surrounding Dali and Er Hai, may be attributed to the perennial need for cooking fuel and building material, but also is evidence of a more modern form of destruction, a legacy, say the Chinese, of Mao Zedong's Great Leap Forward era of the 1950s, when the land was stripped in the name of progress. Anyone who has read Charles P. Fitzgerald's study of Dali culture, *The Tower of Five Glories* (1941),

---

[1] Wiens (1954, chap. 1, part 5), citing D. G. E. Hall, *Burma* (London: Hutchinson's University Library, 1950, p. 9) and Chen Bisheng, *Tianbien sanyi* (Chungqing, 1941, pp. 25–26), notes that Ko-lo-feng (Mandarin: Geluofeng), second king of Nanzhao, conquered the Burmese Pyu kingdom in 760. In 832 Nanzhao plundered the Pyu capital and carried off thousands of captives to Kunming. Wiens says that Chen Bisheng takes the latter episode as the beginning of Nanzhao control over Burma.

now outdated but still wonderfully informative, will recall the author's descriptions of bamboo, pine, and fir forests found thousands of feet above Dali, covering the mountains. Today, the mountains are mostly bare. Along the road between Dali and Lijiang, one daily sees scores of logging trucks bearing heavy loads south, evidence of extensive cutting of big timber in northern Yunnan. An encouraging sign along the same route is the aerial planting of pine seedlings in some mountainous areas. Well aware of the acute need for reforestation, the Chinese government and citizens' groups are sponsoring annual tree-planting campaigns.

## Yunnan National Minorities

The Chinese sense of a nationality or nation, whether a minority or the Han majority, accords roughly with what Western anthropologists or sociologists would term an ethnic group (Hsieh 1986, 4). A nationality is distinguished by significant social and cultural characteristics, such as language, customs, genealogy, or, sometimes, geographical location, but not by racial differences. Clothing or hair styles may mark a nationality, but are not generally considered of central importance (Wu 1982, 279–80). To a certain extent, the modern Chinese notion of a nationality is analogous to Stalin's idea of a nation as having a common language, economy, psychology, and culture (Hsieh 1986, 4). Interestingly, the Chinese model of ethnicity does not place as much emphasis on self-identity as theorists in the Western tradition do (see Jiang Yongxing 1985). Furthermore, many groups—such as the Yi, Naxi, Miao, and Tibetans—do not have a self-identity that encompasses the whole category. A further contrast is that, within modern China, once one's minzu (ethnic identity) is determined, it is generally fixed and unchanging. Western social science theories are more amenable to the idea of ethnic change—as identifying characteristics such as language and customs alter, and as one's self-identification and the identity granted to oneself by a group evolve, both ethnic identity and nationality can change. For example, in contrast to Chinese attitudes regarding ethnic identity, a Korean living in Japan who has the ethnic characteristics of a Japanese person, will be able to pass as a Japanese—unless family genealogies are checked, as they might be in the case of a proposed marriage (Wu 1982, 283–88).

Classifying tribes in China according to cultural similarities, as Chinese scholars traditionally have done, Wolfram Eberhard lists sixty-two tribes named in Chinese historical sources that belong to one common cultural type alone, the Qiang, a northern Tibetan or Tangut people who are the ancestors of numerous nationalities in West and Southwest China (Eberhard 1942, 86–87; Wiens 1967, 36–37, 49–54). While ethnicity is commonly a cultural construction, ethnic identity is not synonymous with culture. Even where cultural differences hardly exist, ethnicity may be important in social organization. David Wu suggests that this occurs when there are important social issues at stake, such as legal status, or common interests, such as economic survival. Extending his cross-cultural examples to Yunnan national minorities, we may identify ethnic groups by their common interests, their continuous and exclusive identity with their group's characteristics, the degree to which members recognize one another in a consistent way, and by the centrality and sense of self-other difference through which they organize their lives and achieve common goals (Wu 1982, 287–94). Some national minorities may share cultural features, customs, and even language, but they see themselves as ethnically distinct in terms of interests and structural organization.

The People's Republic of China has identified fifty-five official minorities, and of this number, twenty-five are found in the province of Yunnan. Also in Yunnan are others, such as the Kucong and Kemu, that are not yet recognized. The whole question of the identification of minority nationalities is a complicated one, and presumably there could be many more minorities in China, depending on how one went about making distinctions. Fei Xiaotong notes that when the Chinese government invited minorities to come forward and identify themselves in the 1950s, hundreds did so (Fei 1981, *Toward a People's Anthropology*, 60–61; Hsieh 1986, 1). The large number may be attributed in part to a desire for some of the special privileges that accompany being known as a minority. The distinctions accorded the minorities by the government, and recognized by the minorities themselves, generally follow ethnic lines, rather than racial differences, and are supported by the general agreement of Chinese anthropologists and linguists and, to some extent, by Chinese historical tradition as well. Traditional perspectives have, of course, altered and developed significantly over the thousands of years of contact and relations between Han Chinese and various minorities, some of whom, such as the Mongols and Manchus, ruled China for hundreds of years. Because of this, and because many of the minorities are located along China's borders with Korea, Mongolia, the Commonwealth of Independent States, India, Burma, Laos, and Vietnam, relations with the minorities are politically important.

According to the national census made in 1982, the minority population in China is 66.5 million, which is approximately 6 percent of the total population (Guowuyuan 1983). National minorities may be found in 50 to 60 percent of China's territory, each province and autonomous region, and in 70 percent of Chinese counties (Hsieh 1986, 2). The system of national minority regions, prefectures, and districts has generally proven itself an effective means of government. By the end of 1985, there were 132 autonomous minority areas in China: five autonomous regions, thirty-one prefectures, and ninety-six counties or banners.[2] In Yunnan itself, roughly ten million people, or one out of three persons living in the province, are members of national minorities.

The history of the origin, migration, and lineage of the Han majority and the minorities in China is extremely complicated and convoluted, and well beyond the confines of this essay. Closely detailed investigations may be found in the works of a number of Western and Chinese scholars (Eberhard 1942; Dryer 1976; Fitzgerald 1941; Moseley 1973; Ruey 1972; Wiens 1967). Ninety-four percent of Chinese today are known as Han, a collective term for a people formed through the integration of a number of ancient tribes and ethnic groups in North China

[2] Statistics cited in lecture given by Huang Guangxue, vice minister, State Nationalities Affairs Commission, People's Republic of China, at the East-West Center, Honolulu, 6 August 1986. "Banner" is a term used for a Mongolian minority district, an area smaller than a prefecture and larger than a county.

who were first active along the Yellow River and gradually occupied the Yangtze and Zhujiang river basins in the south, and the Songhua-Liao River plain in the northeast. The language of the Han Chinese belongs to the Sino-Tibetan family. During the Han dynasty (206 B.C.–A.D. 220) the name Han was adopted (Ma 1989, 2). There is no such thing as a purely Han person—most Chinese have minority origins or mixed ethnic ancestries, even though they may be unaware of the fact, and commonly consider themselves Han.

An example or two will serve to illustrate the complexity of ethnography in China. In his review of Chinese sources that cover three thousand years of Chinese history, up to about A.D. 1800, Wolfram Eberhard has found names of eight hundred tribes, 345 of which live in Southwest China alone (Eberhard 1942; Wiens 1967, 29, 37). The complexity of minority history is well known in folklore studies. For example, Xu Kun has discovered that variants of the "Fish-Maiden" (Yu guniang) tale, originally found among the pre–Han dynasty Qiang minority in northern Tibet, are told by nineteen different minorities today. The variants may be traced by following the historical migration of the Qiang as they moved south from Northwest China and evolved into various tribes now distributed from the Jinsha River area in northern Yunnan to Dianchi Lake near Kunming (Xu Kun 1986). Indeed, the difficulty of unraveling tribes, ethnic groups and minorities sometimes leads to absurd but entertaining speculation: "Lao-tzu, the founder of Taoism, no doubt was a Sinicized tribesman of Ch'u, probably of Miao or T'ai stock. His fondness for the mountain wilds of South China and the lonely communion with nature points to such an affinity" (Wiens 1967, 82).

Two additional points worth noting about minority history in general are, first, that prior to the southern expansion of the Han majority, all of South China was occupied by different tribes (Wiens 1967, 268), and second, that despite obstacles such as climate and topography, Han expansion over many centuries was inexorable, and took a course that is somewhat analogous to the history of the western movement of the European, Irish, and British populations into the land of Native Americans in North America. Harold J. Wiens's description, although not applying to the last thirty-five years of Chinese history (his book was originally published in 1954), presents the general historical picture:

... Han Chinese culture has been gradually overrunning the minority cultures of the South. The non-Han tribesmen have found an increasingly restricted sphere for the free development of their cultures. The Han Chinese advance has led to a scattering of tribal settlements and their retreat into the less accessible and less productive mountain slopes and ravines and a pushing out toward and across the border regions of China. (Wiens 1967, 267)

Historically, non-Han groups have resisted Han expansion, but for the most part they left for remote, mountainous areas thought undesirable by the Han Chinese, who were largely interested in good farmlands and trade. In earlier eras before Han influence, many ethnic groups were plains dwellers. I was reminded of this when I asked a member of the Yi where he came from, assuming he would name some mountainous region. Instead, he said his ancestors came from the plains surrounding Kunming, but were driven out by the Han.

## Folk Literature, Children's Literature, and Chinese Intellectuals

The phenomenal interest in minority folk literature in general, and children's literature in particular, on the part of contemporary Chinese intellectuals, may be traced back to the May Fourth movement of 1919, which ushered in an era of radical cultural, social, and political change.

As regards children's literature, long before the May Fourth era, within several thousand years of Chinese literary history, innumerable materials are to be found in the classical canon and vernacular literature that may be considered children's literature, or literature of interest to children: myths and legends; stories about gods, demons, and animals; popularizations of Buddhism; puppet plays; folk epics; serial stories; and jokes and riddles. Literature written explicitly for children became a central concern of Chinese scholars and intellectuals in the late nineteenth and early twentieth centuries, when a consciousness began to arise that children have their own special educational and recreational needs (see Scott 1980, 109). Children's literature, per se, accompanied the recognition that children were no longer to be viewed simply as little adults, and a new concept, "the child," began to have significance (Hung 1985, 113).

Many Chinese attended schools run by missionaries or studied abroad, and were influenced by Western views of children and children's education, especially as espoused by Jean-Jacques Rousseau and his Swiss disciple Johann Pestalozzi, and Pestalozzi's German follower Friedrich Froebel. Their ideas about child-centered education, childhood, children's play, and psychology were considered revolutionary by Chinese intellectuals, while Rousseau's anti-authoritarianism in Emile was music to their ears (Hung 1985, 114–15). Important figures such as Zhou Zuoren, brother of the celebrated writer and social critic Lu Xun, tended for a time to view children as primitives—probably because of the influence of the writings of Andrew Lang. Guo Moruo, writer and scholar, held to a sentimental opinion that the language of primitive people and children was poetry (Hung 1985, 118). The concept of children's literature was itself uncertain. Ertong wenxue (children's literature), or the simpler phrase tonghua, borrowed from the Japanese, also meant "fairy tale." The writer Mao Dun called his translations of Western fairy tales tonghua. There was also debate about the purpose and source of children's literature: was it literature told or written by adults and intended for children, as many Chinese folklorists thought, or was children's literature the songs and stories children sang and created themselves? (Hung 1985, 111–12). Whatever its definition, the writing of children's literature was accomplished or encouraged by a number of the leading Chinese writers of the 1920s and 1930s, among them Ye Shengdao, Lao She, Bing Xin, Zhang Tianyi, and Shen Congwen. Lu Xun promoted a woodcut revival and picture books. Likewise, writers well known for interpreting China to the West, such as Lin Yutang and Chiang Yee, also encouraged children's literature (Scott 1980, 122–24).

This special concern with children's literature during the May Fourth movement, an interest of a relatively small body of intellectuals, grew astronomically after the Communists came to power in 1949. Children's literature came to be underwritten by the government. Millions of books were published, village book stands for children appeared everywhere, and children's recreation centers and "palaces" were built, providing library, music, and dance facilities for children. Children's literature became a mainstay in the curriculum of teacher's colleges (Scott 1985, 132–37). Most of the children's literature produced in the People's Republic of China until recently may be viewed as a mass culture artifact. It upholds, or at least never threatens, the dominant social order, is produced for mass consumption, and has a generally clear political and moral message. There seems to be little high-culture children's literature, that is, a literature that an elite need to be taught in order to appreciate, and that is written for a special sector of society. In contrast to the Han mass-culture children's literature, marked by ideological message and socialist realism, the children's literature and folk literature of the national minorities belong to popular culture. In other words, as can be seen in our collection of tales, myths, and legends, minority literature is often produced by a particular ethnic group (e.g., Miao, Tibetan, Dai) which has its own distinctive cultural values, separate from both other minorities and the Han majority.

The rapid development of interest in children's literature during the May Fourth era was part of the vernacular (*baihua*) literature movement which was central to the time, and was part and parcel of intellectuals' growing fascination with folklore and folk literature. The collecting and utilizing of folk songs and folktales are ancient enterprises in China, evidenced by the classic anthology of poetry, *The Book of Songs* (*Shi jing*, sixth cent. B.C.), originally of vernacular or folk origins, and the Han dynasty's *yuefu*, songs and lyrics reputedly gathered from the common people by the government's music bureau (Dorson, in Eberhard 1965, xi). Often the motivation for such collecting was political—those in power could listen to what the folk were saying. What is significant about the modern trend is the tendency to see folklore, like children's literature, as a political alternative to elite culture, which was considered stultifying and decadent, and to romanticize the folk (peasants) as the source of oral traditions. These tendencies have been amply demonstrated by Hung Chang-tai in his comprehensive study *Going to the People: Chinese Intellectuals and Folk Literature, 1918–1937* (1985).

During the May Fourth period, interest in folklore and collecting was unprecedented in the enthusiasm of its participants and the breadth of their inquiry. Intellectuals were energized by a resistance to Confucian culture and traditional forms of authority in general, and by an idealistic commitment to the common people. Initially, they "went to the people" as participants in lecturing corps to educate the masses, much like those in the *narodnik* movement in Russia, which intellectuals had learned about through Li Dazhao, one of the founders of the Chinese Communist Party. In the process of participating in this educational effort, they "discovered the importance of the folk, and ultimately discovered themselves" (Hung 1985, 10, 162). Intellectuals also felt guilty about their own privileged position in society, and under an obligation to educate peasants and raise them from ignorance. Summing up his findings, Hung says, "I would argue that the folklorists' commitment to 'go to the people' was one of the most important developments in modern Chinese intellectual history" (Hung 1985, 173).

Originating among scholars and students at Beijing University around 1918, and spreading soon thereafter to Zhongshan University in the southern province of Guangzhou, as well as to several other universities, the movement included such leading figures as Liu Fu, Zhou Zuoren, and Gu Jiegang, who founded journals and inspired collecting and research. Again, as in the example of children's literature, Western influence provided a stimulus. Important sources were the Chinese collections of Baron Guido Amedeo Vitale (*Pekinese Rhymes*, 1896; *Chinese Merry Tales*, 1901), Isaac Taylor Headland's *Chinese Mother Goose Rhymes* (1900), theories of mythology and fairy tale collections of Andrew Lang, James G. Frazer's *Golden Bough* (1890), and the writings of Western folklorists such as Charlotte Burne (Hung 1985, 12–25, 161).

Critics of the folklore movement held that peasants were ignorant, superstitious and badly motivated. To the Chinese Nationalists, folklore was a dangerous field, promoting local cultures in the face of the government's official view of a monolithic Chinese culture, and many conservatives considered folk literature obscene. Folklorists were in error, they argued, for they kept alive superstitions and peasant ignorance (Eberhard 1965, xxiv; Hung 1985, 160, 164). On the other hand, intellectuals committed to folklore studies praised the folk vociferously and voluminously. Their descriptions of what they encountered now read like romantic, rhapsodic litanies. Folk literature was termed primitive, innocent, creative, free, simple, earnest, genuine, colloquial, natural, open, bold, explicit, and erotic, while the folk were considered joyful, lively, and uninhibited. Supporters readily assumed that folk literature mirrored the life and minds of country people, and much like William Wordsworth in his preface to the Lyrical Ballads (1798), they often thought that the language of the folk was sheer poetry, or at least a model for poetic discourse. Minority oral art was especially well esteemed. Since minority oral traditions frequently existed far from the restrictive confines of a Confucian world, folk songs and stories were all the more delectable (Hung 1985, 172–73).

The golden era of Chinese folklore studies and collecting of songs, poems, and tales ended in 1937, with the outbreak of the Sino-Japanese War. After World War II, and the subsequent establishment of the People's Republic of China under Mao Zedong, the collecting of folk materials was resumed in earnest and received special emphasis periodically through the 1950s and early 1960s. In Yunnan, for example, a team doing fieldwork for six months in 1958 gathered one hundred thousand items of folk literature, and sixteen folk epics were published, generating attention among Western scholars interested in oral formulaic research of the type carried on by Milman Parry in Yugoslavia (Lord 1960, Introduction; Dorson in Eberhard 1965, xxiii). A lengthy hiatus occurred during the Great Proletarian Cultural Revolution (1966–1976), and team collecting did not occur again on a wide scale until the late 1970s. Currently, there is a vast folklore project underway in Yunnan. One hundred volumes are to be published over the next ten years, covering the twenty-five minorities in Yunnan, with four volumes of stories, narrative poetry, songs, and music devoted to each minority.

# Textual Issues

A number of issues must be raised in order to understand the nature of the present collection of Yunnan minority folk materials. Without extensive fieldwork, access to archives, and knowledge of minority languages, some of these issues cannot be resolved at this time. Generally speaking, the prevailing viewpoint among Han and minority specialists is that the Chinese translations of Yunnan folk materials, which are the source of our English translations, are literary works. My own perspective is to understand these literary works—the tales, myths, and legends—as redacted narratives that reveal fascinating aspects of both oral and written art.

The first general problem of which a reader needs to be aware is the perennial controversy that exists between fieldwork-based folklorists and folk-literature archivists regarding their work. Those interested in oral art privilege oral over written narrative, and fieldwork over archival work, and are fond of pointing out that archival materials lack the spontaneity and validity of live, oral performance. On the other hand, archivists are concerned with written folk narrative and its preservation, and center their attention on the relation between performance and written text, listening versus reading audiences, and questions of aesthetics regarding written art (Bottigheimer 1987, 68–69).

In a marvelous series of studies on the Kammu (Chinese: Kemu) in northern Thailand, Kristina Lindell exemplifies the folklorist's approach to oral performance. She describes the presentation style of the storyteller, noting tangents and confusion, where these exist. Writing about the recording of stories told by one teller, she says: "Every word uttered by the story-teller, even his mistakes, explanations, pause markers and asides, are included. The text has not been touched up in any way, either regarding the content of the stories or the wording. If a phrase is faulty in the original this will show in the translation, and if a point is clumsily taken it will be rendered clumsily in English" (Lindell 1980, 22). This description may be taken as a rough approximation of the data or workbooks Xu Kun refers to in his "Introduction to Yunnan National Minority Folk Literature" in this volume, the field texts that are the source of the redacted literary texts we have translated. Strictly speaking, story telling is an oral art that is uniquely dependent on individual performance and audience, and such details as gesture, voice, inflection, the level and type of language the storyteller uses, and his or her popularity with the audience. Were this a folkloristic study, we would need to have access to the raw materials cited, and to do fieldwork in which we tape-recorded, transcribed, and translated the storyteller's language. The number of languages spoken by the twenty-five minorities in Yunnan represented in this collection make such a task formidable, if not impossible. Furthermore, while the folkloristic text provides a fascinating apparatus for the appreciation of story telling, it cannot substitute for performance or duplicate the storyteller's art. For the reader of literature who is looking for an interesting story, the inclusion of variants or a teller's memory lapses or clumsy rendering can be positively irritating.

In relation to the folkorist versus archivist controversy, the translators of the present volume should be considered archivists concerned with the dimensions of oral art embedded in literary tales. The starting point in our translation of Yunnan minority oral folktales is written materials. At the point where our work begins, collectors and editors have already decided basic questions regarding fieldwork and archiving. Although Xu Kun is a well-known folklorist in Yunnan and has extensive experience with fieldwork, the present collection is not a folkloristic text made from his recording of live oral performances, but from materials he selected from forty volumes of folk literature published in Chinese translation. Our objective has been to produce English translations that are dynamically equivalent to the oral minority folk literature translated from various minority languages into Chinese.

Another issue of central importance is the authenticity and reliability of written folktales in general, and the Yunnan minority tales in particular. In the recording, writing, and publishing of folk narrative, there invariably arise aesthetic problems that are solved quite differently, depending on the purposes of archivists and translators. Tales do not fall from the sky dictated on Sony tapes, or as leather-bound notes from a storyteller. If they did, no one, save for a handful of oral folklore buffs, would care to listen to or read transcripts of the unedited tapes. In order to broaden our perspective on the textual nature of the Yunnan minority folktales found in this collection, let me point to some of the problems and creative solutions faced by all transmitters of folk literature.

To cite a celebrated Western example, that of the brothers Grimm, recent research indicates that instead of traveling among the German folk and gathering their stories, as was commonly thought, the Grimms collected tales of a generally European—rather than German—origin from educated, middle-class informants, members of the aristocracy, and books. Rather than being interested in literal, word-for-word recording of peasant stories, they adapted their collection to accord with their idealized notion of what a folktale should be, expurgating all reference to sexual and other matters considered contrary to middle-class tastes. They embroidered the prose with proverbs, emphasized the Protestant ethic, and synthesized variants to form their own version of a tale. While their works continue to be read as folktales today, generically speaking they ought to be considered artistic or literary tales (Zipes 1987, 23–24). The significant point to be gleaned from such research is not that the Grimm brothers' tales are somehow unreliable or inauthentic, but that written folktales reflect particular cultures and classes, as well as the purposes of their transmitters.

The rewriting of folk, literary, or historical materials to fit the needs and interests of audiences, reflect world views, embody political objectives, or improve style occurs in practically all literate cultures. For that matter, in the oral tradition (depending on the particular culture), the dynamic relation between storyteller and audience may change the content and direction of a tale at the moment of its telling. Historian Winston Hsieh claims that in China the domination of political philosophy and myth in the writing of history has been prevalent because of "a long-continued and intimate association of history with politics." There "history has often been used by rulers as a source of legitimation, by ministers as a means of remonstrance with their emperors, and by leaders of political movements as an ideological tool" (Hsieh 1975, 3). China's earliest anthology of folk songs, The Book of Songs, is a collection of folk poetry modified and rewritten by literati. The love songs of folk lovers in the anthology have been interpreted by Confucian commentators throughout Chinese history as political allegories about the relationship between prince and prime minister.

A twentieth-century Chinese example of the adaptation of folk materials to suit artistic or critical purposes is found in the regionalism of the writer Shen Congwen, and is revealed in a masterful study by Jeffrey C. Kinkley. Drawing on childhood memories of folktales narrated by his Miao (Hmong) nursemaid and relatives, Shen wove street talk and legends to construct his creative stories set in the western countryside of Hunan Province. He made his own fairy tales out of Miao stories, inventing folklore references, mythologizing the tribespeople into a vigorous, primitive folk set apart from the decadent world of Confucian society during the early decades of this century, and sitting in judgment of modern China (Kinkley 1987, 8, 111, 147–48, 150–55). While his example of rewriting folk materials is interestingly analogous to the work of the brothers Grimm, in contrast to them Shen Congwen provided a critique of his contemporary society, rather than an affirmation, through his recreation of Miao tribe folktales. The conscious artistic recreation of folk materials by the brothers Grimm or Shen Congwen need not surprise us. Even the unconscious shaping or interpreting of historical or literary materials according to political myth or ideology is to be expected. Whether intention is conscious or unconscious, the oral and written word enjoy a dynamic relation with both progenitor and culture, and this fact should be borne in mind.

Another significant point is the evolution of folklore research in China since the early years of the twentieth century. From 1918 until the folklore movement came to a halt in 1937, with the onset of World War II, almost none of the participants and collectors were themselves professional folklorists, or had knowledge of folkloristic methods and approaches to fieldwork. In most cases, they had little actual contact with peasants whose oral art they were studying. Raymond Jameson introduced the Finnish historical-geographical method while teaching in China in the 1930s, but had minor impact, and the application of historical or comparative approaches to folklore studies was scant (Hung

1985, 52, 61). Nonetheless, the collections amassed by scholars such as Gu Jiegang and now held in Taiwan are highly esteemed by mainland scholars, partly because they are inaccessible, but mainly because they are thorough, comprehensive materials from the golden era of modern Chinese folklore studies.

After the war and the revolutionary years leading to the establishment of the People's Republic of China in 1949, folktale collecting resumed. However, a number of Western scholars and folklorists question the reliability of folk literature texts published in China in the 1950s and early 1960s. Over twenty-five years ago Wolfram Eberhard, a leading Western authority on Chinese folklore, criticized the compilations made through the support of the Communist government, as these were not done by trained folklorists. No complete collections were made of all variants of a tale from a single place, told by one person, noted Eberhard, and he considered the contents biased. Heroes and heroines were invariably common people, and young women were unusually prominent, while praise of emperors or the imperial system was virtually nonexistent. Such biases or lacunae do not square with folk collections made prior to Communist rule, and Eberhard suspected that editors or redactors had emphasized negative views of the upper classes, while preferring stories that lauded the lower classes, landless peasants, or females (Eberhard 1965, xxxv–xxxvi).

In his foreword to Eberhard's book, Richard M. Dorson holds that the collections were marred because the Communists used folk materials for political purposes: "The propaganda possibilities of folklore for Communist ideology, first appreciated in Soviet Russia in 1936, did not long escape the Chinese Communists, who perceived in folklore a splendid opportunity to identify their cause with the great anonymous mass of seven hundred million people" (Dorson in Eberhard 1965, xii). Dorson noted that Chinese scholars who called for scientific folkloristic research, and who were against the use of folklore for socialist propaganda, were severely criticized (xiii–xiv). The Communist approach was to sharpen the class struggle perspective through stories of conflict between peasants and rulers or foreigners, to rationalize the presence of supernaturalism and magic, and to acclaim peasant revolts and uprisings, especially since such stories were especially dear to Mao Zedong (xiii–xiv, xvi, xviii). Dorson refers to an article in the *Journal of Folk Literature* (December 1959) by Zhang Shijie, a mainland Chinese folklorist, in which Zhang talks about collecting and processing folktales as an example of the Chinese Communist technique of redaction:

His [Zhang's] argument proceeds from the premise that folk literature contains two sets of values: one, the scientific recording of data; the other, the artistic refining of the material for the people. This latter process, aimed at elevating the masses through popularization of collected folktales and folk songs, must precede scientific international research, because of the immediate needs of Chinese society. (Dorson in Eberhard 1965, xv)

The situation regarding the collection, use, and redaction of minority folktales has changed considerably from what it was three decades ago, as noted in contemporary accounts by foreign and Chinese folklorists. While it is beyond the confines of this introduction to discuss the history of China's political policy toward the minorities, suffice it to say that since the Cultural Revolution—when performers were terrorized and folklore society activities were suspended (Honko 1986, 7)—the challenging task of the Chinese government has been to help minorities modernize while preserving some aspects of native culture, such as art, music, literature, and dance.[3] In terms of understanding the nature of the present collection of written folktales, what needs to be clarified is the state of contemporary research as well as current ideas about collecting and redacting among Chinese folklorists.

Reporting on a Sino-Finnish joint folklore project held in Nanning, Guangxi Province, in April 1986 (see Huang 1986), Lauri Honko, director of the Nordic Institute of Folklore, writes:

[3] For studies in English of China's zigzagging policy toward minorities, see: Deal (1976); Dreyer (1976); Eberhard, *China's Minorities* (1982); Fei (1978; and *Minzu yu shehui*, 1981); Grunfeld (1985); Hsieh, *China's Policy Toward the National Minorities* (1984); Moseley (1966, 1973); Solinger (1977); Wiens (1954); Yin (1977). Grunfeld provides an objective overview. For Chinese studies, see: Fei (1981); Guo-jia minwei (1979, 1981); Li (1980, 1981); Liang (1980); Liu (1980); Ma (1980); Peng and Tang (1981); Sichuan minzu chubanshe (1980); Zhou Enlai (1957); Zhou Zheng (1983). Hsieh (1986) gives a sound analysis in English of studies written in Chinese.

The state of research [in China] may be described as "opening up," "increasingly international" and "cautious experimentation with various theoretical views." The Marxist legacy is strong but not constricting. There is little tiresome cant and plenty of self-assurance, respect for folklore work and research optimism. Enthusiasm for fieldwork runs high, at the academies, the universities and among the people in general. Folk materials are published immediately with little editing in colourful monthly journals. (Honko 1986, 7)

Noting differences in objectives—Finns emphasize archiving folk products while the Chinese aim in collecting is to publish findings—Honko also observes a Chinese quadripartite concept of folk literature:

1) products transmitted orally from one generation to the next, 2) versions of these products transferred in writing (in notebooks or print) and often edited by some talented individual, 3) products adapted to folk literature on the basis of works by writers proper and stories based on the contents of local folk operas, and 4) products of folk literature borrowed from neighbouring countries, such as Buddhist writings. In the West folklore would include only the first category and products from the second whose editor is unknown. In China the author and date are known of a surprising number of orally transmitted folk songs or tales. The right of folklore editors to their products is recognised and their work is valued both by the people and by researchers. (Honko 1986, 7)

Our collection of written narratives is mainly a development of the first category, oral tales, while a few tales belong to the second category, as they were collected and redacted by writers well known in Yunnan, such as Li Qiao, Lan Hongen, Liu Shu, and Chen Guipei. While the concept of folk literature found in this collection may be broader than that in Western collections, it does not seem to include the bias or political propaganda mentioned by Eberhard and Dorson. Skeptics may say that tales about the poor defeating the rich or humans shooting the sun (see "The Gold Pig" and "Myths Concerning the Creation of the World") are but more versions of basic revolutionary parables depicting peasants outsmarting landlords or man conquering nature, yet I would argue that the moral didacticism and accounts of the origins of things we find in such tales are typical of world folk literature, and it would be simplistic to attribute their telling by oral storytellers, retelling by redactors and translators, and selection for publication by Chinese or minority folklorists solely to political ideology.

Redaction or collation is a necessity, of course, if there is to be a written text from oral sources. For an explanation from a Chinese viewpoint, readers are referred to Xu Kun's "Introduction to Yunnan National Minority Folk Literature," which emphasizes that in China two texts are produced in the process of collecting: a folkloristic text or field book (*kexue ben*) without redactions, and a literary text (*wenxue ben*) redacted from transcriptions and workbooks for publication. While the former is an unpublished research text unavailable to the general public or to foreign scholars (Chinese researchers are given first access to unpublished materials and the archive system is underdeveloped for public use), the latter is widely disseminated and is the source of the folktales, myths, and legends in the present collection. In a paper written for the Sino-Finnish seminar at Nanning on Chinese folklore, Jia Zhi, vice president of the China Society for the Study of Folk Literature and Art, identifies three categories of collation: literal collation that makes a text read more easily by eliminating unnecessary words, repetitions, and grammatical errors and providing paragraph divisions and punctuation; collation that deletes detrimental aspects of folk-literary works that have "vulgar or politically harmful contents"; and comprehensive collation of different versions of the same story (Jia Zhi 1986, 25–26). Xu Kun also speaks in his essay of deleting or changing things that are "unhealthy or unsound." Examples of "politically harmful" or "unhealthy" material are stories about the late-nineteenth-century Bai hero Yang Yuke and his Hui enemy, Du Wenxiu. Stories that speak favorably of Yang's defeat of Du (Yang's army surrounded Dali, leading to Du's suicide) may not be published. The Chinese government's official policy promoting the unity of minorities and the Han prohibits the publication of tales by one group that are deleterious to another. On the other hand, many Hui stories are published about Du Wenxiu, as he was a leader of peasant uprisings, viewed favorably by the government. A museum in Dali is named after him. My own impression is that economics, rather than politics, may play the more significant role in the redaction of tales and the formation of literary texts from scientific texts. Editors may lengthen stories, thicken plots, and insert more descriptive, literary vocabulary to sell tales to literate readers.

Political or moral views of collation may be unfamiliar to a Westerner involved in folkloristic work today, and leave him or her feeling uncomfortable. Such views are not set in stone in China, but are significant in terms of marking East-West differences in cultural perspective on written folktales. In China, collation is an ancient phenomenon, as Lauri Honko reminded me in a letter, whereby the oral and written processing of texts have gone hand in hand for thousands of years. In both the past and the present, authors of folk literature are often known by name, and folk poems are modified and restructured by famous poets (Honko to Miller, 14 April 1988). These different views of what constitutes folk literature, collation, and redaction need to be remembered when contrasting Chinese and Western approaches to written folktales.

In considering with my Chinese colleagues minority folk materials as literary works, I have had in mind the dynamic relation between the spoken and written word and between author and culture, evidenced to varying degrees in the brothers Grimm, Shen Congwen, ancient Chinese historical and literary writing, and twentieth-century collecting and redacting. As noted previously, neither the materials nor our approach is folkloristic. Rather, our objective has been to understand and translate Chinese redactions of Yunnan minority tales, myths, and legends as combinations of oral and written art.

## Translation Strategies

In regard to the actual work of translation, Guo Xu had the most difficult task. He would prepare the initial draft translation from Chinese to English, in consultation with Xu Kun. I would then take this draft and check it against the Chinese text, raising questions in the margins and writing alternative interlinear translations. Next would come our discussion sessions. We would discuss the texts in Chinese (Xu Kun does not speak English), getting Xu's advice and input on questions of folklore, then Guo and I would move back and forth discussing the Chinese texts and English translations in both Chinese and English, always checking with Xu to be sure our English wording accorded as closely as possible with the meaning of a story as he understood it from a folklorist's perspective, and with the values, customs, and material cultural of the particular minority. Bearing this discussion in mind, and with the copious notes from our session before me, I would then prepare the next draft translation. In comparison to Guo Xu's literate restructuring, this freer version incorporated discussion and notes, and had as its objective smooth, readable prose for English readers. Guo Xu took this draft and again checked it against the Chinese text, this time watching for places he might consider deviations in the freer translation. I then incorporated his emendations into the final polished version. All along, the objective of the three of us was to produce what in contemporary translation theory is called "dynamic equivalence," which Eugene A. Nida terms an attempt to mirror in the target language the dynamic reading or listening experience that is shared by the audience of the original language (Nida and Jin 1984, 85).

To help the reader appreciate the meaning of dynamic equivalence in the present volume, there follows an example of three strategies of translation we used which may be compared to corresponding dynamically equivalent passages in our collection. (For translation strategies, see Bassnett-McGuire 1980, chap. 3.) While the sample is a somewhat idealized model, it does give the reader an idea of the process behind dynamic equivalence. (Generally, we did not write out separate translations. I would juxtapose my colleague's versions to the Chinese text and write over or edit it, then we would compare versions and discuss folklore and cultural questions with Xu Kun in order to produce a translation we agreed was dynamically equivalent.) In the first translation—a "literate restructuring" by Guo Xu—the word order, syntax, literal meaning, metaphor, or rhetoric of the source language is altered to accord with the target language. My "literal" rendition attempts to match the target language (English) with the source language (Chinese) word-for-word in terms of word order, syntax, and literal meaning. Lastly, my "creative" translation is a freewheeling effort to recast the source language and story in its oral-performance context by altering structure, implanting English colloquialisms, and privileging or emphasizing an American cultural idiom in an effort to imagine the minority storyteller at work. Pertinent examples of this are bracketed for the reader's attention. In the "dynamic equivalent" stage which is the ideal of our collection, Guo Xu, Xu Kun, and I seek to parallel in English the experience of the reader in Chinese by conveying the functional equivalence of Chinese language, metaphor, style, structure, and culture. Readers are encouraged to compare these examples with those in our collection, as an exercise in cross-cultural exploration.

## From THE MAGIC SHOULDER POLE
### Literate restructuring (Guo)

"Pah! Take your trash away! What a magic pole this is! You are simply daydreaming!"

The rich man was still elated. He then said to his wife, "Can a woman tell what a magic thing really is? Now look!" He added scores of jin to the load at each end of the pole and bent over to carry it. "Ah! What's wrong?" The magic shoulder pole had really changed.

He took up his pole and beat her, scolding, "You scum, you always bring me bad luck. You have dispelled the magic of my pole!"

### Literal (Miller)

"Pei! [It's] still your stir-shit-stick, eh? What precious shoulder pole! In broad daylight what a dream!"

Still the rich man, feeling hugely pleased, said, "How can women recognize [what's] precious? Look!" He again added many jin to each end of the shoulder pole, [and] bent [his] waist, lifting. "Ai-ya! What's happened?" The precious shoulder pole had really changed.

Beginning to swing the shoulder pole, on the one hand he beat his old woman, on the other hand cursing, "Spendthrift woman! Gloomy spirit thing! You chase off the precious spririt of old boy's precious shoulder pole."

"Bah! This [ain't nothin'] but a shit stick! [Whadya] mean, magic pole? Daydreaming in broad daylight. [Pooh!]"

Undaunted by his wife's taunts, the greedy man was still [as pleased as punch] with his shoulder pole. "What's a woman know about magic?" he jeered. "Just you watch!" With that, he piled on pound after pound at each end of the pole, then squatted underneath, giving the load a [heave-ho].

["Son of a bitch!] What's wrong?" What do you know, the magic shoulder pole had lost its [punch]!

With that, the man began flailing his wife with the pole, yelling all the while, "[Money-blower! Bad luck woman! You've gone and wrecked] my magic!"

## Oral Art and Folk Literature

The literary materials in this collection combine oral and written forms of art, and it is this combination that fascinates and intrigues the reader. The tales, myths, and legends are originally from oral sources, told by storytellers, and were translated into Chinese from a variety of minority languages, most of which do not have a written form of their own. As oral-written narratives, they are a repository of folk art told, collected, and read by minorities and Han alike. To appreciate the special appeal of these minority stories, we need to discern the ways in which the oral and written traditions are joined. In his insightful and creative study *Orality and Literacy* (1982), Walter J. Ong delineates the distinctive characteristics of oral and written art, as well as the relationship between them, and we shall make use of his approach to assess folk literature from Yunnan.

We need, first of all, to realize that there is a difference in consciousness between oral, or preliterate, cultures and literate cultures. "Readers whose norms and expectancies for formal discourse are governed by a residually oral mind set relate to a text quite different [sic] from readers whose sense of style is radically textual" (Ong 1982, 171).

Writing restructures consciousness, and the "verbal performances of high artistic and human worth . . . are no longer even possible once writing has taken possession of the psyche" (pp. 14, 78). While literacy can destroy oral art, we can make use of it to reconstruct "the pristine human consciousness which was not literate at all" (p. 15). We can also use our literacy to discern the oral and written art of the folktale, and suggest some ways in which they interact.

In the Yunnan folktales there are many signs that we are in an oral world. Time, for example, is unspecified, except for vague references to "long, long ago," or "once there was," or "legend has it that." Space, too, is usually unclearly defined, unless the teller is presenting a legend about a particular location, such as the area of Sipsong Panna in "The Nanxi River." The emphasis, rather, is homeostatic, with a concern for living in equilibrium with the present, and forgetting whatever aspect of the past is no longer meaningful (Ong 1982, 46). In "The Nanxi River," one would imagine that the names of the tribal enemies who destroyed the Dai people would be important, but we are told only that at some time in the distant past, "there was a cruel war between the Dai and people of a different race." There is practically no evidence of abstract or analytical thinking, definitions, or syllogisms in the stories, all of which are found in literate cultures and are facilitated through the use of written texts (pp. 49, 54–55). One possible exception is the Dai tale "The Rhinoceros Hornbill," in which the close parallel drawn between the behavior of the jealous lover who imprisons his wife, and the male bird which seals his mate in her nest, borders on being analytical. If this analogy is abstract or analytical, it is evidence of a writerly text, one that has been rewritten by the redactor or editor to serve a *reading*, rather than a *listening*, audience.

Generally speaking, our stories are situational and subjective, and rarely interpreted by the teller. In "The Rainbow," we learn that the father sees a snake in his daughter's coffin, while the mother sees instead her daughter's smiling face. The teller raises no questions about differences in vision. His unreflective role is complemented by the absence of self-awareness on the part of characters. The Bai princess in "The Cloud That Longs for a Husband" is not aware of why she loves to walk beyond the city walls, or how it is possible for her to be cold in a magic cave, when she ought to be happy with her husband of divine origins. Psychological motivations—her hidden desire for sexual union, her resistance to parental authority—must be ferreted out by the listener or reader. Similarly, Yange, the hero of "The Rhinoceros Hornbill," is never introspective about his jealousy, which leads to his wife's death and his own suicide.

Another feature of oral art in the Yunnan folk narratives is the predominance of action, rather than elaborate description of physical appearance or motivation, as a way of defining character. "The Nine Brothers" follows an exaggerated pattern of such character definition. In the series of episodes in which the brothers triumph over the emperor, what matters to the tale-teller is action—overcoming hunger, torture, freezing, fire, and flood. The sheer abundance of the brothers' feats delights us, not their introspection (Ong 1982, 150–51). Similarly, we remember the hero of "Five Tales about Ayidan" because of what he does to his lord—wins his rice-pounder, forces him to swallow ice water, convinces him a lake has run dry, and tricks him into eating excrement.

Conversely, it is precise descriptive language in some of the Yunnan folktales that is a sign of written art (Ong 1982, 106). In "Asking Permission," the bride explains exactly to her husband her father's "lies," and thereby defends his honor, underscoring the story's theme of the importance of honesty and truthfulness: " 'He said I was blind,' she explained, 'because I had seen no evil. He said I was dumb, because I had never sown discord among people. He said I had no feet, because I had never stepped in any indecent place. He said I had no hair, meaning I have never been seen in public.' " We find vivid and elaborate visualization of the seven princesses and seven princes in "The Nanxi River." The women's soft, delicate arms are likened to amber-colored wax candles; the men wear yellow caps made from bamboo shoots, inlaid with white jade, and tied with a spray of golden flowers and green leaves. In "The Gold Pig," details about the old couple's care for a pig and a peach tree, the bird that proclaims the pig's gold-bearing proclivities, and the drowning of the rich man in dung are graphic and exact.

Such close attention to the visualization of scene and character suggests a literary reworking of an oral tale.

Most of the characters who originate in oral traditions, and who perform marvelous feats, are marked by a single personality characteristic or physical feature, often bizarre (Ong 1982, 69). Of the many examples of such types found in nearly every Yunnan story, the following come to mind: the beautiful heroine of "The Girl with Tufted Eyebrows," whose birthmark leads to her eviction by the village shaman; the girl in "The Rainbow" who dies of anguish, waiting for her lover's return, then transforms first into a snake and then a puff of smoke; and the wife in "Asking Permission" who is allegedly blind, dumb, bald, and a paraplegic besides. And who can forget the pig that defecates gold bars in "The Gold Pig," or the boa that swallows his bride in "Two Sisters and the Boa," or the wonderful Thunder God in "Stories about Bubo," who drinks indigo dye and fascinates children with his protruding tongue?

Typically, an agonistic tone is found in these oral narratives about wonderful characters who are remembered for their actions, and much bragging and verbal combat takes place. As Walter Ong points out, this agonistic feature of oral art is pretentious or insincere only to persons who are literate, and who are not used to elaborate forms of praise and blame in their cultures. The reason for the agonistic tone in oral art, he argues, and for its frequent celebration of violence and physical behavior, is the dominance of direct word-of-mouth communication in oral societies, where sound dynamics are high. For those who live a "verbomotor" life-style (term coined by Jousse [1925] for oral cultures and personalities), human interaction and the effective use of words are central. Food bartering is not just a matter of getting the right price, for example, but is an important form of human interaction in which speech is dominant and informal verbal contests are commonplace (Ong 1982, 43–45, 68–69). The most obvious examples from our tales of flyting (verbal quarreling) are those in which there is also physical combat between protagonists. In "Stories about Bubo," the hero must outwit Thunder God to keep his harvest, and eventually is destroyed by the god in a cosmic battle; in "The Magic Shoulder Pole," the verbal battle between husband and wife ends with her being beaten; and in "The

Arrogant Tiger," the tiger is killed by peasants and animals after being outwitted by the clever speech of the anteater. Frequently, strained encounters give way to verbal contests that are just plain fun. One thinks of the witty flyting between landlord and servant in "Five Tales about Ayidan," but especially of Longsi's strategical cry in "Longsi and the Third Princess": "Ai-ya! I've cut myself! Oooh! It hurts! My thumb, my thumb!" The timing of his speech is perfect, for he prevails upon the princess to climb ever higher, to where he is repairing the palace roof, forcing her to look up at him, and become his bride.

In other examples of verbal art in our Yunnan collection, an agonistic tone is coupled with schizoid behavior. In oral cultures, such behavior is commonly externalized rather than internalized (Ong 1982, 68–69). Instead of withdrawing into an interior world after an aggressive verbal exchange, a character may act out anger or jealousy. In "Mr. Crooked and Mr. Straight," the silly argument between the protagonists leads Mr. Crooked to gouge out his friend's eyes. When he learns Mr. Straight has been helped by the gods, he gouges out his own eyes. "Two Sisters and the Boa" is a delightful case of the power of argument run awry, and of externalized madness. A talking boa wins a verbal contest with a mother, forcing her to give him one of her daughters to be his bride. The second daughter initially refuses to marry the boa, then becomes insanely jealous when her sister's boa turns out to be a prince. Finding a boa of her own, the second daughter insists on sleeping with him (it is significant that this boa cannot talk), and is swallowed, inch by inch, while her mother listens to her agonistic cries, imagining the sexual play of young lovers. In "The Rhinoceros Hornbill," the husband's words convince his wife he is protecting her by locking her up, when actually he is externalizing his jealousy. Discovering she has starved to death, he acts out his grief through suicide.

Stylistically, the importance of speech in the Yunnan folk literature extends well beyond flat characters and agonistic tone to the realms of structure and memory. Everybody and everything talks—people, gods, devils, animals, trees, and rocks—for we are in a cosmos of sound in which one thing is manifested to another through sound, or speech. The community is aware of its existence through the interchange of sound, the only place where the word exists (Ong 1982, 71–73). Words are word-events to oral peoples, writes Walter Ong, and have a powerful, magic potency precisely because spoken words are sounded, and seem power-driven (pp. 32–33). The sound of a bird's cry (suma!) in "The Rhinoceros Hornbill" evokes the community memory of a man's sorrow for killing his wife. The right words must be spoken in "Asking Permission" for a man to be considered a true member of the Hui nationality. The cosmos of sound in "Two Sisters and the Boa" is what makes the tale amusing and dramatic, from the sha-sha and hua-hua swishing sounds of the boa's tail and the falling mangoes, to the daughter's terrified screams (which sound delightful to us) as she is being eaten by the snake: "Mama, it's up to my thighs! Mama, it's up to my waist! Mama, it's up to my neck now . . ." What is important to note about this oral world is that we do not see the boa in the tree, or the daughter in her bed. We hear them. In "Five Tales about Ayidan," the folk hero knows about the effective use of sounds: he convinces his lord that the clicking noises of a new rice-pounder are saying "clan de-cline" to the lord, thus leading his master to trade away his brand new machine.

When animals talk, and human beings listen, as they do in "The Guileless Man and the Trickster," human beings become very powerful. Oral sounds in the form of oaths are powerful too. The princess in "Longsi and the Third Princess" vows she will never look up at any man, and she never does, until Longsi wins her with his own series of clever sounds and exclamations. The cultural heroine of "Daughter of a Slave" cards wool, spins yarn, and weaves cloth by singing magic verses. The central question to the Dai community in "The Ancestors of Dai Singers" is, Which form of oral performance is more important and attractive: singing folk songs or chanting Buddhist sutras? In this instance, singing wins, and a new tradition begins. The sound of singing voices in "Why Sui People Live in Two-Story Wooden Loft-Houses" tells an old couple they should settle by a magic pond. The sound of talking rocks terrorizes a community in "A Blang Youth," while the youth terrorizes the rock-ghosts by getting cocks to crow in the night. Lastly, the power of the spoken word—its ability to identify a people and evoke a communal memory—is exemplified in "The Origin of Making Offerings to Ancestors." Here the storyteller playfully informs his audience that the name of their people, Jino, means "last squeeze." They were the very last people to squeeze out of a magic gourd during the creation of the world.

Such examples convince us of the predominance of sound, rather than vision, in the oral world, and the magic, evocative power of words when they are voiced.

In a culture dependent on sound, memory complements spoken language, and remembering through telling is central to community life. Verbatim memory is extremely rare. The way one remembers or thinks in an oral world is by thinking memorable thoughts, that is, through the use of mnemonic patterns marked by rhythm, repetition, antitheses, epithets, sayings, formulas, and standard thematic settings (Ong 1982, 35). Mnemonic devices are evident throughout Yunnan minority folk literature and are a key to the overall structure of most of the individual stories, as well as a reflection of the worldview out of which the tales are woven. What we find in these examples of oral art often is reminiscent of what Milman Parry showed was characteristic of Homer— the repeating of formula after formula—or what Walter Ong terms the stitching together of prefabricated parts (p. 22).

Among the many mnemonic devices found in the Yunnan folktales, standard settings or situations are the most obvious: encounters with women washing clothes or bathing in a river ("The Girl with Tufted Eyebrows," "The Rhinoceros Hornbill"); the beautiful, wealthy young woman who prefers to marry a poor man against her parents' wishes ("The Rainbow," "The Cloud That Longs for a Husband"); the poor, childless old man, woman, or couple ("The Gold Pig," "The Head-Baby," "The Gathering of the Birds"); the orphan ("Daughter of a Slave," "Nabulousi, the Life-Restoring Tree"); the old man or woman who saves an animal that transforms into a child or a god ("Wine-Flavored Spring," "Why Sui People Live in Two-Story Wooden Loft-Houses"); the village beset by ghosts ("A Blang Youth"). Such recurring events and figures, which are easily remembered by the oral tale-teller, are international folktale motifs.

Often the tale-teller intersperses sayings, epithets, or proverbs not only to point a moral, but also to orient himself or herself within a narrative. A girl with tufted eyebrows "will cause her husband to die young." The heroine of "The Rhinoceros Hornbill" loves to "scold the dog but mean the chicken," that is, criticize indirectly. Much of the humor of "Five Tales about Ayidan" lies in the ironic use of conventional phrases such as "It's a boy!" "Though the snake dies, its tail lives; though the bee perishes, its sting is still felt," says the storyteller in "The Formation of Heaven, Earth, and Humankind," making the point that devils will never give up their quest to overcome the gods.

Formulaic endings, repetitious sequences, series of tests, and numbers are further means of organizing stories in a memorable way. Much of the time, tales end happily with a marriage and the birth of children, the support of elders, and the overcoming of previous barriers or injustices. In the creation myths, we find interesting variations on a generally uniform sequence: once the earth and heaven were one; division came, then a great flood, followed by the scorching of the earth and the shooting down of many suns and moons; the sole human survivors, a brother and sister, are urged by gods or animals they encounter to enter into an incestuous relationship and propagate the human race. The hero of "Longsi and the Third Princess" must fill a palace with gold, cover the earth with satin, and procure a mansion before he may marry the princess. Set numbers, like uniform creation sequences and series of heroic tests, structure ways of telling. There are nine sisters who come to the well in "The Clever Sister," eight of whom act identically, and wrongly, in seeking a gold ring. In "The Guileless Man and the Trickster," both characters overhear the same series of reports from an identical set of animals as the latter address their tiger king. The two celestial maidens in "Myths Concerning the Creation of the World" are easily remembered: one has exquisite eyes, but never washes her face. The other has one eye, but her face is clean.

Yunnan minority folktales also reveal their oral origins structurally in the way they begin, move forward, and end. Usually, they start in medias res, allowing the teller to catch the attention of the audience. Aside from a "long, long ago," we are plunged into an immediate situation: two men arguing about whether crooked or straight is better; a thirsty old woman claiming she is willing to trade her daughter for a succulent mango; a magic bull and a fairy who keep appearing and disappearing among a herd of cattle. The stories themselves unfold in series of clusters, like beads on a string, in a way that is additive and aggregative (Ong 1982, 37–40). Typical examples of the additive or episodic structure are "Five Tales about Ayidan," "The Clever Sister," "The Arrogant Tiger," "The Nine Brothers," and "Why Sui People Live in Two-Story Wooden Loft-Houses," as well as the creation myths. Another formulaic way of structuring oral narrative is through a causal sequence, or a series of transformations. In "Asking Permission," the hero quenches his thirst without asking permission of a landowner, leading to a test to see if he is fit to marry the landowner's daughter. A relatively long tale can be advanced by several transformations. In "Why Sui People Live in Two-Story Wooden Loft-Houses," the old man saves a snake from an eagle; the snake transforms into smoke, and returns later as the dragon king's daughter, who leads the old man to the waters of eternal youth. She then becomes a fish, and finally the dragon king's daughter again, saving the old man from a flood. There is no particular logic to these transformations, except that they reflect a worldview in which this is possible, and they enable the storyteller to change the direction of the story and move it forward.

As mentioned previously, a story ending is normally positive, although there are a significant number of exceptions, such as "The Rhinoceros Hornbill," "The Cloud That Longs for a Husband," "The Nanxi River," "Water-Splashing Festival," and "Wine-Flavored Spring." What is more common in tales that are clearly marked as examples of oral art is a vague sense of closure. The ending of "The Girl with Tufted Eyebrows" is upbeat, but an addendum. The hero finds his lost mate in the jungle (how, we do not know), villagers help them build a house, and they live happily ever after. "Stories about Bubo" seems to end with a coda that, to the reader looking for some sort of denouement or climax, appears to be tacked on simply to explain the characters' fate.

Uncertain closure in our collection of tales is a sign of oral tale telling, but the almost complete absence of inconsistencies indicates their literariness. There are two odd exceptions, "The Origin of the

Sixth Month Sacrifice" and "Nabulousi, the Life-Restoring Tree." In the former, Moon Princess floods the world and destroys crops while her son tries to protect the people. We never know in "Nabulousi" whether the orphan boy marries the girl he restores to life. The general lack of inconsistencies in the stories is evidence of the backward scanning that occurs in written texts (Ong 1982, 104). The writer's task, and the redactor's as well, is to go back over a text and make it consistent. In our Yunnan stories, situations and motifs in an individual work usually do not repeat themselves, as we expect them to in a strictly oral world where the teller may pile up descriptions of mighty heroes, exquisite beauties, and evil ogres. In oral art, the tale-teller tends to override inconsistencies, and may not even be aware they exist, because he or she is interested in relating clusters of episodes. Inconsistencies do not really matter; what does is maintaining a dynamic relation with the live audience.

There are other signs of writerly texts. "The Gold Pig" unfolds in a linear direction, rather than in a sequence of clusters, from the discovery of the peach pit to the pig and the carp that make the poor rich. In "The Head-Baby," there is a writerly plot with a series of climaxes subordinated to one another, and well-placed dialogue. "The Rhinoceros Hornbill" has a clear, definite sense of closure, in the love-death of the couple, and the interesting etiological coda accounting for the behavior of hornbills. The coda works aesthetically as well, allowing the reader needed time to adjust to the tragic ending, and see the sorrow of the couple gently played out in the natural world of birds. Further evidence of writerly structuring is the development of episodes subordinated to one another, leading to a climax or denouement, instead of the sequence of beads on a string more typical of oral art. The theme of a man destroying what is both beloved and beautiful structures the juxtaposed sequences of tracking a bear, wounding a deer, and mistakenly killing one's wife.

Examples of clusters of formulas, clichés, standard settings, and aggregative episodes clearly suggests that the world of memory is largely conservative and traditionalist, and the oral storyteller's or singer's concern is not originality, but "a conventional realization of traditional thought for his listeners, including himself" (Peabody 1975, 176). Another indication of the conservative or traditionalist world of oral narrative is that the stories are full of wise old men and wise old women. They are significant not simply because they are transformations of deities and thus can perform useful feats of magic, but because they carry knowledge in their minds—in their memories, not in books—and therefore are revered by youth who depend on them for help (Ong 1982, 41). A wise old man in "Longsi and the Third Princess" knows how to assemble woodpeckers to bang on the palace roof and make the king imagine his residence is caving in. An elder in "Why Sui People Live in Two-Story Wooden Loft-Houses" saves his people from poverty and old age, and an old widow in "The Head-Baby" faithfully nurtures her monster child. Apierer, the grandma figure in "The Origin of Making Offerings to Ancestors," is revered because her sacrificial death in a gourd brings life to all the nationalities.

Another characteristic of the oral world, in which the remembering of tradition is a public act, is its duality. Like oral art elsewhere, Yunnan minority tales reflect a polarity, or "twoness," in their worldview, and follow what David E. Bynum calls the "two-tree pattern" in their structure. Dual vision, in which the world and events are readily divided into polar opposites, is a mnemonic device. More significantly, the two-tree pattern is more than a means of making things memorable. Not only does it reflect traditional values, it also embodies a simple, dualistic vision of reality that is distant and distinctive from the complicated ambiguity found in literate culture. Tales may be easily broken down into rhythms of opposites—good and evil, or praise and blame—but more significantly, episodes in sequence are parallel or opposite to one another, and tales as a whole are patterned around two trees. Separation, gratuity, and unpredictable danger cluster around one tree, while unification, recompense, and reciprocity cluster around the other (Bynum 1978, 145; Ong 1982, 25).

In "Mr. Crooked and Mr. Straight," two men who have been blinded have their eyesight gratuitously restored by a god, and are warned to stay in their homes at night. Mr. Straight heeds the warning, and is rewarded with gold and a pen full of animals. Mr. Crooked disregards the warning, and finds his food has turned into dung. The two-tree pattern of "The Guileless Man and the Trickster" is patently clear in the innocence and meanness of the two protagonists, the heat of the fire and the cold of the night, and the parallel series of animals they both overhear while sitting in a tree. "The Magic Shoulder Pole," "Why Sui People Live in Two-Story Wooden Loft-Houses," and "Nabulousi, the Life-Restoring Tree" are other full-blown examples of a polar world-view and structure, but the outstanding example of duality and the two-tree pattern is "Daughter of a Slave." Here we find two mothers, one rich and mean, the other poor and kind, each with a daughter born on the same day, one daughter ugly and stupid, the other beautiful and intelligent. The mean mother gives both daughters the same impossible tasks, which the poor daughter miraculously fulfills, and the rich daughter miserably fails.

This two-tree pattern is reflected in the union of oral and literary modes hidden within examples of communal remembering. In "The Girl with Tufted Eyebrows," the teller, like other oral artists, evokes a communal sense by recalling a taboo. In our written version of the tale, a writer's presence may be seen in the criticism of the taboo. Community values are questioned by marking the pathetic situation of girls born with a particular birthmark. "Asking Permission" reaffirms the centrality of what the Hui community considers moral behavior in a husband or father. The bride's explication of the moral logic behind her father's deceit may well be a writer's touch. The veiled symbolism of "Water-Splashing Festival" is set against the wife's clever wit. The festival is a joyous holiday of the Dai people, while the oral tale itself celebrates ancient Dai women who liberated the people from an oppressive king. Another dimension to the written narrative, symbolized in the king's severed head, which circles from wife to wife, is that evil is something impossible to eliminate, and must endlessly be cleansed from the community.

# Conclusion

While one would not claim that these Yunnan minority narratives in Chinese translation are "pure" oral tales, the evidence of oral art in them is overwhelming, and their combination of oral and literary elements is aesthetically compelling. As the variety of examples reveals, each teller's public remembering is different and inventive, though his or her real creativity can be fully seen only in the oral performance, in which the teller's dynamic relation to an audience is manifested. The artistic shaping we have noted—detailed description, a developed visual sense, precise language, backward scanning, the subordination of episodes to a plot climax—is characteristic of written narrative and creative redaction, and indicates ways in which the stories become aesthetically appealing to us as literary texts. But it is the blending of oral and literary art that delights us in the end. As was noted earlier, we need as readers of such a narrative blend to restructure consciousness. Information and analysis provided here—about Yunnan province, Chinese minorites, the response of Chinese intellectuals to folk and children's literature, textual issues and translation strategies, oral art and folk literature—are not meant to suggest that we need only objectivity to appreciate the world of minority folk literature in China. Conversations I have had with minority storytellers and Chinese intellectuals invariably bring out another dimension, and that is—as is commonly the case in cross-cultural and interpersonal relations—that we see the same things differently because we constitute them differently, depending on our cultural conditioning and personalities, even when we are in agreement about facts and data.

A case in point: when I asked Yunnan tale-tellers and singers about the importance of folk literature in the education of children, invariably they spoke about morality. Folk literature helps children to distinguish between right and wrong. Besides hearing about the how and why of life in their community, the origins of things, or relations with animals and spirits, they learn the importance of upholding the common good, and are guided in doing good. While there is a general moral vision of good and evil in the animistic world of the tales, they are full of wild stuff too: children who reject the fears and taboos of their elders, girls who quarrel with their fathers, handicapped newborns who are gifted, lovers who cannot exist in the world as it is, people crippled by emotions such as greed and jealousy, men who are tricked into marriage, mothers who sacrifice their daughters for a piece of fruit, clever folks who torture their masters and test their wives' fidelity, and strong men who do not play fair when they wrestle. When the gods or animals do not encourage the incest of siblings in order to repopulate the world after a flood, as they usually do, a brother takes up the responsibility on his own.

The Yunnan stories are a gift to the imagination. There are magic objects, shamans, and animal helpers that provide ways of overcoming obstacles, gaining power, defeating enemies, and creating a life that may not be possible in the real, everyday, hard world, but that are essential to the human imagination. Barriers can be overcome, or at least survived. The origin of the world, birds, beasts, and humans makes sense, or at least a delightful story. There is a sense of awe before the beauty and terror of the earth. Gods and people can be mean, but funny too. Life may be unfair—there are wicked people and natural calamities—but the imagination provides hope that something good will happen to barren old women and handicapped children.

What is intriguing about the cross-cultural and interpersonal encounter that occurs in the study of minority folk literature is that when we "go to the people" or "return to the folk," we discover aspects of our own culture and self that we would not be aware of otherwise, much like the Chinese intellectuals of the May Fourth movement. To return to the question of ethnicity with which this essay began, perhaps intellectuals should be considered an ethnic group, with Westerners and Chinese forming separate tribes. Each of us has cultural values that identify us, mark us, and control how we hear oral art or read folk literature. We do not awake to them, however, until we encounter the other culture or other self.

The question of the reliability of texts, folkloristic or redacted, may be less important than it seems, once we become aware of the cultural and ethnic contexts out of which we and others listen to, read, redact, write, and interpret folktales, or, in a word, talk-story.

LUCIEN MILLER

# Introduction to Yunnan National Minority Folk Literature

## Myth, Legend, and Tale

Amidst the vast body of folk literature in Yunnan, myth, legend, and tale are of central importance, noteworthy for their variety and aesthetic appeal. Such oral art goes back to the beginning of human society and has continuously developed since earliest times. In Yunnan, verbal art is a window to the particular ways and habits of each minority people, and profoundly reflects their spirit and psychology. It also mirrors the course of their historical development, and may be likened to a painting in which one sees a panorama of mountains and rivers, and within that large landscape, a detailed revelation of a certain hill or river, a tree, bird or animal, or even a single blade of grass.

Prior to Liberation in 1949, when the Chinese Communists won the revolution, the majority of Yunnan national minorities did not have a written language, owing to a variety of historical factors. The richly varied legacy of folk literature was completely dependent on the collective creation of each minority, down through the years, and it was through this creative activity that oral art was preserved. The oral nature of this folk art, and the collective way in which it was produced, fostered in the various nationalities a deep appreciation for the beautiful—a profound aesthetic sense—and gave rise to the development of whole societies in which nearly everyone was able to sing and tell stories. Today, most national minorities in Yunnan have a custom that is expressed in a common saying: "When you eat the new, tell the old" (chi xingu shuo jiuhua). In other words, whenever the rice is cooked, it is time

UNIVERSITY OF SHEFFIELD LIBRARY

for the old people in the household to call the children and grandchildren around the central cooking fire, or the hearth, and drink and tell stories. Beyond this general custom, each generation has its singers and storytellers who are recognized by all for their natural gifts and intelligence, and who sing and tell stories for everyone during festivals and special events in the life of the people. These songs and tales fuse with the life of the people and are handed down generation after generation. Over a long period of time, additions to this material are made collectively by each people, and the body of folk art is revised and polished, over and over again. As a result, the language we encounter is, on the whole, lively and vivid, and the imagination is rich, so that individual pieces appear to us well-knit in structure, their vision daring and bold.

To the person who knows the languages and cultures of the national minorities, the verbal art of each people has its unique style and special flavor, and is a precious object within the treasury of Chinese literature. As for myth, legend, and tale, these are among the oldest genres of oral art, and all of the Yunnan peoples have many versions and examples within their respective traditions. In a broad sense, myth, legend, and tale all can be termed "story," but if we are to speak more exactly and fittingly, there are certain basically different characteristics found in each of the genres, and mutually exclusive oral styles. In what follows, I should like to provide a general explanation of these distinctions, by selecting and elaborating upon some significant points that have been explored by Yunnan minority peoples.

## ANCIENT MYTH:
## WORLD, PEOPLE, AND CREATURES

In regard to myth (shenhua), it would seem that in primitive times, everything in creation had a mysterious coloring for humankind. The phenomenon of change in nature baffled human beings, and natural calamities filled them with fear. In need of some way to explain such things to themselves, they used their imaginations and personified nature, and ended up creating the gods and deities. They took their human experience of life and projected it onto a divine world, the world of the gods. As this process took place, every kind of strange and marvelous story began to be woven. This then is the world of myth. In Yunnan, the primitive ancestors of the minorities were expert weavers of myth. A vast number of myths of every sort were passed down among the people. Most of this corpus has an ancient history. The majority are origin stories, telling of the creation of the sky (heaven) and the earth, the beginnings of humankind, the roots of myriad creation, and the source of the individual minority peoples. All this is depicted in a lively, telling way through myth.

In Yunnan, the primitive ancestors of each of the minority peoples created all sorts of wonderful stories revolving around the mysterious origin of the sky and the earth, and their separation. According to the Naxi myth "The Ancestor of Humankind, Li'en" (Renzu Li'en), before sky and earth were separated, the universe was green gas (air). In time, a bright light appeared and became a lovely sound. The sound transformed into a god who bore a white egg, from which came a white chicken. The white chicken then bore nine gods who created the sky, and seven gods who formed the earth by splitting it off from the sky, thus separating heaven and earth. And that is how the world came to be. The Naxi myth reminds one of a wild dream. Another example is the Achang myth "Zhepoma and Zhemima" (Zhepoma he Zhemima), which holds that originally, only chaos (hun luan) existed. There was no light or darkness, no above or below, no tangible form to rely on for support or to push against, and no border or boundary. At some later, indefinite time, a white light issued forth from chaos. Then there was light and darkness, and the sun and moon appeared. Together, light and darkness produced Zhepoma and his wife, Zhemima, along with thirty divine generals and thirty divine soldiers. Thereupon, Zhepoma, the lord of heaven, and Zhemima, the mother of earth, created the world. When one hears this kind of colorful, imaginative material told by the minority peoples, or reads it for the first time, it seems fantastic. In fact, such myths reflect common views about creation held by primitive peoples. Sky and earth may be small in size, but the imagination employed in conceiving them is vast.

Still other Yunnan minority myths contain all sorts of fascinating hypotheses about the origin of humankind. Dai, Miao, and Drung myths say that a god of heaven kneaded humanity from mud. The Wa claim that human beings were first born from a cave, while the Jino tell of a gourd's being the source. The De'ang describe a god of heaven blowing a great wind, scattering 120 tree leaves. These leaves form husband and wife couples who propogate a flourishing human race. No matter what the theories of origin may be, all these myths share several common motifs: a great flood, the incestuous union of a brother and sister pair who are the sole survivors of the flood, and the shooting down of suns and moons. The will of heaven is always seen as requiring this union to propagate the human race. These origin myths may reflect humanity's earliest memory of consanguineous marriages, and suggest that our primitive ancestors approved of such unions on a large scale. The brother-sister incest motif, as well as other human origin stories, should prove to be a valuable area for research.

In the course of humanity's subjugation of nature, questions about sowing seeds, planting crops, and raising animals were always central. The earliest peoples did not know the source of grains and animals, but using their powers of imagination, they thought grains and animals must be the gifts of the gods. Thus we find the practice among many people in later eras of making offerings of grain to the gods, and sacrificing and praying to them at planting time. But what happened if the god to whom they sacrificed refused to give the people grain? The Blang (Mandarin: Bulang) have an agricultural or farming myth, "Ailuobuwo," that gives one answer. Once a god, Payatian, would not give grain or animals to the Blang, so their king, Ailuobuwo, sent a white ant to bore through Payatian's defenses. Payatian was defeated, and the white ant brought back to earth the five grains, poultry, and domestic animals. Women, being bright and careful by nature, were given the poultry to care for, while men got the livestock. Men are stupid and careless, so most of the livestock ran off to the woods. Ever since then, men have gone hunting in the forests, taking their crossbows and arrows.

What this myth tells us is that, although humankind must ask the gods for seed, crops, and animals in a farming society, people may use strategies to defeat the gods if they do not grant human wishes. Here we see human beings discovering their own power. Clearly, "Ailuo-buwo" reveals the elevation of agricultural production in Blang society. There are many such myths in Yunnan depicting fights between human beings and the gods. The Lahu myth "Zhanuzhabie," for example, shows humankind's ardent hope of casting off the domination of the gods, following the rising importance of agriculture in society. In terms of tracing the rise of a positive human spirit that conquers nature and resists the domination of the idea of fate, this phenomenon of war between humanity and the gods encountered in Yunnan origin myths is extremely interesting.

There are many Yunnan myths about relations between human beings and animals, indicating an intimate bond in primitive society. In initial encounters between human beings and animals, animals appear as both people's bag, or kill from the hunt, and as the enemy. Animals are thought to be more fierce than humans and are held in awe. Thus animals came to be worshipped. As [Georgy] Plekhanov (1857–1918), the Russian Marxist philosopher, has noted, primitive humans not only thought that they were possibly related to certain animals, but often traced their genealogies from these animals. In fact, primitive people had no awareness of any difference between themselves and animals. Particular characteristics peculiar to human beings were thought to have been added to the bodies of animals. Prompted by a contradiction in thought, that is, a desire to subjugate animals, along with a fear of them, primitive people fantasized about friendships between human beings and beasts, going so far as to imagine marriages in which humans united with animals and assimilated them. In Yunnan, one finds many myths about marriages between human beings and snakes, dogs, bears, or monkeys. It is not unusual for animals to become the totems of a people. This practice deserves careful research, for it reflects humankind's earliest thought.

# WONDROUS LEGENDS:
## EVENTS, PERSONS, AND PLACES

Legends (chuanshuo) are narratives and commentaries on the past that take as their basis historical events, persons, or sites, or else the actual customs and habits of a people. To a certain extent, legends reflect a people's hopes, as well as its needs, and they tell us about a minority nationality's attitude and viewpoint toward historical situations. The Bai legend "The Burning Tower" (Huoshao songming lou) is woven from a celebrated event in Bai history. It portrays the story of Bojie, the wife of a prince, and has so moved Bai people that for hundreds of years she has been commemorated in the annual Torch Festival.[1] Other important Yunnan historical happenings about which there are legends are the uprising of Lisu peasants led by Heng Zhabeng during the Jiaqing era of the Qing dynasty, or that of Hani peasants led by Tian Zheng in southern Yunnan, which lasted half a year, or the Hani uprising led by the woman warrior Dosha'apo, in the Yuanyang District in 1917. These events left in their wake many legends that still are sung and wept over today. They serve to educate and inspire a people, and enable us to understand their historical struggles and aspirations.

Legends about historical figures have considerable influence among each of the minorities. In these legends, we find those persons whom a people especially needs to remember, of which there are many. One thinks, for example, of Zheng He, the famous Hui navigator, or the Hui hero Du Wenxiu, who led a peasant uprising, or the Bai leader Duan Qicheng, who liberated his people, or the Bai hero Du Chaoxuan, a person of unparalleled bravery who killed a giant python. There are many colorful accounts about these figures. In all these legends, the

[1] The Torch Festival (Huoba Jie), celebrated by Bai, Yi, and other ethnic minorities in early summer (a parallel festival is held in late summer), commemorates Bojie, a legendary faithful widow who committed suicide to resist the advances of the Nanzhao king, who, by means of a banquet fire, had murdered her husband and four other princes of the Er Hai region. During the Torch Festival, people set afire a log tower erected in the village square, or walk the fields holding burning torches, to invoke a good harvest and ward off evil spirits and agricultural pests. Bullfights and wrestling matches are held.

storytellers identify examples of positive, heroic behavior, reflect their people's appraisal of these historical figures, and clearly express their group's thoughts and feelings about what behavior, persons, and events are to be loved or hated.

Most minorities in Yunnan live in mountain and river areas that are naturally graced with exquisite scenery. The lovely natural landscape inspires them to express their feelings about what they see around them, and they have created many legends about local scenery. One type of legend depicts famous historical sites, such as Dali, the ancient capital of the Bai people. These might be termed "magnificent place" legends, evidenced, for instance, in those stories about the breezes at Xiaguan, located at the lower end of Er Hai; the flowers at Shangguan, at the upper end of Er Hai; the snow in the Cang Mountains to the west of Er Hai; or the moonlight over Er Hai. Such "wind and flower, snow and moon" legends about four kinds of landscapes have long been famous. Other parallel examples enjoying universal praise are "The Cloud That Longs for a Husband" (translated in this volume), "Cart-Rumble Village" (Lujiao Zhuang), "Bird-Perch Mountain" (Niaodiao Shan), and "Dali Marble" (Dali shi). These local legends about specific places are well known among the Bai people, who find them deeply moving. In other parts of Yunnan, such as Sipsong Panna, a similar phenomenon is found.

Another type of legend about place reflects the customs and habits of a people. Examples that come to mind are the Bai legend "The Origins of Raosanling" (Raosanling de laili) and the Naxi legend "The Origins of the Seven-Star Shawl" (Qixing pijian de laili). Three to be found in this collection are the Dai "Water-Splashing Festival," the Yi "Torch Festival," and the Yao "The Gathering of the Birds [on Yao Mountain]." Such legends describe the origin of certain customs and practices. They are rich in romantic flavor as well, and the feeling of a particular region is so pronounced that the special character of the people of that area seems clearly present. Such legends are a wonderful source for humanistic studies.

# FOLKTALES: FAIRY TALES, ANIMAL AND PLANT STORIES, TALES ABOUT LIFE

In addition to myths and legends, folktales (minjian gushi) from each of the twenty-five national minorities found in Yunnan are also translated in this collection. On hearing or reading these stories, you feel as though early one morning you had entered a primitive forest, and suddenly there comes into view an ancient tree reaching to the sky, with vines all around it covering the ground. You simply stare, tongue-tied. In the scene before you, there are also unfamiliar flowers and exotic fruits, rare birds, and strange animals. You feel as though you cannot stop looking. Because there are so many tales, I cannot introduce them one by one. Instead, I shall emphasize special features that differentiate three types of tales.

In the minds of children, there often resides a particularly happy memory, that is, the remembrance of a fairy tale. Among the minorities in Yunnan, one finds a common desire and lovely objective in regard to the use of fairy tales. Things that could not possibly exist in actual daily life are made real through the marvelous power of the storyteller's imagination. These fairy tales, which are woven for generation after generation of children, include, in passing, vivid descriptions of the natural scenery in Yunnan, but their main importance is that they reveal the singular, educational value of the imagination. Utilizing bird and animal talk, the magic art of fairies and monsters, and wild exaggeration to present ideas and ideological perspectives, these tales let children know the world and know life.

The Bai tale "The Divine Flute" (Shen di), the Yi "The Precious Shoulder Pole" (translated here as "The Magic Shoulder Pole"), the Zhuang tale "Zhuang Brocade" (Zhuang jin), the Jingpo "Precious Lantern" (Bao deng), and the Lahu "The Head-Baby" (translated in this collection), are fairy tales that are outstanding in terms of imagination and romantic color. They exhibit one common feature: the characters they depict do not exist in the real world, but may be likened to human forms that do. For example, the mountain witches, monsters, devils, spirits, and shamans of the fairy tale are found in actual life in the form of cruel, oppressive rulers. Dictatorial personalities are especially in evidence. Fairy tales, then, are the projections of certain kinds of evil power. Conversely, the white-headed old people, fairy maidens, dragon girls, and strong men are truthful, good, hard-working, and brave, and they are the personifications of justice in the world. In the fairy tale, good and evil worlds are clearly distinguished.

Other common features in fairy tales for children are magic and magical objects—a flute, a lantern, a dragon-pearl [a large pearl held in the mouth or claw of a dragon], or the feathers of a white bird. These magical objects are found only in the hands of people who are honest, good, and industrious. It is only because of their goodness that they are able to manifest miraculous powers. However, the magical object can be lost as well as acquired. Often we see that a person who is rich and who sits idly, enjoying the fruits of others' labors, soon loses the magical object. There is an additional moral for children: magic and magical objects that bring money are not reliable. Only wealth that is created through diligent effort is secure.

Being a province with range after range of blue mountains, a veritable paradise of thick forests, and every kind of rare animal and plant, Yunnan naturally has many tales about animals and plants. In these we find a type of fairy tale in which an animal or plant is the protagonist. Involved disputes in the animal kingdom and the plant world reveal the way of the world in human society. Often the rich content has a profound moral. Taking some particular feature or characteristic of an animal or plant as a starting point, farfetched analogies may be drawn, leading to strained interpretations or erroneous conclusions on the part of the characters within the tale. Such tales are invested with a certain instructive quality. The animal or plant character is a human personification with a lively personality, and the resulting psychological portrait is often both specific and general in its significance. One example of the lively feeling found in animal and plant tales is the Jingpo story "The Bat" (Bianfu). The special characteristics of the bat are that it does not go out during the daytime, and it is half [like a] bird and half [like a] mammal, as there are two sides to its form. At one time, wanting to meet the sun, it used false analogies. Among birds, it would open its claws and reason that it was an animal. Among animals, it would stretch out its wings and reason that it was a bird. In order to punish the clever bat, people thought it best to let it go out only at night, forever unable to enjoy the sunlight.

Stories about plants are often similar. The Bai tale "The Palm Tree and the Cassia Tree" (Zongshu he guishu) tells of two trees, which originally were good friends, living together beside a cliff. They became bored with their location, and decided to move. The palm was to find a good place and come back to tell the cassia. The latter never expected that its friend would find a lovely garden with just the right soil and water, and stay there, without caring about the cassia. Through this tale, people understand why, every year, the bark of the palm tree strips off. It is being punished for being unfaithful. Here we see an example in which a characteristic of a plant is given a farfetched interpretation to illustrate an important moral, in the context of an interesting tale that has emotional value and a philosophical viewpoint.

Stories that are lifelike in their style or their reflection of actual life are called "realistic tales about life" (guanyu shenghuo hen xianshi de gushi). In Yunnan, these tales about life touch every aspect of human existence, and realistically reveal the living circumstances of a people, as well as their attitude toward, or their criticism of, these circumstances. Among these tales, stories that reflect struggles between workers and the ruling class occupy an important position. In such stories there are seldom many characters—usually just a single farmhand or slave and a landlord who is his master. The plot usually revolves around a battle of wits. Generally, the narrative tone is light and humorous, but the issue at stake is significant. In the Bai tale "Suffocating the Living King of Hell" (Qisi huo Yanwang), an intelligent, clever, calm peasant character matches wits with Yama, the king of hell. A landlord's stupidity and avaricious nature are mercilessly exposed, and, unable to move his limbs or differentiate the five grains, he is asphyxiated. "Five Tales about Ayidan," translated in this volume, and the Yi series "Four Tales about Luomu'azhi" (Luomu'azhi gushi size) all are of this type.

Among the tales about life, the one that receives the most attention from people is the romantic love story that has as its theme a conflict with the feudal, or Confucian, ethical code. In the oral art of each of the minorities, this is the theme that is most frequently encountered in tales of romance, and the most moving. In Yunnan myths and legends, love and marriage are seldom central, probably because in the lives of primitive people, there was little talk of such things, and they knew little about them. After humankind passed from the stage of arranged marriages, concepts about individuality and love gradually developed, and accompanied changes in the marriage system itself. In feudal society, young men and women were subject to the patriarchal system and the prevailing ethical code, along with the pressures of bought marriages or marriages that could not be self-determined. These social factors resulted in a great many tragedies. Phenomena such as the avoidance of marriage, elopement, and burial or cremation of the living along with the dead were much in evidence. Tragic tales about such events easily penetrated people's hearts. They were developed over time, passed down, and loved by the people.

The Yi story "The Rainbow" is an example (a De'ang version is translated in this volume). It tells of a young herdsman who loves a beautiful girl. The son of a wealthy man also loves her, but the girl loves the herdboy and rejects the rich family's offer of marriage. The rich man then conspires with a shaman and uses sorcery to kill the herdboy. As the youth is being cremated, the girl takes advantage of a moment when no one is looking, and throws herself into the fire. Two columns of smoke float aloft and join together, forming a rainbow, and the hearts of the boy and girl are one. The lovely rainbow in the tale is an expression of sympathy on the part of the Yi people for the two lovers, and it is also an expression of Yi opposition to feudal marriage, and the hopes of a people for a way to share genuine love. This kind of story is found among all the minorities, and is socialistic in attitude.

## On Collecting, Recording, Translating, and Redacting

China is a country of many nationalities, each of which has its own extensive history and ancient cultural traditions. Under different cultural conditions, each nationality created its own distinctive and original culture, as well as numerous outstanding works of oral art. Questions about how to preserve this precious heritage and disseminate it are of central importance. In 1958, at the first general meeting of representatives of the Chinese Writers Association, held in Beijing, a policy was passed in the plenary session providing the following general guidelines regarding folk literature: "Establish comprehensive collections, emphasize redaction work, disseminate material on a large scale, and strengthen research activity."

In accordance with these guidelines, each province organized literary workers and university students, and sent them to minority localities where they collected, recorded, translated, and redacted a vast quantity of folk literature. The success of these groups was phenomenal. In the course of their work, they developed a methodology that was particular to China.

## COLLECTORS AND RECORDERS

Each province was divided into districts, and folk literature investigation teams were set up for the various areas where minority nationalities were located. The responsibility for collecting a certain part of the oral material was shared among team members. Stories told by storytellers from each nationality and folk songs sung by singers were recorded in this way. As for the investigation team's work of going from the oral presentation to a handwritten copy, we required accurate recording. We wanted to be faithful to whatever the teller or singer said or sang, and we used means such as phonetic symbols, musical notation, and tape recorders to record exactly the speaker's entire language. We also required that accurate records be made of the district in which oral materials were passed down; the time and place in which a piece was recorded; and the name, age, place of birth, nationality, social status, and degree of literacy of the teller or singer. Recorders were not permitted to make any changes at their individual discretion. In order that there be no question later as to who was responsible for this work, the names of the collectors (shouji) or redactors (zhengli) were appended to each piece.

# TRANSLATORS

In the process of making faithful recordings of the oral materials, another question that arose was how to translate accurately into Chinese. The method we adopted was to find an intellectual or cultural worker who was a member of the minority, who was proficient in the minority language, and whose level of Chinese was comparatively high, and then ask that person to assume the responsibility of translation. If a particular national minority had its own written script, the translator would first use the nationality's language to record the piece. Then, word by word and line by line, this written record would be compared alongside one made by still another person whose job it was to record the piece in Chinese. From this comparison, the Chinese translation would be made. If a nationality did not have a written language, the translator could make an oral translation into Chinese only, following the words in the original spoken language, and thus make an accurate record.

The responsibility involved in such work is formidable. At times, depending on where folk art is produced and evolves, it is conditioned by a nationality's particular social history. Different works have their own ideological content and linguistic forms which develop in accordance with unique patterns of expression found within each minority. If one is the least bit careless, a Han form of expression will be substituted for that of a minority. That is why it is vital that both the recorder and the translator stop their work, temporarily, and first understand the way of life of a minority people and their customs, how they think about a problem, and what their psychological qualities may be; and know their aesthetic sense and patterns of expression. Once they become familiar with these things, the recorder and translator can sit down once again and resume their work of comparing their translations. In this way, the meaning of the original can be accurately conveyed.

As an example of the sort of problem to which I am referring, I might cite the phrase "breaking off flowers" (panzhi hua), which Han people are fond of using as a metaphor for living a passionate life, or to describe a girl glowing with youthful beauty. But in Jingpo folk songs, "breaking off flower branches" has a different implication—it is a dirty phrase used to curse someone. If such a fact is not understood, and the phrase is translated directly from Jingpo into Chinese, the meaning will be nearly opposite that of the original. Because such a phenomenon occurs in translation, the name of the translator should accompany the work. In this way, responsibility is made explicit.

## REDACTORS

Why is it that the names of redactors are listed following each piece in this collection? The reason for this is found in the method by which folk literature is collected in China. According to this method, two works are produced in the process of collecting. The first work is a kind of data or reference book used for scientific research. The sole focus of the data text is faithful recording and accurate translation. There are no redactions. Essence and dross are recorded, as well as both positive and negative materials. Whether the original oral presentation is fragmentary or complete, everything is collected in this reference book. Not one phrase is omitted. No single word is changed. This kind of text is distributed only internally, and is not for sale on the open market.

The second kind of book that is produced is a literary textbook or reader. In regard to the pieces that have been collected, what is needed now is to make selections and to focus on redaction work for the purpose of publication. Here arises the question of sifting the grain from the chaff. In redaction, things that are unhealthy or unsound are deleted or changed. Among a number of dissimilar variants, one is selected, and the work of redaction is carried on. When doing redactions, redactors need to have a serious, discreet attitude. They may take a loose, fragmentary structure and tighten it up, but they may not add to the contents just as they wish. They may make minor revisions, or polish a word that is written incorrectly, but they may not substitute Han language, or the language of intellectuals, for the way of expression of the national minority. In order to make explicitly clear who is responsible for a redaction, the name of the redactor is always appended to a text.

Thus, when readers look at a book of Yunnan folk literature, they always see included the names of collectors, translators, and redactors.

## Conclusion

Yunnan minority myths, legends, and tales are like a treasure house containing objects of art. In such a place one can go about uncovering one precious object after another that has been selected and collected previously. Similarly, one delights in Yunnan's oral art.

In closing, it is important to point out that our work is based on that of many, many Yunnan minority intellectuals and writers who have been unearthing and promoting Yunnan folk literature for a long while. Our effort is dependent on the vast foundation they have built. Were it not for their work collecting materials for so many years, we would have nothing from which to make our selections for this book of translations. Naturally, we scholars from China and America too must make a great effort to complete this cooperative project. We have but one goal, and that is to do the job well, to the best of our abilities.

Owing to limitations of time and other factors, our work has its shortcomings. This is our first cooperative venture, and we hope to hear the opinions of experts and readers. If there is a possibility of continuing our work together in the future, we want to improve on what we have done before.

XU KUN
Translated and edited
by Lucien Miller

# STORIES

## ABOUT

### CREATION

# Myths Concerning the Creation of the World

## DRUNG MYTH

## » 1 «

## The Big Ants Separate Heaven and Earth

In ancient times, heaven and earth were directly linked. They were connected by nine earthen terraces. In those days, people on earth could go to heaven simply by climbing up these terraces.

Legend has it that in Mukemudamu, there lived a man by the name of Gamupeng who often visited heaven. One day, Gamupeng wanted to go to heaven to make gold and silver. He strode on the terraces and walked, step by step, up toward heaven. Now it happened that a big swarm of ants turned up unexpectedly, and blocked his way, and they shouted at Gamupeng and demanded leggings. Gamupeng had the utmost contempt for ants, and he told them off. "Your bodies are tiny and your legs are even thinner. What do you need leggings for? Get out of my way!"

Seeing Gamupeng's attitude, the ants sang in chorus, "Never mind that our legs are thin, and never mind whether our size is small. Though the earthen terraces are as high as heaven, we can pull them down." Gamupeng thought this was impossible, and he persisted on his way, going straight up to heaven, *thump, thump, thump.*

Once Gamupeng had reached heaven, the huge swarm of ants descended underneath the earthen terraces and made a mighty effort to loosen the dirt. During the night, a loud roar was heard, and the nine earthen terraces came tumbling down. From then on, heaven and earth were separated. Heaven was so high up in the sky that people could not get there anymore.

Gamupeng, who was making gold and silver, got really worried when he saw that suddenly, heaven and earth were splitting apart, and there would be no way to go back to earth. He shouted to the people on earth, "Please hurry up and fetch me a ladder, fast! I want to come down." The people on earth quickly set up a ladder for him, but no matter how hard they tried, the ladder would not reach heaven, and Gamupeng had no way to descend.

He turned again to the people on earth. "Hurry along and grow palm trees. I'll come down holding on to the palms!" The people on earth promptly did as he bid, but no matter how tall the palm trees grew, they could never reach heaven. So Gamupeng still could not come down to earth.

Then he addressed the people on earth once again. "Go and grow rattan and bamboo. Hurry! I'll climb down grasping them!" After the people on the earth heard what he wanted, they hurriedly grew rattan and bamboo. But no matter how long the rattan and bamboo grew, they could not reach as far as heaven.

Gamupeng could not find any way to come back to earth. Seeing that the people on earth had no way to help him descend, he decided he should make ropes out of gold and silver so he could lower himself down. But his gold and silver ropes were not long enough, so he still could not return to earth.

Countless years passed by, and lonely Gamupeng became a blang spirit in heaven. He would spend entire days calling to the people on earth, "Oh, you people on earth! I have nothing to eat, nothing to drink. You eat and drink your fill every day. Hurry, please! Give me something!" After hearing his pleas, the people on earth decided to kill bulls to offer a sacrifice to the heavenly spirits on Kaquewa, Spring Festival Day, and other festivals. Thus they might give Gamupeng something to eat and drink so that he would not get angry with them and cause them calamities.

# » 2 «

## A Hunter Shoots the Sun

In ancient times, there were two suns which always appeared side by side in the sky. The scorching sunlight burned the earth and made it as hot as a cooking fire. Trees and grass withered. Poor little children were burned to death, one after the other. People cried pitifully, and the entire earth became dreary and desolate.

There was a hunter who was a superb shot. When he saw that the two suns were bringing calamities upon the people, he was furious. He made up his mind to shoot one of the wicked suns. He climbed the peak of a mountain, bringing along his big crossbow made of Yansang rock maple, drew his bow, and aimed at one of the suns. *Sssst* went the arrow, straight and true, hitting its target dead center. With a mighty crash, the sun rolled down the mountain. As a matter of fact, these two suns were a man and a woman. The one shot by the hunter was the male, and when the female sun saw how bad the situation was, she fled in a panic, and hid behind the mountain.

Instantly, the earth became pitch black. People could not go out of their houses, or do any work at all. Worse still, they were afraid of running into *blang* ghosts and monsters. For nine days the situation went on like this, and people found it impossible to live. By the tenth day, a dim light appeared in the east, yet the sun still did not come out. People thought that it simply would not do to be without the sun—it would be far better if they could just find some way to ask her to show her face.

After a lot of talking, they got a rooster to crow for the sun. The rooster stood on the crest of a mountain and called in the direction of the light, "Cock-a-doodle-doo! Oh, Miss Sun, Miss Sun! Please give me a small earring!" No sooner did the rooster finish his crowing, than a small green earring dropped from the sky. Putting on the earring, the rooster again called toward the light, "Oh, Miss Sun, Miss Sun! Thank you so much. From now on, I'll crow three times a day at the first break of dawn. Wait until I'm finished—then you can come out."

Immediately, the rooster cleared his throat and flapped his wings, then raised his head and crowed loudly three times. Before long, a round red sun was seen rising slowly from the other side of the mountain.

This rising sun was the female sun, while the male, who had been shot and blinded by the hunter, became the moon. Ever since, the sun and the moon have taken one another's place, appearing by day and by night. It is said that the hunter's soul ascended to the moon after he died. The black spot that people see there today is the shadow of the hunter as he moves about on the moon.

## » 3 «

# Humans Fight the Blang

In the ancient Lizhemuzhe era, human beings were found everywhere. There were also many blang, who, in those days, intermingled with humans. The children of human beings were looked after by blang, and blang children were looked after by humans. People were very careful about taking care of blang children and, as a result, every one of them grew up. But when the blang helped look after the human children, they found all sorts of ways to eat them. So the blang grew greater and greater in number with each passing day, while humans became fewer and fewer. Humans began to realize they could no longer live with the blang, so they put their heads together and made up their minds to drive them off. They took branches and chased the blang all over the place, and beat them. Although the blang were driven away, and were no longer allowed to live with humans, they would not give up, and were always waiting for an opportunity to eat people. When people went out to cut firewood, the blang were there, hiding behind the trees. When they went to fetch water, the blang would be hiding by the river. Human beings were terrified, lest they fall prey to the sinister schemes of the blang.

There was a young man by the name of Peng who so hated the blang cannibals that he was ever working on ways to conquer them and rid the people of this scourge.

Peng was very brave and a crack shot—his every arrow hit its mark. One day, when Peng was walking along, he found himself closely followed by the blang king. No matter where he went, the blang king was always right behind. Once Peng had a glimpse of the king, his burning rage knew no limits, and he lifted his crossbow and took careful aim.

The blang king opened his big mouth and roared with laughter. "You cannot kill me with but one arrow," he said, arrogantly. "Try your luck if you don't believe me!" On hearing his words, Peng thought to himself that misfortune would indeed be his lot if one shot were not enough. He must find the right moment to kill the king. Peng said to him, "All right, I will shoot just once. If I fail to kill you, I will sit right here so you can eat me." The king, laughing heartily, agreed to let Peng shoot, confident that no matter what the man did, he could not kill him with merely one arrow.

Just then, Peng jumped up into a big tree. Taking advantage of the moment when the blang king was laughing with his mouth wide open, he drew his bow with all his might, took good aim at his throat, and let his arrow fly. It was squarely on target, and the blang king fell dead in an instant. Ever since then, all blang have been afraid of human beings, and dare not harm anyone rashly.

## » 4 «

# Penggenpeng Gets Married in Heaven and the God of Heaven Presents Him with Grain and Cattle

After the time the earth was flooded, people gradually grew in number. But there were neither the five grains nor cattle on the earth, and they had to live on wild vegetables and fruits.

In Mukemudamu there was a young man named Penggenpeng. Though he was old enough to take a wife, he did not know how to do it. He had great physical strength and was very diligent. Every day he would go up the mountain to cut firewood. One day, he found that the wood he had cut up previously had become trees again, growing just as they were. He thought this was quite strange, and he wanted to get to the bottom of it.

That night, Penggenpeng secretly hid himself in the woods to see if there was anything suspicious happening, and he spotted an old man approaching from afar. When the old man came to the fallen trees, he lifted them up and placed them back on their stumps. Immediately, the trees were whole again. Penggenpeng was so angry that he charged forward and tackled the old man by the waist, intending to give him a good beating. The old man turned around and grinned: "I am the god of heaven, Mubengge. I am here today to propose a marriage to you."

Right away, Penggenpeng let go of the god of heaven and asked him how this could be. Mubengge said, "If you can accomplish the few things I ask, you may come up to heaven and take my daughter for your wife." Whereupon Mubengge pointed at a huge, towering tree. Penggenpeng was to climb to the top and descend to the bottom in less than a breath. He nimbly made his way up and back in a flash. Mubengge ordered a tiger to come near, and told Penggenpeng, "Follow this tiger. If you can reach the end of the earth, you may come up to heaven to take a wife." With that, Mubengge floated away.

Now Penggenpeng set out following the tiger. Along the way, the tiger would roar with anger, or charge wildly all about, but Penggenpeng was never the least bit afraid, and always stuck right behind. How long they trekked is uncertain, but suddenly they reached the end of the earth. Only then did the tiger turn around and speak to Penggenpeng: "The place you want to go to is right ahead. Go quickly! Mubengge, the god of heaven, is waiting for you." Looking up, Penggenpeng saw ahead a broad stretch of land, with all kinds of crops. In the woods was every kind of bird and animal. He had not gone far before he saw Mubengge, the god of heaven, waiting for him, just as he had been told.

Mubengge led Penggenpeng home to heaven and called his two daughters to come forward so that Penggenpeng might make his choice. One of these celestial maidens had exquisite eyes, but she had never washed her face. The other had only one eye, but her face was quite clean. The celestial maiden who had only one eye was called Mumeiji. She deeply loved Penggenpeng and was willing to be his wife. The other maiden, however, wanted to marry a fish. Accordingly, the god of heaven gave his daughter Mumeiji to Penggenpeng in marriage, and let him take her home. Hence the beginning of the earthly custom that men take wives, and women marry men.

As Penggenpeng and Mumeiji were about to return to earth, the god of heaven presented them with seeds of millet, buckwheat, corn, and oats, along with birds and animals of every kind, and a bamboo pipe full of bees, and another pipe of medicinal liquor. Clever, quick-witted Mumeiji found that her father had not given them rice seeds, so she stole some and hid them beneath her fingernails to bring them to earth. Before they set off, the god of heaven warned them, time and again, that they must not look back, no matter what they heard along the way.

Penggenpeng and Mumeiji brought with them all the things the god of heaven had given them, and they came back to earth in high spirits. As they were walking along, the birds and animals following behind suddenly began making an uproar. Mumeiji was startled, and could not refrain from looking back. Damn! As soon as the birds and animals that had been following them saw Mumeiji look back, they began running away and crying out. Penggenpeng and Mumeiji panicked and tried at once to grab them, but all they caught were a few cows, pigs, sheep, dogs, and chickens. The rest escaped to the ancient forest, deep in the mountains. That is why the Drung have always had only a few kinds of domestic animals and cattle to raise. In their rushing about, Penggenpeng and Mumeiji let go of the bamboo pipe of bees. So bees now build their honeycombs only in cliffs and rocks. That bamboo pipe of medicinal liquor was spilled into the water. That is why, in the past, the Drung people had no medicine to cure disease, and only knew how to ferment light wine. Luckily, they did not lose the seeds of the five kinds of grain, and they began to grow millet, sweet buckwheat, corn, oats, and rice with these seeds after they got back to earth. From then on, people on the earth have known how to grow crops.

Seeing all kinds of crops growing on the land made Mubengge pleased, but he thought if too much edible grain was produced on the earth, people would become lazy. He scattered from heaven many weed seeds, and weeds grew in the fields. Only if people weed will the crops grow well.

One day, Mubengge discovered to his surprise that rice was growing on the land. He was shocked to realize his daughter, Mumeiji, must have stolen his rice seeds. Accordingly, when the rice ripened, he ordered the gods to bring some back to heaven. The reason why empty husks of rice exist is that they have been reaped by the gods of heaven.

It is said that when Penggenpeng and Mumeiji were leaving heaven, Mubengge gave them a book made from animal skins, on which many words were written. Later the children of Penggenpeng cooked the book and ate it. Hence there was no written language, and people had to use their brains to remember things. As a result, the Drung people cannot read and write. They can only tell stories and sing songs.

## NOTES

"The Big Ants Separate Heaven and Earth" (Damayi ba tiandi fenkai), "A Hunter Shoots the Sun" (Lieren she taiyang), "Humans Fight the Blang" (Ren yu Bulan zhengdou), and "Penggenpeng Gets Married in Heaven and the God of Heaven Presents Him with Grain and Cattle" (Penggenpeng shangtian qu xifu—Tianshen gei wugu zhongzi, shengchu), included in "Myths Concerning the Creation of the World" (Chuangshi shenhua liuze), from *Yunnan minzu minjian gushi xuan* 1982, 582–91. Storytellers: Dangse. Ding, Kong Meijin, Lula. Ding, and Bu Song (Drung). Translators: Meng Guocai, Zhang Lianhua, and He Quan (Drung). Recorders: Li Zixian, Zhang Wenchen, and Li Chengming (Han). Redactor: Li Zixian. Area of distribution: Drung River valley, Gongshan County, and Gongshan Drung-Nu Autonomous County, northwestern Yunnan.

**Mukemudamu.** Legendary place in Drung mythology.

**leggings.** Worn by the Drung in the warm, wet climate as protection against leeches.

**blang.** According to traditional Drung belief, everything in creation has a spirit. All spirits, ghosts, and monsters are called *blang* (Mandarin: *bulan*). *Blang* are omnipresent. The spirit or *blang* of Gamupeng is not his individual soul, but the personification or transformation of a natural force. This spirit is equivalent to a god.

**Kaquewa.** The three-day New Year festival which takes place during the first month of the lunar calendar. During this festival, Drung dance the "beef pot" dance while meat is cooking on a fire, and stick and sacrifice bulls to the spirits of heaven, whose protection is hoped to be secured.

**Lizhemuzhe.** A mythical era.

**fingernails.** In some versions, a dog follows Mumeiji carrying rice seeds pressed against its belly with its tail.

**Mubengge.** A Drung god of heaven and an ancestor, similar to Amoyaubu (the Jino god of heaven) and to Pan Gu, the mythical Han creator of the world. In the mythology of many Chinese minorities, heaven is inhabited by several gods, one of whom may rank higher than the others. Gods of heaven often are considered to be the ancestors of a people.

# The Origin of Making Offerings to Ancestors

## JINO MYTH

Whenever we Jino people sing a tune, we sing the word "Apierer" first. When we tell stories, we chant "Apierer" at the beginning. Before we take a meal, we offer it to Apierer [Mandarin: Api'e'e]. There is never a time when this word is not on our lips. Visitors who come to the Youle Mountains for the first time do not know what it means. Now let me explain it to you. Apierer is our ancestor, our very first ancestor. In speaking of the origin of our making offerings to Apierer, we have to start from the time of the great flood that drowned the world.

Ever since Amoyaobu separated heaven and earth, the myriad things gradually came into being. In those days, human beings lived in harmony with all of creation, and their lives were peaceful and happy. But suddenly one year, there came a mighty flood that inundated crops and villages. Many people were drowned, and cattle too.

At that time, there were a twin brother and sister, Mahei and Maniu, who lived with their parents. Seeing that the flood was rising higher and higher, and that all of humankind was on the brink of extinction, the parents felled a big tree, hollowed it out, and covered both ends with cowhide to make it into a big wooden drum in which grain and seed could be stored. A string of tinkling brass bells was attached to the drum from the outside. Then the parents gave a knife and a cake of beeswax to the twins, saying, "Now climb on in and flee for your lives! Remember, don't come out before the water from the flood dries up. Keep an eye on the flow of the water by looking through the hole you cut with this knife. And after you take a look, stop it up tight with the beeswax. When you hear bells tinkling, you'll know for sure that your drum has touched ground, and the water has gone down. Then you can break open the drum and come on out."

Mahei and Maniu did exactly as their parents told them. They climbed into the wooden drum and were carried away by the flood. Hours and hours passed, and Mahei began to get fidgety. He cut a tiny hole in the drum and peeked out. Help! Muddy waves were surging in every direction. Dead people and dead animals and dead birds floated on the water. What a terrible sight! Mahei quickly filled in the hole with beeswax. On and on they floated with the great drum, without a clue as to how much time had gone by. Then it was Maniu who couldn't bear waiting any longer. She, too, cut out a small hole in the drum and peeked out. Wow! What a huge expanse of water—nothing but waves out there. Maniu hastily filled in the hole with beeswax. On and on they floated, not knowing at all how long they had been in the wooden drum. Suddenly, *jingle-jingle-jangle*, the brass bells were ringing! Mahei and Maniu knew the drum had touched ground and the water was gone. Boy, were they happy! They speedily sliced open the cowhide at one end of the drum with their knife and walked out together.

As the twins began to walk on land, a desolate scene lay before them. The mountains looked barren and so did the earth, with mud and silt everywhere. Their parents were nowhere to be seen, and there was not a person, animal, or even a tree leaf in sight. They bawled their eyes out. Why, they were the only people left in the whole wide world, and would have to depend on one another to survive! They threw up a makeshift shed, and started reclaiming the wasteland and planting grain. Life wasn't easy.

Many, many years went by. Mahei's hair turned white. So did Maniu's. They realized they were both old. Only then did it dawn on them— if they should die, there would be no people left on earth at all. What could the twins do? Mahei was really worried. So was Maniu. When they were young, they never even thought of such a thing as getting married because they were brother and sister. But now, there wasn't anyone else except them. For there to be children, they simply had to marry.

Mahei said to his sister, "Hey, let's get married!"

Maniu was ashamed to hear such talk from her twin. "How could that ever happen? We are brother and sister. Can a brother and sister become husband and wife?"

"If we two don't get married," said Mahei, "that will be the end of people!"

Maniu thought about this for a while. "We'd better go and consult the magic tree at the fork in the road. If the tree god says no to your idea, we can't get married."

Mahei said, "Fine with me, go ahead and consult the tree god."

After saying this, Mahei took a shortcut and got to the fork in the road ahead of his sister. He hid himself behind the tree and waited. Along came Maniu, walking up to the magic tree. "Oh, Tree God," asked Maniu, most respectfully, "there are only two people left on the earth, my brother and I. To prevent people from completely disappearing, would it be possible for us, a brother and a sister, to get married?"

Pretending to speak as if he were the tree god inside the magic tree, Mahei made his voice rumble. "You and your brother are the only people in the whole world. It simply won't do if you don't marry. Without your marrying, there will be no more people. So get married!"

Mahei returned home ahead of his sister, again taking the shortcut. He asked her deliberately, "Did you consult the magic tree?"

"Yes," answered Maniu.

"Well, did he approve?"

Maniu had to report that the tree god approved.

And so, brother and sister married and became husband and wife.

But now that they were old, they were unable to have children. Through all the many years, they lived a lonely, dreary life.

It happened that the sole gourd seed they had picked out of the wooden drum grew very profusely, once they planted it. The vines of the gourd climbed over seven mountains, and its green leaves covered seven valleys. All sorts of gourds, big and small, hung from the vines. Strangely enough, these gourds dried out and rotted as the days went by—all except for one. This one gourd got big and ripe, with a round belly and a hard golden-yellow shell. The old couple picked it and hung it on the eaves of their shed, so that later on it might be used for seeds.

One day, when they came back from working in the field, they thought they heard voices talking faintly. Now how could there be voices, since they were the only people in the world? At first, they did not believe their ears, thinking they must have heard something else. Yet, for several days in a row, just as they passed under the eaves, they did hear people talking softly. The old couple searched all over the house, trying to find where the voices were coming from. They looked and looked, until finally, they realized that the voices were coming from the gourd hanging from the eaves. Mahei and Maniu took down the gourd and heated their fire tongs red hot, thinking they would burn a hole in the gourd to see what on earth was in there. As they moved their tongs toward the upper side of the gourd, a voice shouted, "Don't burn me!" Then they changed position, and tried to burn a hole in the bottom of the gourd, and again a voice was heard, "Don't burn me!" No matter from which side they approached the gourd—upper, lower, left, or right—the same voice would shout, "Don't burn me!" Mahei and Maniu were in a fix, not knowing what to do. In the end, they simply did not have the heart to pierce the gourd with hot tongs, so they only stared at it, perplexed. Just then, an old and weak but pleasant-sounding voice was heard. "Do burn me! Otherwise, not one of them can get out!" Clearly, it was an old woman talking.

"Who are you? Where can I burn you?" asked Mahei.

"I'm Grandma Apierer. How about on my belly button?" the voice replied.

Turning the gourd upside down, Maniu found a big, black navel on the gourd's bottom.

At this point, the voices they had heard before cried out with grateful glee, "Grandma Apierer, we will never forget you after we get free!"

Mahei did as Apierer told him, disregarding whatever the consequences might be, and burned a hole through the navel of the gourd. As soon as an opening was made, several people jumped out, one after the other.

The first one was called Apo. Because he happened to come out first, his skin was smeared by the black carbon at the mouth of the hole, so he had dark skin. (He is the ancestor of the Konge people now living in Xiao Mengyang, a county in Sipsong Panna.)

The next one was a Han. As soon as he left the gourd, he went about all over the place. That's why Han people now occupy the greatest part of the land.

The third one who came out was a Dai. As soon as he got out, he ran into a banana grove. That is why the Dai people's skin remains white— they are seldom in the sun.

The very last one to squeeze out of the gourd was our Jino. Ji means "squeeze," and no means "last."

After all the people came out, the gourd died and disappeared. Now when the Jino person came out, every place had already been occupied by other brothers who got out before him. So, he had no place to go, but stayed where Mahei and Maniu lived. That was the same place where the gourd had grown. There they worked and lived together. The place was called Bi'enmuxi, and is now the mountainous Youle region.

We Jino are a people that originally lived and flourished in Bi'enmuxi, the descendants of Grandma Apierer. Our ancestors have never forgotten the kindness of Grandma Apierer. It was she who gave her life so that we Jino people might live. Nor did our ancestors ever forget the promise they made to Grandma. Whenever they ate newly harvested rice in the autumn; celebrated the New Year and other festivals; killed pigs, chickens, cattle and sheep; worked in the fields; ate their lunch in the open fields; went hunting in the mountains; or sat around the table for dinner, our ancestors would first set aside a handful of steamed rice and put some vegetables on it, humming fervently, "Grandma Apierer—please come back! Please come back!"

After calling her this way, they would invite other departed ancestors to return. What this means is that the ancestors were asked to eat first; their living descendants ate afterwards.

This custom has been handed down from generation to generation, up to now. In recent years, though, fewer and fewer offerings of rice are made to Apierer. Still, when we come home at the end of a day's work, and gather around the cooking fire talking about the past and present, or when we open our mouths to sing with joy in our hearts, we never forget to invite our most respected ancestor, Grandma Apierer, to come and share our happiness. A fervent and solemn "Grandma Apierer," said with a nasal drawl, is the starting point of story and song.

## NOTES

"Jingxian zuxian de laili," from *Yunnan minzu minjian gushi xuan* 1982, 592–96. Storyteller: Sha Che (Jino). Collector and redactor: Yu Chi (Han). Area of distribution: Sipsong Panna Dai Autonomous Prefecture, southern Yunnan.

**Amoyaobu.** The legendary ancestor of the Jino, and creator of heaven and earth. Equivalent to Pan Gu in Han mythology.

**brother-sister marriage.** Many minority creation myths contain an incest motif. A great flood is followed by the marriage of a brother-sister pair of survivors, who are the progenitors of a particular people. The parallel in Han mythology is the incestuous relationship between Fuxi and his sister Nüwa.

# The Formation of Heaven, Earth, and Humankind

## LISU MYTH

## » 1 «

## Mubupa Kneads the Earth Out of Clay

According to legend, in ancient times there was a heaven, but no earth. The four sides of heaven lacked pillars, and there was nothing to hold them up and make heaven secure. Heaven itself could be likened to a flat layer of floating clouds, wobbling to and fro, or to a dugout canoe tossed and bumped about by pounding waves.

At that time, there was an extraordinarily hardworking, able god by the name of Mubupa. So powerful and strong was he, loads as heavy as mountains were nothing for him to carry. His walking pace was so fast, he could make it all the way around heaven in a single day. Now when he saw that heaven had no supportive structure underneath, and just might collapse at any moment, he made up his mind to take clay and make a ball of earth to bolster up heaven. Instead of seesawing back and forth, heaven would hold steady and secure. So Mubupa bid farewell to his parents, wife, and children, and bearing clay from heaven on his back, he went to knead the earth.

Mubupa traveled many days, penetrating clouds and finding his way through thick fog, before he had broken through to clear, blue skies where he could settle down to work. He molded his ball from dawn to dusk, and from nightfall to the moment the morning star vanishes. He drank nothing but a mouthful of dew to quench his thirst, and he ate only small handfuls of fried, dry rice-flour to allay his hunger. Night and day he worked, soaked in sweat, shaping the ball. Once he had

74

formed a section of level ground, he planted a flower bed, grasslands, and woods, and molded the birds that fly and the beasts that roam. Thus, flowers bloomed and bees buzzed on this plain, while in the forest, tigers roared and apes cried, and the myriad birds tried to outdo one another with their songs. The land was bubbling with new life and bustling with activity.

At one point while Mubupa was toiling away, the prince of devils, Niwadi, source of all disaster and affliction, suddenly appeared before him. Niwadi set upon a wicked scheme to shake Mubupa's resolute ambition. Pretending to be breathless and alarmed, he addressed Mubupa with an air of deep concern. "Oh, my dear Mubupa! You shouldn't have gotten so involved in this business of yours. I feel if I don't tell you what I must, I'll feel bad. But if I do say anything, you're bound to be hurt. Still, here's the truth: Your only son is dead."

Hearing such dreadful news, Mubupa's heart began beating violently, as though pierced by a needle. But he quickly calmed himself down, raised his head, and cast a glance at the sky. "Though my son is dead, I can have more sons. But I must carry on my task of kneading the earth." Mubupa went right along molding clay, without glancing up at Niwadi. The devil realized that the god of heaven was like a wooden stake stuck in the ground, firm and sure, emotionally unruffled, and as immersed in his work as ever. Realizing that Mubupa had not fallen into the trap he set, nor stepped on the bamboo spikes he planted, the devil went away, crestfallen. But, as the saying goes, "Though the snake dies, its tail lives; though the bee perishes, its sting is still felt." The prince of devils would not admit defeat, and continued to plot against Mubupa.

Before long, he again pretended his heart was heavy with sorrow, and he came back to see the god of heaven. "Oh, Mubupa! What a pity! Your wife took sick and dropped dead! Last time, when your only son died, and you didn't even go home to see him, your wife cried her heart out, saying you were born with a heart of stone. Eh! Once your luck turns bad, misfortune piles high! Think of your poor parents. They're all alone and uncared for. There's no one to look after them. How long they have been expecting you to come home. Now that your wife has died, why not act like a husband and go see her?"

Learning that his wife had passed away, Mubupa felt as though stabbed by ten thousand daggers. He was overcome with grief. But then he realized, "The work of molding the earth out of clay isn't complete. How can I give it up, halfway?" Bearing his grief, he looked up at heaven with tears in his eyes, and expressed his sorrow to his wife. Then he said to Niwadi, "There's no salt in chicken feed, and no medicine for regret. Since I left wife and child to mold the earth, I won't turn back now, whatever the disaster!" And he went on kneading the earth. Seeing he had not changed Mubupa, the devil had to leave, his head hanging down in disappointment.

Hoping to be soon finished with his job of shaping the earth, Mubupa went on working. Always bent over and engrossed in what he was doing, he would never stand straight or look up. Though his body was soaked with sweat, and his feet were raw from the rubbing of his rough shoes, he kept on kneading.

When Mubupa's work was near completion, Niwadi tried once more to carry out his evil plans. Knitting his brows and pulling a long face, he ran up to Mubupa in a panic. "Alas! Alas! Both your parents have died! When your wife died, you refused to return home. If you don't go home this time, that would be outrageous. Not being present when your parents breathed their last simply means they brought you up for nothing! If you don't take a handful of dirt and bury them after they've died, you aren't worthy to be their son." With that, the devil left.

The god of heaven had loved and respected his parents ever since he was a child. On hearing of their deaths, he felt as if he were struck by lightning, and fell in a swoon on the ground. "Though my son died, I could have another one. Though my wife died, I could marry again. But a man has only one father and one mother in a lifetime. When they die, shouldn't their son bury them himself?" Thinking this way, Mubupa picked up the clay that he had yet to finish kneading, and he molded it into lumps which he threw down towards the plain he had made earlier. Some lumps sunk into the land, forming canyons and gorges. Others landed on the surface of the land and became high mountains and mysterious peaks. It is said that, even now, a small part of the edge of the earth is still missing, because the god of heaven had no time to finish his task of molding the earth before hurrying home. Since Mubupa's work was left undone, rivers flow toward the hollow, low-lying places at the edges of the earth. From that time on, the earth itself, with its uneven surface, has supported heaven, while heaven has covered the earth. Heaven is male, and the earth is female. They make a nice couple.

## » 2 «

# The Macaques Give Birth to the Human Race

Soon after Mubupa kneaded the earth, he molded a pair of macaque monkeys, using mud. Gradually, the pair grew up. They mark the appearance of the human race on the earth. As time went by, the number of people slowly increased.

One day, Mother Macaque carried her nursling son on her back to collect wild fruit. The scorching sun burned down so fiercely that the baby monkey would not stop crying. Mother Macaque stopped picking fruit to nurse her baby and coax him to sleep, then before going back to picking fruit, she put him in a cradle in the shade so he could be comfortable. Just then, a parrot flew to the pine tree above mother and baby, and it began pecking a pine cone and eating the pine nuts. It happened that one of the pine cones fell and hit the baby monkey squarely on the temple, and immediately he stopped breathing. Mother Macaque cried so loudly that the sky darkened, the earth grew dim, and there were landslides and earthquakes.

After weeping hard, she chanted a curse: "May trees fall, so new trees may grow; may people die, so there is room on the earth for others." And that is the origin of birth and death.

## » 3 «

# The Great Flood

As a result of the macaque's incantation, all things that are born are bound to die. After death, heaven's blue sky seeks the human soul, while earth longs for human bones. That is how the great flood began.

In an ancient time, in a stockaded village of some ten thousand households, there once were a brother and sister whose parents died when they were still young. As they were without friend or support, they stayed in a shed made of wormwood branches near the village, and they lived just like the wild boar and wild ox.

One day, as the brother and sister were passing time putting wild vegetables they collected into their earthen cooking pot, adding buckwheat flour, and stirring with a pair of wormwood chopsticks, a pair of dazzling, golden-colored birds flew down from the sky and alighted on the top of their shed. These birds were able to speak human language. "What poor orphans you are!" the birds exclaimed. "As the saying goes, 'Rotted wood makes a lot more smoke; orphans and widows have a lot more tears.' You two have had your taste of suffering. You've experienced enough sorrow. But your bitter days have not yet passed. Greater sufferings are yet to come. A huge wave will flood the earth. Go quickly now and find a gourd to use for your shelter. And don't come out till you hear us birds singing, and we've alighted on the gourd and are calling you." Then the birds flew up into a cloud and disappeared.

Hearing this terrible news, brother and sister were terror-stricken. It was a case of "you wait for me to move, and I wait for you," for they were so scared they did not know what to do. They gathered their wits and decided they should let the villagers know of this threat to the human race, so that others might avoid disaster. They called on one household after another. One family said these orphans were so starved they were talking nonsense, while another claimed that, because they had no parents to teach them better, they were mistaking their dreams for reality. Others just laughed after hearing their story, saying, "Even if what you say is true, we live in a house made of fir. It doesn't shake in the wind, or rock when the earth quakes. It has pillars of iron and walls of brass. Why should we be afraid of some flood drowning us?"

Brother and sister could do nothing but go home and pick out a huge gourd. They sawed off the top to make a cover so they could hide inside when the flood came.

That year, the sun, which ordinarily hung high up in the sky, seemed to be much lower and closer to the earth. Its golden rays disappeared, and it was more like a burning, fiery ball, rolling across the sky. For seventy-seven days, there was not a breath of wind stirring, nor did a single drop of rain fall for ninety-nine days. The earth was so scorched, it gave off tongues of fire. The surface of the earth eventually cracked, forming vast, deep crevices. Then the underground water at the bottom of the crevices dried up, leaving a layer of burnt, dried moss. The tree leaves withered away, and the branches in the once dense forest looked bald. People felt like they were being steamed in a pot, unable to distinguish their tears from their sweat. Their dry mouths looked like fields split into endless ruts, while the skin of their tongues peeled as though they had taken poison. Everybody was as thin as a dried bamboo shoot.

Ninety-nine days and ninety-nine nights passed by. Suddenly, a mountain breeze began to blow, there was a clap of thunder and a flash of lightning, and the rain poured down as dense as a hemp forest. The water in the rivers, puffing and blowing deep breaths, began climbing the banks, ruining crops and houses, sweeping away people and cattle.

Brother and sister had hidden away in their gourd, and they floated about the world riding the surging waves. From time to time, they could hear the gourd ringing as it bumped against the bottom of heaven. On and on they floated, unable to tell from within the gourd whether it was day or night, or how much time had gone by. At long last, the crashing of the waves could no longer be heard, and the endlessly floating gourd came to a rest. Brother and sister dared not climb out. They waited for the singing of the birds. They waited, oh so quietly, for good news from two golden birds.

By and by, they heard the joyous twittering of the golden birds. "Come out quickly, you orphans!" the birds called. "The terrible flood is over. There's no need to be afraid or worried any longer. You're free to wander anywhere on this wide earth you wish, to the edge of the sky, or the corners of the sea." Brother and sister lifted off the cover of the gourd. Lo! They had floated to the top of a mountain. The flood had completely receded. The earth was quiet. They were ecstatic, yet afraid. They had escaped catastrophe, but they were the only survivors on earth. There was not even a sign of chimney smoke on the distant horizon, as far as the eye could see.

## » 4 «

## Shooting the Sun and the Moon

After the flood receded, rolling mountain ranges came back into view. But now there appeared nine suns and seven moons in the sky. They scorched the earth so severely during the day that it smoked. At night, a cold wind blew fiercely, covering the entire earth with white frost. Brother and sister were melancholy—it was as though their hearts were overshadowed by darkness, and they were frightened by this bad sign in the sky. Just then, the two lovely golden birds returned, singing happily, bearing a golden hammer and silver tongs, and speaking of a bottomless pond belonging to a dragon. "In the pond there is a reef, half of which stands above the water," they said. "Below the reef is the palace of the dragon king. On his head are nine forked horns, and his beard is seven arm lengths long. Once you have a way to get his golden bow and silver arrows, you will be able to conquer the burning suns and the freezing moons." The birds pointed out the direction to the pond, and taught the brother and sister a strategy whereby they could subdue the dragon king.

Brother and sister went to look for the dragon pond. After three days and three nights, a dark-green dragon pond came into view. They quickly found the reef, and struck it with their golden hammer, exactly as the golden birds instructed, making a long *dong-dong* sound. They struck so hard and deep that flames shot forth, and spray flew all about, causing the dragon pond to heave. The dragon king, who was sitting comfortably with his eyes closed, was jolted by this disturbance. He opened his eyes, twisted his silver-grey beard, and said in a nasal voice, "Who dares to make trouble on these premises? Drive him away fast!" The little whitefish received the command from the dragon king and left in a hurry. Enough time went by for smoking two pipes of tobacco, and still the whitefish had not come back. The *dong-dong* noise kept right on reverberating through the palace. The dragon king then sent a crucian carp to investigate what was going on. Again, like the little whitefish, once it was gone it was gone. Instead of diminishing, the deafening din grew worse. The dragon king had to send his most bellicose fish, the wolf herring, who had fins like sharp saw teeth. Once he, the dragon king's most capable assistant, was gone, he never returned either. In fact, when brother and sister saw the small whitefish, the crucian carp, and the wolf herring, each with a murderous look on his face, come roaring and howling, they gripped them with the pair of silver tongs, one at a time, and threw them onto the sandy beach.

In the end, the dragon king had to go in person. As soon as his head popped above the surface of the water, he saw a young man and woman hammering away at his reef. Furious with rage, he roared and shook his beard. "You two idiots! Were you born deaf? Are your ears stuffed with maggots and pus so you can't hear my orders?" The dragon king was all set to keep yelling, and had no idea he was the vulnerable one. Suddenly, something silvery and glittering came at his nose, pinching so hard and hurting him so much he couldn't even cry out. His thrashing about in the pond stirred up terrible waves, like water boiling in a pot. The waves crashed against the beach, knocking off chunks of land and rolling rocks all about, darkening the sky and obscuring the earth. Still, brother and sister would not loosen their grip in the least. The dragon king could not stand it any longer. He nodded deferentially, and admitted defeat. "We do not wish you any harm," said brother and sister. "We'll be glad to let you go if you will just give us your bow and arrows." The dragon king had no choice but to politely offer his golden crossbow and silver arrows.

Taking the dragon's glittering crossbow and silver arrows, brother and sister joyfully climbed the highest peak there was. Brother drew the bow, and sister set the arrows. Together, they shot down eight suns, one after the other, leaving the brightest. Then, they shot down six moons, again leaving behind the brightest. After that, gentle breezes blew, and withered trees turned green again. The earth returned to what it had been before.

## » 5 «

# Brother and Sister Become a Couple

After the eight suns and six moons were shot down, there were no more calamities on the earth. But neither were there any sounds of dogs barking, nor cocks crowing, let alone any sign of people. The earth was as silent as death. Brother and sister were so sad they decided to search for people separately.

As they parted, brother worried about his sister traveling by herself in high mountains and on dangerous trails, with no one to assist her. As for sister, she was worried that her brother would have nobody to mend his clothes torn by thorn bushes in the dense woods.

Brother sighed deeply, then went north, while his sister headed south, with tears in her eyes. He searched north of the river, but did not see a soul. She went south of the river, but did not meet anyone either. On the way back, he turned downstream, while she went upstream, each hoping to find someone. In the end, they met one another. Both hung their heads, feeling despondent.

Just then, the pair of golden birds flew back. They urged these good, honest siblings to marry, since there were no other people in the world. But they refused, saying it was not proper for brother and sister, born of the same womb, to get married. They had nursed at the same breast, and drank soup out of the same cooking pot. If they became spouses, without regard for what was right, the stone axe from heaven would chop them in two, and rocks would roll down from the mountain and crush them in half.

Brother and sister were adamant.

The golden birds informed them it was the will of heaven that they should marry, and this could be proven by divining with two tortoise shells. "Try this!" urged the golden birds. "If one of the tortoise shells lands facing up after you throw it, and the other faces down, then you two can become husband and wife." Not believing that such a thing could actually happen, the brother took up the tortoise shell to divine, with his sister watching closely by his side. What do you know?—the bottom of one shell faced up, and that of the other faced down. He did this three times, and always the results were the same. Even so, brother and sister were reluctant to get married.

Then the golden birds said, "If you don't believe that divining with tortoise shells reveals the truth, use the two halves of a millstone. Each of you take one half, and let it roll down from the mountain top. If the two halves come together to make one millstone, that means you should be husband and wife."

Brother and sister could not help but follow the birds' advice. Each of them took one part of the millstone—the brother got the upper stone, while his sister got the lower stone. They climbed two steep, high mountains and let go of the two stones at the same time. When the two halves rolled to the foot of the mountain, they came together and made a single millstone. They repeated this three times, and each time the two pieces became one millstone. Still, brother and sister were determined never to marry.

Then the golden birds spoke again: "Whenever something works three times when divining, you have to accept it, whether calamity or happiness. Now sister, hold up this needle as a target. Brother, take your crossbow and shoot your arrows through the needle hole. If the three arrows pass through the needle hole one after another, three times in succession, then it shows heaven approves, and earth assents. You'll have to get married quickly and raise a family."

Brother and sister did what the golden birds told them. He raised his crossbow, and aimed at the needle hole. The three arrows all passed through the needle hole. Thus, following the will of heaven, brother and sister got married.

After they were married, they gave birth to twelve children, six sons and six daughters. These children grew up, and each made a living. The pair that went north are the Tibetans. The couple that went south are the Bai. The couple that went west are Keqin people. The pair that went east are the Han. The couple that went toward the Nu river are the Nu. The couple that stayed with their parents are we Lisu.

## NOTES

"Mubupa Kneads the Earth out of Clay" (Mubupa niedi), "The Macaques Give Birth to the Human Race" (Mihou yuhai), "The Great Flood" (Hongshui fanlan), "Shooting the Sun and the Moon" (She ri yue), and "Brother and Sister Become a Couple" (Xiongmei jiehun), included in "The Formation of Heaven, Earth, and Humankind" (Tian di ren de youlai), from Zhu (Lisu), Zuo (Yi), and Shang (Han) 1985, 1–6. Collectors and redactors: Liu Huihao (Han) and Hu Gui (Han). Area of distribution: Bijiang and Lushui counties, Nujiang Lisu Autonomous Prefecture, northwestern Yunnan.

**Mubupa.** One of the divine ancestors in Lisu mythology, a god of heaven similar to the Drung Mubengge and the Jino Amoyaobu.

**Niwadi.** A wicked divine headman, or chief, in Lisu mythology, and the source of evil in the world.

**dragon king.** Dragons and dragon kings, wondrous embodiments of divine power in minority folklore, dwell in mysterious or hidden places such as lakes, rivers, and ponds; inaccessible mountain caves; underground regions; and in the cosmos. As in Han mythology, they may be benevolent or malevolent, depending on whether they are worshipped respectfully and on whether their creaturely egos are manipulated skillfully.

# Sunbird Creates the Sun and the Moon

## MIAO MYTH

In ancient times, there was neither sun nor moon in the sky. Darkness covered the earth and it was freezing cold all year round. In order to obtain light and warmth, wise Sunbird constructed nine stone plates and transformed them into nine suns. Then he fashioned eight more stone plates and converted them into eight moons. Having completed his work, he flung the suns and moons into the sky with a mighty heave.

Suddenly, light scattered the darkness, and warmth drove off the cold. The earth became a glittering globe filled with sunlight. From then on, the nine suns and the eight moons circled round and round in the sky, one chasing the other, coming and going, never stopping for a single instant. The fiery suns began to sear the earth, withering the woods and grasslands. With the exception of one lone hemp tree, all the trees in the whole world were scorched to death.

Seeing what had happened, Sunbird chopped down the hemp tree and made a bow with its trunk and arrows with its branches. Then, summoning all his strength, he drew his bow and whish!—a volley of arrows shot toward those eight suns and seven moons in rapid fire. In the twinkling of an eye, all that could be seen were suns and moons falling down pell-mell from the sky, one after another, and shattering like golden plates and silver platters. Sensing trouble, the remaining sun and moon hurriedly hid themselves in the dark depths of the clouds, not even daring to show their faces. By and by, heaven and earth were again obscured by gloomy darkness.

Sunbird gazed up in the sky for a time, then smiled and said to himself, "It doesn't matter. Everything will be all right—if I can just find a way to get them to come out!"

At first, Sunbird sent Brindle Bull to encourage the sun and the moon. When Brindle Bull went up to the sky, he flourished his two pointed horns and stared at the sun and the moon with his big bulging eyes. "Moo!" he bellowed loudly, three times in a row. "Moo! Moo-oo! Moo-oo-oo!"

Hearing the bellowing of Brindle Bull, the sun furtively bored through the clouds and had herself a look. "A spotted bull has come up to the sky," she told the moon. "He is mooing rudely, and two sharp swords are stuck in his head. He looks fiendish. No doubt he's up to no good. Let's get out of here fast!" So they broke through the clouds and flew to the faraway horizon, where they hid.

Seeing that Brindle Bull had not come back for a very long time, Sunbird sent Flying Horse to bid the sun and the moon to come out.

Chin up, tail raised high, Flying Horse soared up to the sky and pawed the ground with his hoofs. "*Whee-nee!*" he neighed loudly three times at the sun, his mouth wide open. "*Whee-nee! Whee-nee! Wheeee-nee!*"

When the sun, who was hiding behind the horizon, heard the neighing of Flying Horse, she stuck out her head and quietly stole a glance. "Both the spotted bull and this flying horse look the same," she said to the moon. "They are fierce. Quick, let's go hide!" So they rushed to the foot of a high mountain and there securely hid themselves away.

Realizing that much time had passed, and still Flying Horse had not come back, Sunbird pondered for quite a while. Finally, he called for the cock. "You have an amiable disposition, and you're reliable at handling things," he said. "I'd like you to make a trip to the sky."

Big Rooster smiled and nodded in agreement, and flew off up high. He stood on the fleece of a cloud and made a polite bow, then he cocked his head, looking this way and that. Deploying his most ear-pleasing singing voice and wearing a smile, he crowed a mellifluous crow: "*Cock-a-doodle-doo!*"

When the sun heard this intimate sweet cry, she began climbing slowly toward the mountaintop, despite the moon's pleading that she stop. She climbed and climbed and, just as Big Rooster was crowing for the third time, she arrived at the summit.

Noticing that the cock was warm, self-effacing, and sincere, the sun was deeply moved. She turned around and addressed the moon, which still was hiding at the foot of the mountain: "Come on and meet our Big Rooster! Don't be afraid. Come out!"

The moon remained where he was, not daring to budge a step.

"If you are afraid," the sun said, "let me go first. If nothing bad happens to me, you just come along afterward and catch up!" With these words she left the mountaintop and rose up in the sky, her face beaming with a smile.

The next day, when the moon found that nothing had happened to the sun, he too ascended to the summit of the mountain, and chased after the footsteps of the sun.

And that is why the time the sun spends traveling is the day, and that spent by the moon is the night. They have been chasing after one another ever since.

To repay Big Rooster's loving kindness, the moon made a gold comb and presented it to him. Big Rooster treasured the comb so very much that he wore it on his head every day. And so it remains there on the cock's head, its teeth up and its back down, even today.

From that time on, the world has been filled with light and warmth, generation after generation.

## NOTES

"Yangque zao riyue," from *Shancha*, no. 5, 1982, 7. Storyteller: Tao Yonghua (Miao). Redactors: Tao Yonghua and Liu Derong (Han). Area of distribution: Wenshan Zhuang-Miao Autonomous Prefecture, southeastern Yunnan.

**Sunbird.** A Miao totemic ancestor and source of creation.

# Great God Gumiya

Legend tells us that many, many years ago, there was neither heaven nor earth, let alone grass, trees, or humankind. Everywhere, dark masses of clouds and fog floated about, moving to and fro in the sky. Gumiya, the giant god, and his twelve children resolved to separate heaven from earth and create all things. They got so busy running about looking for building materials that they did not rest for a second.

In those days, there was a giant rhinoceros-like beast called a li, which had the clouds and fog for its friends and companions, and which wandered about freely, happy-go-lucky, in the vast expanse of the sky.

Gumiya discovered this li, had it flayed, and used the hide to make heaven. He clothed heaven with beautiful clouds, then gouged out the two eyes of the li to make stars, which he set glimmering brightly in the sky. He turned its flesh into earth, its bones into stones, its blood into water, and its hair into every kind of flower, grass, and tree. Finally, he used the li's brain to form people, and its marrow to make myriad kinds of birds, animals, insects, and fish.

Heaven hung high up in the sky without anything to prop it up. What could be done if it should fall? The earth too was suspended beneath heaven, without support. If it should turn over, what then? Wise Gumiya thought of a way. He made four huge pillars out of the four legs of the li and had them erected on the four corners of the earth to prop up heaven. Then, he placed a great turtle under the earth to hold it up.

The turtle did not want to have any part of all this, and he longed to escape at every moment. But should he move his body the slightest bit, the whole earth would wobble. To prevent the turtle from escaping, Gumiya sent his most loyal golden cock to guard it. As soon as the turtle moved, the cock would peck at its eyes. Sometimes, the cock himself would get so weary that he closed his eyes. Then the turtle would begin to move, thus causing earthquakes. At such a moment, people would rush to scatter some rice on the earth, so as to wake up the cock.

Because of Gumiya, heaven was stabilized, and the earth stood firm. The sky was filled with lovely clouds, and there was a pair of bright, twinkling stars. People on the earth did their farm work happily. Little birds glided through the air, bees buzzed among the flowering shrubs, and yellow muntjacs ran about on the mountain slopes, while fish played in the water. How lovely this vast world really was! Gumiya and his children smiled.

But misfortune befell them! The nine sun sisters and the ten moon brothers, who had always been hostile to Gumiya, were not happy about his success. They intended to destroy all that he had achieved in creating the universe. They came together in the space between heaven and earth created by Gumiya, concentrated all their fiery energy, and emitted an intense, hot light with which they scorched the earth, and tried to destroy everything in existence.

The lovely clouds changed their hue, and the bright, shining stars lost their luster. The earth was so dry that it cracked. The crops died, while flowers, grasses, and trees all withered. The very stones melted. Even today, one can find many footprints on the large stone on Maiyinzipo Mountain, left behind by people and cattle that trod on it when it was melting. Crabs lost their heads, fish their tongues, snakes their feet, and the frogs their tails, all because of that burning heat. That is why today crabs have no heads, fish no tongues, snakes no feet, and frogs no tails.

Now Gumiya wanted to go out, but as it was too hot, he pasted his bamboo hat with wax, and stuck it on his head to protect him from the sun.

But no sooner did he leave his house than the wax melted and dribbled down, drop by drop, into his eyes, making him jump with pain. "If I don't shoot down every last one of you suns and moons, may I no longer be known as the hero who created heaven and earth!" he vowed in a fit of anger.

Gumiya went into the forest to chop down a xinima, a green-bark tree, to make a bow, and he got akajiema, wild rattan, from Chongzibian Hill, and made a bowstring by rubbing its fibers between his palms. Then he whittled arrows out of slender, tough shoots of *alima*, arrow-leaf bamboo. After that, he daubed his arrowheads with poisonous water from the dragon pond.

Having made his bow and arrows, Gumiya stepped on the stones that were as hot as stove iron, and swam across rivers boiling hot like water in a pot. After going through all kinds of hardships and difficulties, he climbed the highest mountain peak.

The sun sisters and moon brothers felt very proud of themselves, and were showing off their skills, releasing heat and sparks over the face of the earth. Just at that moment, Gumiya had reached the top of the mountain.

He was filled with hatred and anger, and without so much as wiping the sweat from his brow, or taking a breath, he placed an arrow on the bowstring, drew his bow, and shot at one of the suns.

There was a loud noise which shook heaven and earth. The sun had been hit. It rolled down to the foot of the mountain slope, giving off sparks. The remaining eight suns and ten moons became desperate. They attacked Gumiya together, trying to burn him to death. Immediately, a second and a third arrow whizzed through the air. One after another, suns and moons were shot dead. A rain of blood poured from the sky, and made the earth much cooler. Withered crops, grasses, and trees sprang to life again. Flowers bloomed. The earth, tree leaves, flowers, and even the feet of silver pheasants all were dyed red by the blood of the suns and the moons that fell on them.

Now all that was left in the sky was one sun and one moon. Seeing that their brothers and sisters had been shot, one by one, they became afraid, turned, and fled. At that moment, Gumiya felt so tired it was as though his arms had no more strength. But his anger had not abated, and somehow he managed to shoot his eighteenth arrow at the last moon. It missed its mark, partly because he had lost his strength, and partly because the moon was fleeing so swiftly.

Though the arrow missed its mark, it brushed past the moon and scared him so much that he broke out in a cold sweat. His whole body turned cold. From then on, the moon could no longer give any warmth.

Knowing how terrible Gumiya's arrows could be, the sun and moon, having succeeded in escaping, quietly hid themselves, and dared not show their faces again.

But now the world turned dark and cold, as there was neither sun nor moon in the sky, and the earth was devoid of light and warmth. One could not tell whether it was day or night. Rivers stopped running. Tree branches no longer swayed. People had to hang their lanterns on the horns of water buffalo to plow the field. If they wanted to just step outside, they had to use a walking stick. Otherwise they would stumble. "How can I live in this darkness and cold?" Gumiya wondered. "I should try to find the sun and moon who are hiding, and get them to serve this beautiful world." And so, he sent a swallow to find out the whereabouts of the sun and the moon.

Several days passed. The swallow flew back and reported to Gumiya: "To the east, at the farthest edge of heaven and earth, there is a big stone cave in which the sun and moon have hidden themselves."

Gumiya assembled all the birds and animals together to have a meeting at which he consulted them about this matter. They all agreed with his proposal to go to the remote place, despite the hardships, and invite the sun and the moon to come out. Everyone except Aduma, the black-capped partridge, and Yijimiguli, the white-capped partridge, went on this errand. Aduma dyed his bottom red, and kidded people by humming, "I'm sick. I've got diarrhea. Look! My bottom has become red from shitting. I can't manage flying, so I'm not going!" Yijimiguli, in turn, painted his head white. He wept and wailed and told everyone, "My parents have died. I cannot leave the house because I'm still wearing mourning clothes. So, I'm not going!" Ever since then, the black-capped partridge's red bottom and the white-capped partridge's white head have become symbols of selfishness, laziness, and fear of hardship. Everybody ridicules and loathes these birds.

The contingent of birds and animals that went to fetch the sun and moon made quite a spectacle. The swallow flew before them all to serve as guide, and right after him came a big swarm of fireflies to provide light. The birds of the air were headed by the rooster, noteworthy for his eloquent speech and loud, clear voice. The beasts of the field were led by the brave boar, who has great physical strength. Gumiya did not go, for the sun was afraid of him.

By this time, the sun and moon, who had hidden themselves in the stone cave, had become wife and husband. Night and day, they worried that if they stayed in the cave too long, they would suffocate, and that without anything to eat, they would starve to death. They wanted to go out, but they feared being shot by Gumiya. As they could not figure out what to do, they just hugged one another and wept.

Just as they were worrying about all this, all of a sudden, they heard a hue and cry. They were more afraid than ever, so they squeezed closely together in the corner of the cave, not even daring to breathe.

The welcoming crew of birds and beasts came to the entrance of the cave with everybody talking, shouting, and entreating at the same time. But all was quiet in the cave, nothing was stirring. The rooster asked everyone to be silent. He fluffed out his beautiful feathers, stretched his neck, and crowed:

> Bright sun
> beautiful moon
> please come quickly forth.
> How about some heat and light!

How sincere, kind, beautiful, and pleasing to the ear was the rooster's crow! The sun and moon felt somewhat relieved. They replied to the rooster's appeal:

> Suffocate and starve we'd rather
> than face Gumiya in a lather!
> Even if we should appear
> no one would feed us, we fear.

The birds and animals all sang in chorus:

> 'Twas Gumiya's wish to seek you out
> he'll never shoot, so never pout.
> Your servant will be his daughter
> she'll bring you breakfast, lunch, and supper!

The sun and moon did not dare to show their faces, for they did not believe that Gumiya would forgive them. The rooster and his companions said many fine words, but it was of no use. Finally, the rooster assured the sun and the moon like this: "From now on, come out when I call you. If I don't crow, don't come out. This way, there won't be any danger." In order to remove their suspicion, the rooster cut a knot into two halves, one of which he threw to the sun and the moon in the cave. He carried the other half on his head. That's why today, the rooster has a comb. From that time on, roosters have taken on the duty of waking up the sun. If any rooster ever fails to perform its duty, people will kill it. Gumishafema, Gumiya's daughter, became responsible for feeding the sun and the moon. She transformed three times a day. In the morning, she was a beautiful girl. At noon, she changed into a lovely, sturdy young wife, and in the evening, she became an old woman with white hair. She never stopped for a single day feeding the sun with gold juice, and the moon with silver juice.

At last, following the instructions of Gumiya, the birds and animals requested the sun to come out by day, and the moon at night. In the evening of the first and last days of the month, they were allowed to meet in the stone cave. As the sun was a young wife, timid and nervous, and afraid of the dark, she was asked to turn up during the day. But she was so shy about being seen that the moon sent her a set of embroidery needles, telling her that if anybody looked at her when she appeared, she could prick his or her eyes with the needles.

Everything was agreed upon, and the sun and the moon were about to come out. But it happened that the mouth of the cave was tightly blocked by a big stone. The animals and birds set to work to move it. They tried to carry the stone, lift it up, and push it, but no matter what they did, the stone wouldn't budge. Then the boar came up, waving his ears, saying, "Everybody step aside. Let me have a try." Using all his strength, and giving the big stone a mighty shove with his snout, he succeeded in pushing it aside.

The sun and the moon came out at last. Day and night were clearly marked. Now the earth had heat. When the sun shone on the mountain slope, animals started running about. When its rays touched the forest, the birds began to sing. When it reached the rivers, the fish came out to swim. When the sun shone upon old men, they came out to repair their plows. When it shone upon old women, they came out to weave. When it shone upon young men, they went to labor in the fields. When it shone shone upon young girls, they went up the mountains to gather firewood. When it shone upon little children, they put cattle out to pasture.

At night, when the bright moon came out and shone upon the old people, they happily began telling stories. As the moon shone upon the children, they had fun playing games. As it shone upon the young people, they would pair off and make music, playing the touching *bawu* flute and the melodious two-stringed *maqie*.

Once again, the earth was full of life, joy, and hope. And this lovely world became even more lovely.

## NOTES

"Gumiya," from Wang 1979, 159–67. Collector and redactor: Zhu Jialu (Han). Area of distribution: Sipsong Panna Dai Autonomous Prefecture, southern Yunnan.

**li.** A mythical animal analogous to the rhinoceros.
**pair of stars.** At the beginning of creation, according to Blang belief, there were two stars. More appeared in time.
**muntjac.** A small deer found in the East Indies and Southeast Asia.
**Maiyinzipo.** Place name in Jinping County, Yunnan, near Sha Yi Po Village. On a nearby slope there is a large stone with holes that look like the tracks of animals and humans.
**knot cut in two.** According to Blang custom, when two sides in a dispute reach an agreement, a knot is cut in half. Each party keeps a half.

# WHY PEOPLE DO
# WHAT THEY DO

# The Origin of
# the Sixth Month Sacrifice

## BUYI LEGEND

In the mountainous region of Pingtan, there is a river that suddenly rises and falls. It has a local name, Luoyu He, "Rainwater Creek." Not far from its bank stands a giant rock, weirdly shaped, which from a distance looks like some old gaffer. People in the area call it Prince of Heaven Rock. In the old society, every year on the sixth day of the sixth month of the lunar calendar, the local Buyi people would go there to burn incense and offer wine and sacrifices to the gods in heaven, to ask for their blessings. Today, the people of that area still tell a beautiful story concerning the origin of this giant rock.

During the ancient period of the great flood, the gods of heaven, human beings on earth, and the demons of hell could intermarry. In those days, in the stockaded village of Bangao there was a nice, cool well that led to an underground, twelve-story dragon palace.

One day, Liuliu, a hardworking young man, went to the pool beside the well to wash vegetables, and he discovered a big white shrimp swimming in the water. He took her home and put her in a water vat to keep her. That same evening, he dreamed a lovely dream in which the goddess of the moon came floating down to earth, looking for her missing moon princess.

Early the next morning, Liuliu woke up and hiked up the mountain to till the soil, just as he always did, a hoe on his shoulder. But all the while he worked, he was remembering the scene in his dream the previous night, until finally he decided to stop weeding and return home early. To his surprise, what should he find but a beautiful maiden cooking dinner for him. When the girl saw Liuliu, she was both startled and delighted, and she lowered her head, blushing.

"Oh, my!" said Liuliu, walking up to her. "Could this be a dream, or is it real? Who are you?"

"Didn't you see my mother looking for me in your dream last night?"

"Ah! Then you are the moon princess!"

Indeed it was true. This beautiful girl was the sixth daughter of the goddess of the moon. She had transformed herself into a big white shrimp to pay a visit to her maternal grandfather, the dragon king, at the dragon palace. On her way back home, she passed through the surface of the earth, and noticed that the sixth month crops were just beginning to bud, but were suffering from a drought. Yet, despite the scorching heat, valiant Liuliu was still out working in the fields. The very sight of him laboring there made her fall deeply in love.

After being married just one year, the moon princess gave birth to an amazing son. He could say "Mama" three days after he was born, walk at seven days, and herd sheep at ten. The boy was ever so much brighter than any other child, so the old people in the neighborhood gave him a nickname, Tian Wang, meaning "Prince of Heaven."

News about this family spread, and when the king learned that among his own people there was a lovely moon princess who excelled all the beauties in the imperial city, he wanted to have her for his very own ninth wife. He ordered his minister to lead a troop of warriors, and take the moon princess by force. When she was about to be parted from Tian Wang, she told him, "My son, you and your father don't need to feel sad about losing me. From now on, whenever you have any difficulty, just go find me on the moon!"

"But dear Mama," Tian Wang cried. "I don't know how to get to heaven!"

"So long as you are honest in your relations with others, someone will point out the way."

Liuliu came home after cutting firewood that day, and was unable to find his wife. When he discovered she had been seized by the king, he was heartbroken. He made a promise to himself and told Tian Wang,

"My son, the king took away your mother. You see that the present world is unjust and good people suffer oppression. I'm going to go and settle accounts with the king. I'm going to find your mother, even if I have to go up to heaven!"

Liuliu left home, seeking his wife. As he came to Rainwater Creek, he encountered a hoary-headed old man. "Grandpa, did you see my wife pass this way?" he asked.

"I wouldn't know who your wife is," the old man said, "but I did notice several people pushing a woman up to the river. She stooped down to scoop up some water with her hands for a drink, then spat out a mouthful. The mouthful of water turned into a rainbow and, all at once, the river rose rapidly, and those men who were there were all swept into a whirlpool. The woman mounted the rainbow, and off she flew!"

"Ah, that's my moon princess!"

"If that woman really was your wife, you ought to go find the streamer she left behind on the river bank. With that in hand, you could make your way to heaven too."

"Many thanks, Grandpa, many thanks!"

Once his father was gone, Tian Wang went on raising crops all by himself, even though he was young. The uplands he planted lacked water, yet his harvest was bigger than that reaped on the plains below.

At that time there was a local official in Bangao by the name of Ransu, the king's flunky. He longed to seize Tian Wang's abundant harvest, so he caught him at the village well, just when Tian Wang's hands were busy lifting water, covered him with a huge iron pot, and sunk him to the bottom of the well.

Strangely, a few days later, people saw Tian Wang bathing in Wai Weng Pool at the base of Bangao Village. Hearing this, Ransu gave another order—this time his men were to bind up Tian Wang and tie him to a big stone next to Gajin Pool, and leave him there for a tiger to eat during the night.

But after a few more days, Tian Wang was seen again, this time helping someone weed their rice paddy below Rainwater Village. Again, Ransu sent his men and had Tian Wang tied to a big fir tree.

"My poor brothers," Tian Wang said to the men, "what's the use of tying me?"

Indeed, what had happened each time passed through everyone's mind: Ransu had Tian Wang sunk to the bottom of the well, yet he escaped; then he left him to be chewed up by a tiger, but that never took place. To these poor men, there seemed no point in binding him yet once more. Wouldn't it be better to set him free and be done with it?

"Save me now," Tian Wang said, "and someday, when I'm in heaven, I'll cause locusts to eat the crops and make moths gnaw the clothes of the wicked. Mark the fields of the good, and I'll protect them from the locusts. Take your clothes and dry them in your courtyards. I won't let them be eaten by the moths."

As soon as some of the brothers had released Tian Wang, he made a huge leap, jumping forward some seven or eight yards, and immediately transformed into an old man. An instant later, the old man became a puff of black smoke ascending into the sky.

Later on, in the place where Tian Wang ascended, there appeared a giant stone, shaped like a man. The local people said it was the incarnation of Tian Wang.

Once Tian Wang reached heaven, he told his mother, the moon princess, all about the injustices on the earth. She was in charge of the weather during the sixth month. After she heard from her son, how she made people suffer every year at that time! She would send either a torrential rain or a drought. Insect plagues became more and more frequent and crops withered with each passing day. It was then that people called to mind Tian Wang's words. They hastily gathered their money together, bought a pig, and sacrificed it before the giant stone as an offering to Tian Wang, the prince of heaven, begging him to drive off the locusts, grant favorable weather, and bless them with abundant harvests.

Gradually, this activity became a widespread custom, and many villagers would come on the sixth day of the sixth month of the lunar calendar, the day of Tian Wang's ascension, to offer him sacrifices in front of the giant stone, asking that he wipe out all calamities. At this time, every household would sun clothing to prevent moths from eating it, and young men would cherish the hope that they too might find a lovely "white shrimp" girl, as Liuliu did, and sing beautiful love songs with her on the banks of Rainwater Creek.

Today, people in certain Buyi areas still hold a grand Sixth Day of the Sixth Month ceremony. They say the festival is held in memory of Moon Princess and Tian Wang for blessing the Buyi.

## NOTE

"Liuyueliu de laili," from Xu Hualong (Han) and Wu (Han) 1985, 135–41. Storytellers: Cen Laoliang (Buyi) and Luo Shiyuan (Buyi). Collector: Yang Luta (Han). Redactors: Cen Yuqing (Buyi) and Yang Luta. Area of distribution: northeastern Yunnan.

# The Ancestors of Dai Singers

## DAI LEGEND

In Mengbanaxi, "the mysterious, happy land," the following story is passed along.

Many years ago, the Dai people, men and women, old and young alike, were fond of going to the Buddhist temple to listen to a living Buddha chant the sutras. Legend tells us that this living Buddha was named Pazhao, and that he was the first monk to come to this land.

One day, a stranger by the name of Payaman came to Mengbanaxi. He did not believe in any religion, but was skilled in singing, and sang moving songs. He wanted to have a competition with the living Buddha to see what the people liked better—listening to his own singing, or listening to the chanting of the living Buddha.

Payaman's singing at the contest was just too marvelous. His voice was now soft and light as a murmuring brook, and now exhilarating as the tempestuous soughing of the wind in the pines. The flowers all bloomed as he sang; the birds alighted on the ground around him, listening quietly. The people, men and women, old and young, all were drawn by his songs. They admired him greatly and longed to see what he really looked like. As there were too many people who wanted to get a look at him, Payaman felt so embarrassed that he had to hide his face with a fan while he sang. Hence, the Dai *zanha* singer has the custom of using a fan to cover his or her face.

Pazhao, the living Buddha, felt very angry because his sutra chanting was no match for Payaman's singing. He threatened the people, saying that anyone who learned to sing from Payaman would be punished. That man or woman would be made to sing from dawn to dusk, without a rest, and the descendants of such a person would have to do the same. In addition, that person would never live a happy life while on this earth, and after death, he or she wouldn't go anywhere, neither to hell nor to heaven.

Despite Pazhao's threats, there were still many people who learned singing from Payaman. Later, he was honored with the title "ancestor of the *zanha*."

## NOTES

"Zanha de shizu," from *Daizu minjian gushi* 1984, 327–28. Storyteller: Bo'aiwen (Dai). Translator and redactor: Chen Guipei (Han). Area of distribution: Sipsong Panna Dai Autonomous Prefecture, southern Yunnan. The late Chen Guipei was a famous translator of Dai stories into Chinese.

**Mengbanaxi.** Han transliteration of the ancient name of Sipsong Panna, in southern Yunnan.

# The Water-Splashing Festival

## DAI LEGEND

During the Water-Splashing Festival, celebrated every year in the spring, people splash water on whomsoever they like.

This is an old custom popular wherever the Dai people are found. When the day for the festival comes around, people sprinkle one another, revealing their good will and mutual respect. But why do they use water? Well, it's not because the weather is hot, or the streets are dusty, as one might think. To explain this practice, let's go back to its beginning.

Way back in the distant past, there lived a fierce, cruel prince of the devils, who had at his command marvelous magical powers, and great natural abilities. Water wouldn't drown him, fire couldn't burn him, and don't imagine that an arrow, a two-edged sword, a broad knife, or a spear could harm him in the least. He lorded over his territory and felt free to run rampant, killing anyone he wished and doing whatever he liked. Often, he went looting, right out in the open—grabbing up gold, silver, and precious objects, taking slaves and seizing beautiful women. He was a scourge, yet no one dared to go against any of his wishes.

At the time of our story, already he had forced eleven women to be his wives, each of them lovelier than the previous one. All of them hated him with a passion, and wished they could destroy this evil prince of the devils, but they were helpless. He made off with still another maiden, and she became his twelfth wife. This girl was not just exceedingly pretty—she was extraordinarily bright besides, and that's how she came to be the prince's favorite. Now she loathed the prince just as bitterly as the other wives, but she kept her composure, hiding her true emotions and intentions, and keeping on intimate terms.

One night, taking advantage of just the right moment when the prince was in high spirits, she probed him with flattery. "Great Prince, I hear it said that you are so naturally well endowed that neither water nor fire, no two-edged sword or broad knife, can harm you. What a blessing, what a joy it would be, to live forever in this world, just like you!"

"But I have my weakness, too," the prince of devils allowed. On hearing the girl's sweet, honeyed words, he felt so elated that he forgot himself, accidentally letting out this revelation.

"But you are so naturally gifted—what in the world would you ever have to fear?" Seizing her opportunity, the girl probed a step further.

"There is something . . ." He hesitated, then went on. "I'm telling only you. Nobody else. Keep this absolutely private!" The prince came close to her ear and whispered softly, "There is just one way in all the world that I can be killed. Someone would have to pluck a hair from my head and use it to strap down my neck."

The twelfth wife was ecstatic to learn this secret, though she did not reveal her feelings. Yet, she could hardly believe the prince of the devils was telling the truth. She bided her time, and before long, the prince dozed off. Ever so gently, she plucked one hair from his head, then tried using it to strap down his neck. As soon as she applied the hair to his neck, his head tumbled down with a thud! And that was the end of the prince of the devils.

On hearing of his death, the eleven wives he had forced into marriage, and the common people as well, went wild with joy. From that time on, no woman would be violated or oppressed, and the people could live freely and happily.

Now the twelve wives decided they wanted to destroy the head. They tried burning it, but as soon as fire touched its skin, raging flames flew all about. They buried it in the earth, but a horrible stench came out of the ground. Then they cast it out into the river, but the river boiled up at once, causing a great flood. No matter what they did with the head, their action led to some earthly disaster. Finally, all the twelve wives could think of doing was to take turns passing the head from one woman to the next, holding the heavy thing against their breasts. In this manner, though they suffered a little for it, they prevented calamities from happening on the earth. Every day, one woman passed the head along to another. And each time the head was transferred, the blood that the prince of devil's head left on clothing had to be washed away.

To show their gratitude to the twelve women who had eliminated this scourge from the earth, the Dai people helped them splash water on their clothes to wash out the blood. As one day in heaven is equivalent to one year on earth, so every year the Dai chose the seventh day after the Pure Brightness Festival to splash water on the women. In later times, this day came to be celebrated as the Water-Splashing Festival, and has been passed down from generation to generation, until now.

## NOTES

"Poshui jie," from Xu Hualong (Han) and Wu (Han) 1985, 82–83. Collector and redactor: Zhang Gongjin. Area of distribution: Sipsong Panna Dai Autonomous Prefecture, southern Yunnan.

**Pure Brightness (Qing Ming) Festival.** The time of annual spring visits to the graves of ancestors, observed by the Han.

# Why Sui People Live in Two-Story Wooden Loft-Houses

## SUI LEGEND

We have heard our elders say that the houses the Sui people had in the past had earthen walls and slate roofs. Wood was rarely used. Why is it that, in later times, the Sui all prefer to live in houses made of wood? There is a legend that explains the reason, which goes like this:

Long, long ago, right alongside our Moon Mountain, there once was a towering mountain called Sun Mountain, even higher than Moon Mountain. It was so tall you could not even see its crest, and never had there been anyone who made it to the top.

At the foot of this Sun Mountain was a stockaded village where a man called Venerable Xiang lived with his wife, Ya. They both were old, and their sons and daughters-in-law had died young, leaving behind two grandchildren who had barely reached the age of reason. At first, people helped the family get along by giving them handouts, but as the days went by, Grandpa Xiang did not feel like being a burden on everybody any longer. So he and his wife, together with their grandchildren, quietly left the village and moved to the foot of the slopes of Sun Mountain, where they erected a low, thatched shed, and just barely got by, their bellies always half-empty, and themselves ever close to starvation.

One day, just at dusk, there was a heavy downpour, and when it was over, a beautiful rainbow appeared above Sun Mountain. Much delighted by the sight, Grandpa Xiang climbed the mountain to pick bamboo shoots, bearing a bamboo basket on his back, and all the while facing the rainbow as he went.

Just as he crossed the mountain pass, he caught a glimpse of a fierce-looking, hungry eagle clutching a tiny red snake in its talons, and about to soar off gaily into the sky with its prey. The poor snake was wriggling and squirming pitifully, trying to escape. Grandpa Xiang simply could not bear the sight, and he let out a mighty roar and flung his basket at the eagle. Startled by this sudden attack, the ferocious eagle flew off, dropping the snake in its haste to get away.

As Grandpa Xiang walked forward, wanting to see how seriously the little red snake was hurt, a dazzling red light suddenly flashed before his eyes, and then a column of black smoke could be seen slowly floating up Sun Mountain. The snake had disappeared, right before his eyes.

After returning home, Grandpa Xiang told Grandma Ya all about what had happened. Both of them were awestruck, not knowing whether good or ill fortune would come from this event. They made guesses and tried to figure it out for quite some time, but to no avail, and ended up drifting off to sleep.

That same night, Grandpa Xiang dreamed a strange dream in which a resplendent golden dragon, majestic and huge, spoke to him: "Venerable Grandpa Xiang. Many thanks to you for saving my daughter's life! Early tomorrow morning, please cross three mountain passes and climb up a long slope to come to my home. I will do my best to return your kindness."

Grandpa Xiang woke up with a start and told Grandma Ya his dream. Who would have expected it, but she clapped her hands and cried, "I too had a dream, exactly like yours!" Early the next morning, the two of them set out, together with their grandchildren, full of expectations as to what was in store for them.

They crossed three mountain passes and hiked up a long slope, according to the route indicated to them by the dragon in the dream. By then, it was already noontime, and they were so weary that their backs ached, their legs were sore, and they were gasping for breath.

They waited and waited, but it was quiet all around, and except for a deep-green bamboo grove nearby, there was nothing in sight. Just as they were beginning to regret coming, a sweet scent wafted in their direction, immediately followed by the appearance of a beautiful, phoenixlike girl coming from the depths of the bamboo grove. Smiling delightedly, she came up and saluted Grandpa Xiang and Grandma Ya.

She told them that two days earlier, she had gone out, entranced by the rainbow, when Venerable Xiang rescued her from being snatched away by the ferocious eagle. After she finished telling her story, she knelt down before them again, bowing respectfully to express her gratitude.

Grandpa Xiang and Grandma Ya quickly helped her stand up and asked where she lived, and why she had come so deep in the mountains all alone.

This lovely girl just smiled without saying anything, and led them through the bamboo grove.

Ah! Once out of the grove, their eyes suddenly brightened. Amidst clumps of flowers, with bees buzzing and butterflies fluttering about, there was a deep pond with crystal-clear water making blue ripples. When they approached nearer to have a look, they saw that the whole pond was full of red carp, big and fat, gliding about to and fro, and wagging their tails. How they were enjoying their carefree lives!

Grandpa Xiang and Grandma Ya were so lost in amazement that they did not notice the abrupt disappearance of the girl from their side. They heard what sounded like voices singing to them across the surface of the water: "Dear old couple, do please settle down here. You may catch fish in the pond when hungry, and drink the water when thirsty. When it is cold you can put up a house amidst the springlike warmth of the bamboo grove."

The two grandparents talked the matter over and decided to settle down there, as the girl bade them, since if they went back home they would not have enough to eat, or clothes to keep them warm.

Grandpa Xiang and Grandma Ya, together with their grandchildren, began to live by the pond. Before long, they discovered a strange thing: the fish caught there tasted sweet after they were cooked. Upon closer investigation, they discovered that the bees of the area built their hives on the rocks above the pond, and the honey they made often fell, pitter-patter, drop by drop, into the water.

After eating the sweet fish for a month or two, Grandpa Xiang and Grandma Ya found their vision becoming sharper and sharper, and their white hair turning shiny black. The wrinkles on their faces even disappeared, and they became young again. The two grandchildren also changed. The grandson grew tall and sturdy, while the granddaughter turned into a slim, delicate-looking beauty. They were all beside themselves with joy!

One year passed by quickly. One day, Grandpa Xiang wanted to go back to the village where he formerly had lived, to pay a visit to his old fellow villagers. When he reached the village, a string of fish in his hand, he was shocked. The houses all had become rundown and cheerless. The village people were equally surprised to see him, thinking that this feeble old couple and their sick grandchildren would have died long ago. Never would they have imagined that Venerable Xiang could be so young and robust looking.

As for Grandpa Xiang, he found that everyone in the village looked pale and emaciated, nothing but bags of bones. He felt so sorry for them, and told them all about the wonderful things that had happened to him, inviting them to come up Sun Mountain with him.

On hearing what he had to say, the people in the village were ecstatic. They led their children and followed Grandpa Xiang up Sun Mountain, where they all settled down.

Up on the mountain, everyone lived happily for quite some time. But then, an evil man appeared among them. He was crazy about fishing. When he had caught more fish than he could eat, he just threw them away. Worse still, he often shit in the pond and peed there too. As a result, the fish population went down and down. Grandpa Xiang and the other villagers tried to admonish him, but he would not listen. On the contrary, he showed off his muscles and lorded over everyone, even forbidding Grandpa Xiang to fish in the pond. And so, the Xiang family found it more and more difficult to make a living. They often thought of the good-hearted dragon's daughter and secretly shed tears, thinking it was they who had brought misfortune to Sun Mountain.

Seeing that the fish were becoming fewer and harder to catch, the evil man made up his mind to poison them all.

He had ten shoulder-pole loads of poisonous herbs dumped into the pond, making the fish thrash about in the water. Before long, dead fish floated to the surface, belly up, a vast, shiny sheet of white.

When Grandpa Xiang saw this scene, he began sobbing bitterly beside the pond. Unexpectedly, the evil man took a fish head and flung it alongside Grandpa Xiang, jeering, "Since you feel so sorry over this waste, have a fish head to gnaw on!" With that, he lifted two buckets of dead fish on a shoulder pole and was off.

Grandpa Xiang picked up the fish head, and his teardrops trickled down. "Oh, fish! Fish!" he exclaimed. "I am the one who caused your death!"

Just at that moment, the fish's mouth began to quiver, giving Grandpa Xiang a fright, but he listened closely to the sound it made. Ah! It was the voice of the dragon's daughter: "Please don't feel sad, Venerable Grandpa Xiang. I'm not blaming you. There is just one thing I would ask you to do. Go and find some corn flour and make me a body. Feed me every day with dew from scented flowers. After eighty-one days, I will come back to life. For the next few days, go find wood to build yourself a house. You cannot live in that stone house any longer."

Grandpa Xiang listened and made up his mind to do just what the dragon's daughter had told him. With the help of his grandson and granddaughter, who by then had grown up, he cut wood every day to build his house. At the same time, he looked for flower dew to feed the fish. Other villagers were also busy at work building wooden houses—all except the evil man, who did nothing but complain that everybody else was crazy.

On the eighty-first day, a fierce gale suddenly blew, carrying sand and driving stones, while lightning flashed and thunder pealed. The sky was so dark and frightening that it looked as if it would collapse on top of the earth.

In Grandpa Xiang's house, the fish gave her corn-flour body a shake and changed into a bouncing, lively, big goldfish. With another shake she turned into a beautiful girl. She seemed to be saying something, and before long, a golden dragon flew from afar. It was none other than the very same dragon that had spoken to Grandpa Xiang in his dream.

Now the girl transformed herself into a red snake, and flew to the side of the dragon. Grandpa Xiang could hear her speaking in the sky: "Venerable Grandpa Xiang! Venerable Grandma Ya! Please move all your things into your new wooden house, close the door, and don't come out!"

Hardly had she finished speaking than a great roar was heard in the sky, and down poured pelting rain, covering the ground in the twinkling of an eye. Everywhere, there was a vast flood. Trapped inside his room in his stone house, all the evil man could do was watch helplessly as the flood rapidly rose to the windows, beams, and roof. The wooden houses of Grandpa Xiang and the other villagers were not flooded, for they floated as the waters rose.

At this moment, that golden dragon, his eyes wide open, shook his body violently. Instantly, *ka-wump!* came the rumbling peals of earth-shaking thunder. Sun Mountain cleaved in two, its upper half erupted into the sky, and the body of the evil man was buried below by a shower of falling stones.

At the end of this punishment sent by heaven, Grandpa Xiang and the other villagers floated peacefully down the mountain inside their wooden houses. In memory of the girl who had saved their lives, they carved a giant stone fish. Today, anyone who drives a car from the town of Shuilong [Water Dragon] in Sandu County to the town of Zhoutan will certainly see on the roadside a statue about sixty feet high which is the clay figure of the dragon's daughter. Not far from the statue is the lower part of a great mountain, the upper part of which seems to have been neatly cut off with a sword. This is the remaining half of Sun Mountain. The other half, as the old folks say, was flung to the scenic area of Huaxi, near Guiyang, the capital of Guizhou Province, where there is much slabstone. From that time on, the Sui people have been especially fond of wooden houses, and from generation to generation they have been living in them peacefully.

## NOTES

"Shuizu weishenma zhu mulou," from Xu Hualong (Han) and Wu (Han) 1985, 213–17. Storytellers: Wei Yurong (Sui) and Pan Zhifa (Han). Collector and redactor: Wang Yujian (Han). Area of distribution: Jiuqian Cooperative, Sandu Sui Autonomous County, southern Guizhou Province.

**stockaded village (zhaizi).** A village surrounded by a protective fence or hedge made of thorns, sharpened bamboo, or wood stakes.

# The Torch Festival

YI LEGEND

Once there were two men of enormous strength, Sireabi and Atilaba. The former lived in heaven, the latter lived on the earth. Both were as strong as mountains, and no one could throw them when wrestling. When Sireabi heard that Atilaba was the strongest man on earth and a highly skilled wrestler, he descended from heaven to have a match with him. It just so happened that at the time Sireabi arrived, Atilaba was away from home on business. Before he left his house, Atilaba told his mother, "When the strong man from heaven, Sireabi, comes to call, please entertain him with a dish of iron lumps. Tell him this is what I eat every day, and invite him to have a taste. Let him wait in the house for me. I will be back soon to wrestle." And off went Atilaba.

After a while, Sireabi came to Atilaba's home, and his mother entertained Sireabi with a dish of iron lumps, as she had been directed by her son. Sireabi bit down hard as he could—now how was he going to chew that? Then he thought, "If Atilaba can eat iron lumps, he must be stronger than me!" Sireabi took off without waiting around for Atilaba.

After Atilaba returned home, his mother told him what had happened. When he learned that Sireabi could not chew iron lumps, he knew for certain that Sireabi's strength could not be greater than his. So he ran out of the house to chase after him. Just as Sireabi was about to step into heaven, he was overtaken by Atilaba.

"Wait, Sireabi! You came down from heaven to wrestle. So let's have a match and see just who is best!"

Sireabi spread out his arms and wrapped them around Atilaba right then and there, and the two strong men started having at it. So great was their combined strength that the earth quaked, making a loud crack. Trees and mountain peaks trembled violently. Gripping Atilaba tightly in his arms, Sireabi gave a sudden jerk and threw him toward the ground, with himself on top of Atilaba. But before Atilaba's back touched the ground, he made a quick flip, like the wheeling of a sparrow hawk, and rolled the two of them over, so that he came out on top of Sireabi, and he pressed him down. This time, Sireabi's back did touch the ground. Even so, Sireabi would not admit defeat, and he demanded another round.

Atilaba took the "riding a horse stance." No matter how hard Sireabi tried to tumble him, Atilaba remained unmovable, as though his two feet had taken root in the ground. Catching Sireabi at a moment when he was off guard, Atilaba grabbed hold of an arm and jerked him with tremendous force, throwing him more than fifteen feet. Sireabi lay on the ground, his mouth shut tight. Walking up to have a look, Atilaba found blood flowing from Sireabi's nostrils and mouth. He lay in a pool of blood, dead.

Atilaba went back home. The pusa in heaven never expected such a thing to happen to their heavenly champion. When these buddhas heard that Sireabi had died in a wrestling match, they were enraged. As they could not find any way to deal with Atilaba, they sent a horde of locusts and moths to eat the crops on the earth.

On the night of the twenty-fourth day of the sixth month of the lunar calendar, Atilaba cut down many pine trees, and led the villagers to make torches and burn the destructive insects. Using fire, they got rid of all the locusts and moths sent by the heavenly pusa, and protected their crops. From that time on, the Yi people fixed the date of the twenty-fourth day of the sixth month (in some places, the twenty-fifth day) as their Torch Festival.

## NOTES

"Huoba jie," from Xu Hualong (Han) and Wu (Han) 1985, 149–50. Collector and redactor: Li Qiao (Yi). Area of distribution: Lunan Yi Autonomous County, southeast of Kunming. Li Qiao is a well-known Yunnan author, and chair of the Yunnan Writers' Association.

**pusa.** Popular name for buddhas and bodhisattvas.

# HEROES AND HEROINES

## OF THE PEOPLE

# A Blang Youth

## BLANG MYTH

On the southern bank of the Yuan River in the southern part of Yunnan, there once were located some twenty households of Blang people in a stretch of dense, big pine trees, in a village called Manyuanpo. At the roadside near the upper end of this village, there is a big stone about three zhang high, which stands tall and erect at the foot of a large stretch of old pines. The dark pine forest in the background makes the stone, which is itself black, look even darker. In former days, when local people passed by this place, they dared not speak, fearing their voices would make the stone god angry, and thus bring them misfortune.

Where did this strange stone come from?

Long, long ago, in the dead of the night, a great wind began to blow in this area. Sand and stones obliterated the sky and covered the earth. Pine trees as thick as a man's thigh snapped in half, broken off by the fierce gale. The howling wind, which rent the heavens and shook the earth, awoke the people of Manyuanpo Village. Everybody was terrified, and no one dared to get up and see what was happening.

At this time, there was a Blang youth by the name of Mixi. This fifteen-year-old boy was not the least bit afraid. He dressed, picked up a three-point spear, and climbed on the roof of his sod house to see what was the matter.

Suddenly, he heard a rumbling sound from the slope behind the village. It sounded like big stones rolling or branches breaking. The sound came nearer and nearer, and got louder and louder. The boy held the three-point spear tightly in his hand, hurried down the sod roof, and ran toward the road at the upper end of the village. The wind hit him full in the face, and the pain felt like he was being cut by a knife. He used his sleeves to brush away the sand that blew into his eyes. After a while, the sound was like thunder, coming nearer and nearer. In the dim moonlight in the pine woods, he made out two huge black monsters running like the wind in his direction, bringing armloads of sand and stone, and breaking off trees by the roadside. The sight gave Mixi a start, but he got control of his panic, calmed himself, jumped into a grove by the roadside, and hid. As these two monsters were approaching, the first knocked down the top of a pine tree, hitting Mixi squarely on the back.

At this critical moment, the first monster suddenly came to a halt, as if he noticed something in front of him. As soon as he stopped advancing, the second one did the same. Mixi fixed his eyes on these two monsters. Now he was able to see clearly that they were nothing but two big stones. They began speaking.

The one in back asked the one in front, "Why don't you hurry on?"

"Ai-ya!" replied the other, much alarmed, "I forgot to lock our door." Then turning around, he said to the one behind him, "Wait here for me. I'll be back as soon as I've locked up."

"You'll have to hurry up. Stones from far and near are waiting for us by the river. As soon as we arrive, we're going to dam up the water. Then the houses and land in this area will be flooded, and all of loathsome humankind will be drowned!" He burst into peals of laughter, feeling well pleased with himself. Then he spoke seriously, in a soft voice, "Dear wife, hurry up, or our time will be up. Once the cocks crow at the break of day, we will not be able to go on!" The bigger stone nodded its head and began dashing up the slope of the mountain. Again the sound the stone made was like spring thunder.

Now Mixi pondered what could be done to stop the stones from damming the river, drowning people, and flooding houses and crops. As he was thinking, he made his way softly through the forest, and took a detour back home. He removed the bamboo cover from his cooking pot, and carried it up to the roof of his sod house. He gave a few taps to the bamboo cover, and began to crow like a rooster several times: "Cock-a-doodle-doo . . ."

The cocks in the village were awakened from their dreams. They thought this might be one of their own companions crowing, and that it was already dawn. So they all began to crow, one after another. All the cocks in the villages were crowing, far and near.

When the stone that was waiting heard the cocks crow, he thought it was daybreak, so he stood still at the end of the road with his head bowed, not daring to move. The big stone that went back to lock her door heard the cocks' crowing too. She was so frightened that she dared not leave home.

When dawn really came, a red sun rose in the east. Now Mixi took the villagers to see this strange big stone. After hearing what had happened the night before, the old people discovered that this was, in fact, a male stone. He was the head of stones on Guanyin Mountain, and the one who went back to lock the door was his wife, a female stone. As they were jealous of humankind's happy life, they led all the stones from the surrounding mountains to dam the water in the river, and thus drown the people. That female stone, about seven to eight *zhang* high, is still standing on Guanyin Mountain near Sanhezhai Village. Because of its solemn and sublime appearance, people have given it the honorary name Lion Mountain.

Today, these two ferocious, strange stones can still be seen towering high, looking like tamed giants. The courageous, resourceful Blang youth who protected the life and property of all of us with his wisdom will always be honored and beloved by the people.

## NOTES

"Bulang shaonian," from *Yunnan minzu minjian gushi xuan* 1982, 514–16. Collector and redactor: Pu Yang (Yi). Area of distribution: Blang Mountain, Menghai County, Sipsong Panna Dai Autonomous Prefecture, southern Yunnan.

**Yuan River (Yuan He).** Unidentified. The Yuan River in southern Yunnan is also known as the Hong He, but it is unlikely that Blang would be found that far east.

**zhang.** Roughly ten feet.

# Daughter of a Slave

## TIBETAN TALE

Yongxi's mother was a maidservant in a rich man's house, where her family had been slaves of this rich man generation after generation. Her mother had done all the hard work for him ever since Yongxi was a little girl, and her life was like that of a beast of burden. The only comfort her poor soul knew was that she had a bright, beautiful little girl—Yongxi.

The very day Yongxi was born, the mistress of the wealthy man's family also gave birth to a girl. Stranger still, the babies were nearly identical—like a peach broken in two. The mistress was dismayed—a slave's daughter looking just like her own child! She longed to kill Yongxi, but kept this vicious intention secret, as she needed to make Yongxi a family slave once the girl grew up.

Poor Yongxi's father died not long after she was born. When she was six, the mistress ordered her to herd sheep. Despite wintry skies and a frozen earth, wind storms and rainy days, Yongxi had to drive some one hundred sheep up the mountain to pasture, and she was not allowed to come back before dark. Though she suffered much, luckily she had a loving mother, and was well looked after. She would forget all her grief and misfortune in her mother's warm, tender embrace. But even this sole source of happiness was snatched away by the evil lady of the house.

One day, while Yongxi's mother was doing the milking, she did not pay attention, and her milk pail was kicked over by a cow. That same moment, it so happened that the fiendish mistress was coming out of her room. When she saw the spilt milk all over the ground, she was so furious that she picked up the pail and beat Yongxi's mother on the head. The heavy blows knocked the woman unconscious, and she fell to the ground in a heap. When she came to, she found Yongxi sitting by her side, weeping brokenheartedly. Slowly, she sat up and held Yongxi in her arms, grieving. "My dear child! There is no hope your Mama will recover. After I die, I will be reincarnated as a cow, for I could never leave you behind to endure this life all by yourself . . ." Her eyes closed before she finished speaking.

The following morning, the old, penned-up cow gave birth to a calf. How lovable it was! As Yongzi stepped inside the pen, the calf came running over and raised its head, mooing to her. Yongxi hugged the calf in her arms. She was as pleased as if she were seeing her own mother again. From then on, she would sleep with the calf at night, and bring it out to pasture during the day.

After a few months, the calf grew into a large cow. Whenever Yongxi felt wronged about being beaten and scolded by her mistress, she would cling to the cow's neck and make tearful complaints, just as if she were speaking to her very own mother. The cow too, seemed to understand Yongxi's words, and would lick her hair lightly with its tongue, while tears dropped from Yongxi's eyes.

Even though the mistress had Yongxi graze the herd of sheep every day, she was not satisfied with Yongxi's heavy load of work. One day, she said to Yongxi, "You damned slave! You get three meals a day just for herding a few head of sheep. Starting tomorrow, I want you to spin wool while you graze the sheep. You must spin ten balls of wool each day. If not, you can forget about coming home for your dinner."

Yongxi walked into the pen, disconsolate. Hugging the cow's neck, she tearfully related what the mistress had said. This time, the cow suddenly started talking. "No more crying, child! Tomorrow there will be someone to help you with this matter." Not only did the cow comfort Yongxi, it taught her a way out of her dilemma.

The next day, the lady of the house gave Yongxi a large heap of wool. She took it with her and drove the sheep up the mountain where she went every day. There she hung the wool on the branches of the wild rose, and sang to the bush, as the cow had taught her:

> Wild rose so fair!
> Dear friend so true
> green slopes we share
> shepherdess and you.
>
> Wild rose so dear!
> with sad tales do you wake?
> Cruel mistress I fear
> ten balls I must make.
>
> Wild rose so kind!
> Pity poor me
> release me from this bind
> with wool combed free.

After singing her song, Yongxi heard the wild rose rustle in the wind, carding the wool. Before long, the big heap of wool was neatly combed, loose and free of knots.

Yongxi hung the loose wool on the pine tree and sang:

> Green pine, lovely sight!
> Dear friend so true
> 'neath mountains snow-white
> shepherdess and you.
>
> Green pine so dear!
> With sad tales do you wake?
> Cruel mistress I fear
> ten balls I must make.
>
> Green pine so kind!
> Have pity divine
> free me from this bind
> with wool spun fine.

No sooner had Yongxi finished singing than the branches of the pine tree began soughing and swaying in the breeze. The wool became fine-spun yarn and hung down in strands. Yongxi wound them together, and in a little while that big heap of wool was spun into ten balls of yarn.

When evening came, Yongxi drove the sheep home and handed the balls of wool to her mistress. Still the woman was not satisfied. "How can you expect to have any clothes to wear if all you can spin is this meagre amount of wool? Weave it into wool cloth by tomorrow night. Otherwise, you can forget about coming home for your dinner."

Once again, Yongxi told the cow what her mistress had said. And again, the cow comforted her and taught her a way out.

At dawn, Yongxi took the woolen yarn along with her, and drove the sheep up the mountain. She did as the cow instructed, and hung the yarn on the willow tree, then sang the tree a song:

> Willow tree so green!
> Dear friend so true
> grow by the clear stream
> shepherdess and you.

> Willow tree so dear!
> With sad tales do you wake?
> Cruel mistress I fear
> ten balls I must make.

> Willow tree so kind!
> To you I must cleave
> free me from this bind
> wool yarn please weave.

No sooner had Yongxi finished singing than the slender willow branches began swaying, and the woolen yarn, floating and swishing in the air, was woven together. After a while, a long, long piece of coarse, woolen cloth was seen hanging down from the willow tree. Yongxi rolled it up, and when evening came, she drove the sheep home and handed the cloth to her mistress. The lady of the house was astonished. "How could Yongxi be so capable?" she wondered. "No matter what I tell her to do, she can do it." Whereupon, she cross-examined her, and Yongxi told her everything, from beginning to end.

The next day, the mistress told her daughter, Bazhen, to go sheep herding. Moreover, she was to take a lot of wool with her to spin. She went out the whole day, but when she came back that night, she brought nothing home, not even a single thread, let alone a ball of wool yarn. The fact is, she had imitated Yongxi by hanging the wool on the wild roses and singing to them:

> Bushy clump, bushy clump
> tiny leaf and thorn
> growing on the mountain slope
> lonely and forlorn.
>
> If you want a friend in me
> comb this wool in time
> otherwise, in the end, tee-hee
> I'll chop you very fine.

Before Bazhen had even finished singing, a gale blew and swept the wool up into the sky.

When the mistress found out that Bazhen had gone and lost all her wool, she was furious. She insisted Yongxi had lied to her. She gave her a terrible thrashing, and refused to let her eat.

Again Yongxi went to the pen and made her tearful report to the cow. "My dear child!" said the cow. "No need to cry! I'll feed you when you're hungry. Just milk me, and my milk will turn into delicious butter and curds."

Yongxi did just as the cow directed. Lo and behold, as soon as she started to squeeze the udders, out came butter and curds! Yongxi ate to her heart's content and fell asleep by the side of the cow. From then on, she ate fresh milk and curds every day, and her face gradually became fair and plump.

One day, while Yongxi was sweeping the floor, the butter box she kept tucked away under her gown fell to the ground, and was noticed by the mistress. She interrogated Yongxi about where it had come from, and Yongxi had to tell her the truth.

Once again, the mistress told her daughter, Bazhen, to go graze the sheep. Moreover, this time, she also gave her a *baba* cake made of wheat bran for her to eat, to try to improve her complexion, for this was the poor food she had allowed Yongxi to eat in the past. Bazhen tended the sheep all day long and she got hunger pangs. She thought of milking the cow so she might eat butter and curds, but not only was she unable to squeeze one drop of milk from the cow, she got kicked besides. She came home starving and wearing a long face. When the mistress heard Bazhen's tearful complaint, she was so incensed that she determined to kill the cow.

That same night, the cow spoke to Yongxi, weeping. "My dear child! Tomorrow the mistress will kill me. I shall no longer be able to be with you. Remember, when they kill me, you must hide my skin in the crack of the wall, put my horns on the roof peak, bury my hoofs underground, and hang my intestines on the branches of the trees. Whenever you are having any difficulties, just take out these parts of my body. They will turn into the very things you need."

The cow was killed by the mistress. Crying bitterly, Yongxi hid away the cow's skin, horns, hoofs, and intestines, as she had been told. From then on, Yongxi was without her beloved cow, and had no one at all to comfort her, while the mistress remained as cruel to her as ever. Thus Yongxi lived a miserable existence, until she turned sixteen.

That year, the king's son wanted to choose the fairest maiden in the kingdom to be his wife, so he issued a decree that all young girls were to be candidates. The mistress was delighted when she heard this news, for she hoped that her own daughter would be chosen. At the same time, she was afraid that if Yongxi participated, she might be selected instead.

On the day designated for choosing a beauty, the mistress dressed up Bazhen, making her look simply lovely. Just as she was about to go out the door, the mistress scattered a basket of turnip seeds on the ground, and said to Yongxi, "Today we are off to join in the prince's selection of a bride. You pick up all these turnip seeds, and don't leave the house until you've finished the job. If you miss a single seed, you might as well stop thinking about living." With that, she left.

Yongxi was beside herself. She sat on the ground, weeping. Ah! So many turnip seeds! How could anyone pick them all up?

Just as she was feeling so upset, suddenly a flock of sparrows flew by, pecked up the turnip seeds, and dropped them into the basket. Before long, there was not a single seed on the ground. How ecstatic Yongxi was! "The turnip seeds are all picked up," she thought to herself. "The prince is about to choose a bride. Why shouldn't I go and see what is happening?" But then she looked down and saw the rags she wore. How could she go to the palace dressed like that? Suddenly, she recalled what the cow had said. So she took out the cow's hide, horns, and everything else. Ah! She was overjoyed, for the hide had become a beautiful, shimmering gown, embroidered with golden thread, and the horns had turned into a scarlet kerchief, while the hoofs were now a pair of shoes with cloud embroidery, and the intestines that had hung on the trees had become a multicolored sash.

Quickly now, Yongxi changed her clothes, made herself up, and left for the palace. As soon as she walked in, all the candidates for selection stared at her blankly in utter amazement. Why she was more beautiful than anyone! Both Bazhen and the mistress looked aghast, and their mouths hung open at the sight of Yongxi in her gorgeous dress.

The moment for choosing began. All the candidates were seated in rows in the palace courtyard. Yongxi sat beside her mistress and Bazhen, to the rear. The king made an announcement: the prince would shoot an arrow up in the sky, and whoever could catch the arrow in her bosom when it fell would be chosen as the prince's bride. Following this message, the prince appeared from within the palace. He studied all the girls for a while with his eyes, and was elated to discover at last Yongxi sitting at the back of the courtyard. Immediately, he took up his bow and shot an arrow in her direction.

Everyone looked up, following the course of the arrow, as it shot straight up, arched in the air, and then slowly fell. All eyes were fixed on that arrow, watching it as it descended precisely toward Yongxi's arms.

When the mistress saw what was happening, she hastily stretched out her hand and caught the arrow, placing it in Bazhen's bosom. The onlookers began shouting, saying that the arrow was rightfully Yongxi's, but the mistress denied the fact, and refused to give it back.

Seeing that the situation had yet to be resolved, the king made a second announcement. "Here now is a magic shoe. All candidates should try it on. The girl whose foot the shoe fits will be chosen to become the wife of the prince." At this, the candidates tried the shoe, one by one, but none succeeded in getting it on, including Bazhen.

Finally, it was Yongxi's turn. Strangely enough, the shoe suited her perfectly, being neither too big nor too small. All the people applauded Yongxi and surrounded her as she entered the palace.

From that time on, Yongxi lived a happy life with the prince in the palace.

## NOTE

"Nuli de nü'er," from *Yunnan minzu minjian gushi xuan* 1982, 505–13. Collector and redactor: Zewangrenzeng (Zang). Area of distribution: Diqing Tibetan Autonomous Prefecture, northwestern Yunnan.

# Wild Goose Lake

## BAI LEGEND

Legend tells us that in Pineapple Village, at the foot of Horse Ear Mountain, there once lived a man and his daughter. Their family name was Jiao and the girl's given name was Haimei, "Sea Sister." One year, a drought made it impossible for people to make a living. Sea Sister used to go with her father to Horse Ear Mountain to cut bamboo, with which they plaited brooms to sell.

One day, Sea Sister was up on the mountain cutting bamboo. She kept chopping away happily, until after a while she had quite a huge pile, having cut a large swath through the bamboo. Suddenly, right through the opening in front of her eyes, a sparkling expanse of lake could be seen. The water looked clear and bright, without so much as a single fallen leaf. The reason the lake was so clean, in fact, was that as soon as any leaf fell in the water, a big wild goose would fly over from the bank and carry the leaf away in its bill. This then, according to traditional accounts, was Wild Goose Lake.

Sea Sister delighted in her discovery of a lake. She quickly put the bamboo on her back and carried it home. The next day, she went to this lake carrying a hoe, hoping she might find some place where an opening could be made, so that water could flow and relieve people suffering from the drought. She walked around the lake for quite a long time, noting that the whole body of water was surrounded by high mountains, forests, and rocks. But there was also a big stone gate at one end. She dug away at the ground nearby for a while, but still could not make an opening with her hoe. Much upset by her failure, she sat down under a big tree, trying to think of some other way. Suddenly, a wild goose flew by and called to her, "Sea Sister, Sea Sister! To open up Wild Goose Lake and release water, you need a golden key." But where was this golden key to be found? Sea Sister was just about to ask, when the wild goose flew away.

She kept strolling along the beach and came to a forest of cypress trees. Standing on top of a cypress were three parrots. "Parrots, parrots! Where can I find the golden key?" she asked.

The parrots answered in chorus, "Sea Sister, Sea Sister! To find the golden key, you have first to find the third daughter of the dragon king!" With these words, they flew away.

Sea Sister kept walking along the beach, intending to find the third daughter of the dragon king. She came to a pine forest and saw a pair of peacocks perched on a tree. She asked them, "Peacocks, peacocks! Where can I find the third daughter of the dragon king?"

"Sea Sister, Sea Sister," they answered. "To find the third daughter of the dragon king, you have to go to the mountain pass in the south." With that, the peacocks flew to a sweet osmanthus tree in the south.

Sea Sister followed after them and stopped under the tree, but she could not find the dragon king's daughter. Then she heard the peacocks up in the tree: "Sea Sister, Sea Sister! The third daughter of the dragon king likes to sing songs. If you sing, she will come out!" And the peacocks flew away.

Sea Sister started singing in earnest. At the end of one day, the snow on the mountains melted at her songs, yet still the third daughter did not come out. The second day passed, during which her singing caused all the seaweed in the lake to turn green, yet the third daughter still did not come out. On the third day, Sea Sister came back to sing again. She kept on singing right until the sun went down behind the mountain, and flowers bloomed everywhere, covering the mountains with blossoms. It was then that the dragon king's third daughter walked out of the lake!

According to the regulations of the dragon palace, no one was allowed to leave at will, and go among the people on earth. But the problem was, the dragon king's daughter was so fond of singing. When she heard Sea Sister singing better than she could, she admired her immensely. By the end of the third day, she could not stand it any longer, and simply had to walk out of the lake, secretly.

"Which is your family?" she asked Sea Sister. "Where do you live? Why do you come here to sing every day?"

Sea Sister answered, "My name is Sea Sister. I live in Pineapple Village at the foot of Horse Ear Mountain. I'm here to find the golden key, so I can get water from Wild Goose Lake to provide relief for the drought-afflicted people."

The good-hearted third daughter of the dragon king informed Sea Sister, "The golden key is locked in the treasury of the palace, guarded by a big eagle. Only the dragon king himself can get it. Any other person would be pecked to death!" But she promised Sea Sister that she would think of some way to get the key when the dragon king left the palace.

One day, the dragon king went on a journey, and his third daughter brought Sea Sister to the palace. They started to take turns singing songs in front of the treasury. At first, the eagle just kept dozing off, feeling sleepy, and paid them no attention. Later, it was so moved by their music that it spread its wings and flew out to look for the singers. At this time, Sea Sister hastily went into the treasury to look for the golden key.

The treasury was piled high with gold, silver, pearls, and gems which dazzled Sea Sister's eyes. To take even a few of these items from the treasury would be enough for one to live a luxurious life. But the one thought Sea Sister had in mind was to find the golden key, so she gave no heed at all to the treasure. She looked all over the entire treasury, but could not find the golden key. Just as she began to get upset, she unexpectedly stumbled over a big box. It fell open on the ground with a bang, and the glittering golden key sprang out at her. Sea Sister grabbed it up and ran out of the treasury at once. She and the third daughter of the dragon king did not sing any more, but walked together out to Wild Goose Lake. With no more exquisite songs to listen to, the eagle returned to his dozing.

With this golden key, Sea Sister tapped on the stone gate three times. The door opened and the water in the lake gushed out. After a while, the entire Pineapple Village plain was full of water. The dragon king's daughter realized that the flow of water was too fast, and that it would spoil the crops below, so she quickly warned, "Sea Sister, Sea Sister. The crops will soon be ruined!" Turning her head to look, Sea Sister became flustered. She hurried to block the water with some straw blinds, but inadvertently stuffed the opening in the stone gate too tightly, so no water could escape, except through the narrow cracks in the blinds. The straw blinds are still there today in Wild Goose Lake, but they have turned into stone.

Having returned home, the dragon king discovered that the golden key had disappeared. He knew no one except his third daughter could be responsible for taking the golden key. For this, he drove her away from the palace. The girl came to earth and lived with Sea Sister, and they sang songs together every day. Today, each year on the twenty-second day of the seventh lunar month, women of all the Bai villages gather together and merrily sing songs.

## NOTE

"Yanchihai," from *Yunnan minzu minjian gushi xuan* 1982, 126–28. Collectors and re-dactors: Du Huirong (Han) and Zhang Fusan (Han). Area of distribution: Dali Bai Autonomous Prefecture, western Yunnan.

# Wine-Flavored Spring

## HANI LEGEND

In the thick forest on the south shore of Hong He, the "Red River," there is a steep cliff that towers up in the sky. A sparkling, crystal-clear spring gushes forth from this cliff. The water is not only sweet in flavor, but tastes mellow, like wine. The local people call it Wine-Flavored Spring. How did this spring come to be?

Legend has it that far back in the distant past, there was a poor old woman who had no children, and who lived a lonely life. One day, she was going up a mountain to fetch water when she saw an eagle fiercely chasing after a little bird. As the eagle was about to fly off with the tiny creature in its beak, the old woman quickly grabbed a bamboo pipe and flung it at the eagle, driving it away. She then returned home, holding this pitiable little thing in her hand.

When she got back, she set the bird on the floor of her house. A moment later, it was gone, and suddenly, a handsome, well-knit young man was standing there before her. He held the old woman's hands and spoke to her: "Auntie, you've just saved my life. Won't you please accept me as your own son?"

The old woman's joy knew no bounds, and she readily adopted the young man, giving him the name Ahli. Ahli was hardworking and capable, so the old woman lived an easier life with each passing day.

One day, Ahli said to her, "Mama, please let me go and tend ducks!" The old woman forced a smile. "My child, I'm so poor that I don't own a single duck's wing. Where am I going to get ducks for you to tend?"

Ahli made ducks himself by cutting up the thick leaves of bamboo shoots. He blew them up with a puff of his breath, and set them in water. These bamboo ducks turned into drakes and hens, and they went all about quacking and calling, making a racket. As the ducks increased in number, the old woman would carry them to market to sell.

On another day, Ahli said to her, "Mama, please let me go herd oxen!"

The old woman shook her head. "My child, I'm so poor that I don't even own an ox hair. Where can I get oxen for you to herd?"

Ahli chopped down some pines with his axe and gave them a lash with his whip. The pine trees were transformed into oxen. He drove them up the mountain to pasture, and they grew in number as time went by.

At that time, the king used to force his people to pay him innumerable cattle and fowl in taxes each year. Some people bought Ahli's oxen and ducks to hand over to the king, but as soon as the fowl were brought into the king's presence, they changed back into the leaves of bamboo shoots, while the oxen became wood.

The king sent his men to make a secret investigation. They got to the heart of the problem and seized Ahli.

Before leaving home, Ahli said to the old woman, "Mama, I'm going now. Please keep a bowl of water and a bowl of wine at home. As long as there is water and wine in the bowls, I will not die." With these words, he went off with the king's servants.

The old woman did as her son told her, keeping a bowl of water and a bowl of wine in the house.

The cruel-hearted king intended to put Ahli to death, so he had him shut in a cave for forty-nine days, without giving him anything to eat. But Ahli did not die. Again the king made a secret investigation and found out the reason Ahli could survive. He sent his toadies to Ahli's home and had the bowls smashed.

Suffering from hunger and thirst, Ahli became completely exhausted in the cave. Making one last effort, he scooped out a hole in the wall with his fingers. Water and wine flowed forth. Then he drank to his heart's content, closed his eyes, and died.

Ever since that time, the spring has been flowing. This is the wine-flavored spring Ahli left behind for later generations.

# NOTE

"Jiuxiang quan," from *Shancha*, no. 5, 1982, 49. Storyteller: Qu Minzhou (Hani). Collector and redactor: Li Rongguang (Han). Area of distribution: Honghe County, Honghe Hani-Yi Autonomous Prefecture, Southern Yunnan.

# Stories about Bubo

## ZHUANG MYTH

## » 1 «

## Thunder God Gets His Share of the Rent

In ancient times, heaven and earth were close together. Tall bamboo could touch the ceiling of heaven—that is why today, bamboo bends as it grows and is pliant. When the gods spoke in heaven, people on earth could hear their voices.

The god of thunder who lived in heaven had eyes like a pair of lanterns. Whenever he blinked, green light flashed all about. He had a pair of wings on his back, and if he flapped them, a gale would blow. His feet—why, they were so heavy that when he walked, they crashed together, making rumbling sounds. In his hands he carried a broad ax and a chisel, and with these he would go around splitting and cutting, whenever his temper flared.

As for the earth, that was the abode of human beings. Once we had a brave man named Bubo as our headman. He was a good man. Not only could he plow fields and grow crops, he was also able to tend cattle and hunt.

In those days, all people had to do for there to be fair weather and seasonable rain for their crops was to burn incense and offer it to Thunder God. Then they could live in peace. One year, Thunder God felt bored with all his heavenly leisure, so he came down to earth to amuse himself. Bubo treated him as a rare guest. He slaughtered a pig and a sheep in Thunder God's honor, and heaped the table with exotic delicacies from mountain and sea. The wine tasted mellow, the rice smelled fragrant. Thunder God's eyes turned red with greed at the very sight of such good food. The more he thought about the delicacies available on earth, the less appetizing were the joss sticks and incense he fed on in heaven.

Thunder God got drunk on the wine and stuffed his stomach, then wiped his mouth slightly and turned to Bubo. "I provide you with clear skies as well as rain showers. You'll have to pay me rent for the crop you grow."

"Fine with me!" said Bubo. "Which part of the crop do you want, the top or the bottom?"

"I live up in heaven," said Thunder God. "I'll have the top part, of course!"

"Fine. Come and collect in the fall!"

That year, Bubo grew taro. In autumn, Thunder God came down to earth to collect his rent. All he got for his share was rotten taro leaves and dried taro stems.

Thunder God was about to vent his spleen, but he had already agreed to the deal. Furthermore, Bubo had been so sincere and treated him so cordially, what with so much wine and meat, it just wouldn't do to get angry. So Thunder God waited until he got drunk again, had his fill of meat and rice, and had wiped his mouth lightly. "Say!" he exclaimed, "next year I'll collect the bottom part of the crop!"

"Fine," said Bubo. "Come and collect next fall!"

That year, Bubo grew rice. When autumn came around, Thunder God descended from heaven for his rent, but all he collected were rice roots. Bubo could not give him even a single rice stalk.

Thunder God was so angry that the veins in his neck popped out. Smiling broadly as ever, Bubo treated him graciously again with wine and meat.

As Thunder God drank, his face got redder and redder. At last he smashed his wine glass, saying, "Next year, I'll have the whole crop for my rent—top and bottom both!"

Grinning delightedly, Bubo replied, "Take whatever you like!"

The next year, Bubo's entire crop was corn. In the autumn each corn-stalk held three to five ears. When Thunder God came down for his rent, he could only stare as Bubo's family broke off the ears, one after another, and stuffed them in the baskets on their backs.

Thunder God snorted with indignation, and his normally dark-blue face turned red. He turned around and ran away, without looking back. Bubo shouted after him repeatedly, asking him to come back and drink some more, but Thunder God paid no attention.

## » 2 «

# Plucking the Dragon's Beard

After Thunder God got back to heaven, he called his thunder general, Lumeng, and ordered him to cease sending rain to the earth.

That year, not a drop of rain fell from the sky, nor a single drop of dew. People went to consult Bubo. "The river in heaven has plenty of water, but Thunder God won't let us have any," Bubo said. "Let's go and lift up the sluice gate a little by ourselves."

Bubo brought his people to the heavenly river and opened the copper sluice gate a crack. Thunder God had closed it tight. A stream of clear spring water began flowing down from heaven to the fields on earth. Though Thunder God did not send any rain, or scatter any dew, the harvest that year was fairly good.

After he learned that Bubo had led his people to heaven and opened the copper sluice gate, Thunder God danced with anger. Fearing that Bubo would come again with his group and make trouble, Thunder God lifted heaven higher, leaving only the sun-moon tree on Mount Bachi as a ladder linking heaven and earth. As a result, not only was there no more rain or dew that year, worse still, easy communication between heaven and earth was over. The crops withered day by day.

People went to seek advice from Bubo once again. "The dragon king underground is Thunder God's brother," Bubo told them. "He has water. Let's go and borrow some from him."

Dragon King, brother of Thunder God, had a great, white, full beard. He already had word from his brother, so as soon as he saw Bubo coming with everyone else to borrow water, he flatly refused, saying, "No water for you!"

"So you want us to die of thirst!" exclaimed Bubo.

Dragon King said, "The water is mine. What's yours is a bad fate. I've got nothing to do with what happens to you."

Seeing that gentle tactics wouldn't do, Bubo got tough. Grabbing hold of Dragon King's horns, he demanded, "Are you going to lend us water, or not?"

"No, no," Dragon King said. "Ten thousand times no!"

Bubo ordered his followers, "Come and pluck out Dragon King's beard. Let's see if he persists in flaunting his power!"

Everybody joined in pulling out Dragon King's beard, hurting him so much that he yelled for mercy. He had no choice but to promise to release his stream. Once he let water out, Bubo released him. Dragon King fled into the watery depths in a panic, with but two tattered remnants of his beard yet intact.

## » 3 «

# Pleading for Rain

By the third year, heaven had yet to send down any rain, and streams had dried up. The sun was so scorching hot that fish were fried on slabstones, and their oil came oozing out.

Some elders complained about Bubo's meddling which had offended the deities, so they assembled together and got Taoist priests to chant scriptures, and shamans to dance in a trance. Still, there was no sign of rain or dew.

"This is all because Bubo offended the deities," these elders said. "If he does not confess his sins, Thunder God will never send us rain."

The people who were pleading for rain insisted that Bubo kneel down before the deities in heaven.

"A man has his dignity," Bubo said. "How can he bow and kneel in front of other people? I won't do it."

The elders begged Bubo, saying, "Please, if you do this, you'll be doing a good deed for all of us!" They all knelt down before Bubo.

Bubo submitted to this humiliation, and knelt before the altar. A few children who saw him get down on his knees jeered at him by singing a folk song:

> Bubo prayed but no rain came
> his beard's a mess and his lips are untrained
> an old waterwheel with a busted frame
> he's got knobby knees with black mud stained!

On hearing the children's jeers, Bubo was so angry that his beard stood on end and his body shook. He went home at once to sharpen his sword, determined to go to Mount Bachi to look for the sun-moon tree so that he could climb up to heaven.

## » 4 «

# Fighting Thunder God

At this time, Lumeng, the thunder general, was supervising his soldiers, urging them to repair the river and cement the bottom of the pond so that not even a drop of water could leak down to earth.

One of the thunder soldiers, Qigao by name, was lagging behind in his work, and Lumeng started lashing him with a whip. Who would have expected that, just as he raised his whip, Bubo would come from behind and nab away the whip?

"What are you doing here?" Lumeng asked.

"Tell me first who ordered you to repair the river in heaven? Who asked you to seal up the pond?"

"None of your business," Lumeng said.

Raising his hand, Bubo pushed Lumeng into the river. Lumeng took this opportunity to swim across to the palace of Thunder God.

Meanwhile, Qigao told Bubo that cruel-hearted Thunder God was determined to kill the people on earth by means of the drought.

Bubo trembled with rage. "Where is Thunder God now?" he quickly asked.

Qigao said, "In the evening he's in the north, in the morning in the east, and at noon he sits in the central hall of the palace."

Bubo said, "I'm going to get even with him!"

As soon as Lumeng made it to the shore, he saw Bubo coming forward in mighty strides. He hurried to report to Thunder God, but Bubo entered the palace hall before Thunder God could prepare for his coming.

Without saying a word, Bubo dragged Thunder God down from his throne and pointed his sword at Thunder God's nose. "Will you give us rain, or not? If not, I'm going to kill you!"

Thunder God quickly kowtowed, pleading, "Let me go. I'll send you rain in three days!"

Seeing that Thunder God had promised, Bubo let him go and returned to earth all alone.

# » 5 «

# Thunder God Gets Caught

Thunder God went back on his promise, once Bubo left the palace hall. He was afraid Bubo would come up to heaven and make trouble again, so he ordered Lumeng to cut down the sun-moon tree on Mount Bachi, and he had the other thunder generals bring out their broad axes and hone their edges keen. *Swish-swish-swish* went the blades as they were scraped over the sharpening stone, setting everyone's teeth on edge.

Having heard that Thunder God had gone back on his promise, Qigao came down to break the news to Bubo.

"Every day, Thunder God grinds his broad ax," Qigao reported, "but I have no idea whether he is going to split wood or people. And every day, he is busy figuring how much water he has, making sure none has been released from the river or pond in heaven."

Knowing that Thunder God had really gone back on his promise, Bubo gave orders to his wife and children to dredge up slippery douli plants from the river, and spread them on the roof peak of their house.

He also had them chop down *sha* trees and peel off their slick bark, then plait a lattice roof. After that, he ordered his son, Fuyi, and his daughter to wait underneath, each holding a flat shoulder pole. He then told his wife to get a fishing net ready, while he himself held an empty chicken coop in his hand, standing under the eaves.

Along came Thunder God seeking revenge. He spread his wings and a gale began to blow, turning the sky murky, and darkening the earth. Riding the wind, he flew at the tip of the clouds. From the heights, he blinked, focusing his eyes, and as he looked down, his eyes shot forth rays of shimmering green light that penetrated the layers of clouds. Stepping upon the lightning, he descended halfway down the sky.

Thunder God spotted Bubo's canopied house, and stamped with both feet. In a split second, thunder rolled and rumbled, the sky spun around, the earth shook, and a torrential downpour pelted the earth. Riding the rain, Thunder God dropped, pell-mell, straight to Bubo's house.

So vigorous was his charge that, as soon as his feet hit the roof peak, he slipped on the *douli* placed there and slid onto the roof covered with slick *sha* matting, now more slippery than ever because it was wet with rain. Thunder God's feet went out from under him, and down he tumbled.

Just as Thunder God was scrambling to get on his feet, brother Fuyi and his sister whacked him in unison with their shoulder poles, one on his middle, the other on his neck, all the while pressing him tightly to the ground. Flapping the wings on his back, Thunder God tried to stand up, but Bubo's wife, Mubo, spread the net over him and entangled his wings so tightly he could not wriggle them. There was still some fight left in Thunder God, so Bubo dropped the chicken coop over him. It fell like a copper bell from above, holding Thunder God fast and making escape impossible.

## » 6 «

## Thunder God Escapes

Having caught Thunder God, Bubo locked him in his granary. Some people advocated killing him, while others wanted to chop him up in pieces after he was dead. "We want Thunder God to give us rain," Bubo pointed out. "If he refuses, then we can kill him."

Bubo was clever and resourceful. He feared that if he should let Thunder God go, he would go back on his word again, so he thought of a strategy. He would get Thunder God to make a cord out of straw by rubbing grain stalks between his palms every day, and then he would use the rope to tether Thunder God's heart. That way, should Thunder God prove disobedient, Bubo could pull him back, no matter where he ran.

Bubo told Thunder God, "If you can fill the granary with a straw cord, I'll let you go. But if you won't twist stalks into rope, I'll kill you!"

Qigao was unaware of Bubo's plan, and furthermore, he feared that Thunder God would take revenge against him if he were freed. So everyday Qigao deliberately bit the cord made by Thunder God into short sections.

Three days later, Bubo came to check up on Thunder God. Bubo was furious. There were only a few short strands Thunder God had rubbed out of straw, and still not a sign of rain. Bubo decided to kill Thunder God. He would have his flesh preserved in salt and give it to the people to eat to dispel their resentment. Off he went to buy some salt to make preserved meat.

Before he left home, he warned his son, Fuyi, and his daughter, "Don't give the ax to Thunder God when he tries to borrow it. When he asks for water, don't give him any. Once he drinks water, he will become mighty, and if he gets hold of an ax, he will bust down the granary." Fuyi and his sister nodded their heads dutifully, and Bubo felt at ease as he left the house. Meanwhile, his wife Mubo went to inform all the relatives to get ready to eat their share of salted Thunder God meat.

Thunder God was really upset when he learned what Bubo had ordered Fuyi and his sister to do. But he was crafty too. He waited until

Bubo and Mubo had left home, then he tried to coax the children to come near the granary, so he might fool them. But they paid him no attention.

He tried to tease them by making a funny face. He stuck out his tongue, and then drew it back, in and out, in and out, now swallowing, now spitting. Lo! A burst of blue-green flame shot forth from his mouth. The kids thought Thunder God was marvelous, so they ran up to have a good look.

Thunder God stopped moving his tongue and the flame disappeared. Finding this great fun, the children wanted Thunder God to do it again. He put on a poor, pitiful face. "Good brother, good sister," he pleaded, "I'm dying of thirst. Just give me a little water to quench my thirst, then I'll let you have another look!"

" 'Don't give the ax to Thunder God when he tries to borrow it. When he asks for water, don't let him have any. Once he drinks water, he will become mighty, and if he gets hold of an ax, he will bust down the granary!' That's what our daddy told us. We can't give you a thing."

Hearing this, Thunder God howled and wept. Fuyi and his sister felt bad, seeing his poor, pitiful face. "There's no use crying," they said, comfortingly. "The rivers are bone dry and the springs are stopped up. It didn't rain a bit the other day when you got caught. Papa and Mama have sealed up the water we had in our house. Where can we get any for you?"

Thunder God said, "Good brother, good sister, just give me something to drink. So long as it's wet, I don't care!"

The kids said, "The only thing left uncovered at home is the vat of indigo dye. Can you drink indigo dye?"

"Ai-ya!" exclaimed Thunder God. "In heaven, I was king, but now that I've been captured here below, what choice do I have? Indigo dye is still water. Give me some!"

Fuyi and his sister began scooping out indigo dye with a bowl. As Thunder God listened to the clink-clink sound of the bowl hitting the side of the vat, he was ecstatic. But when they brought him a bowlful, he became anxious all over again: the opening in the granary was too small for the bowl to pass through.

"Good brother, good sister, I'll have to trouble you a wee bit more. This opening is too small. Would you please find me a hollow rice stalk I can use for a straw?"

The children did as they were told, and fetched a straw. Thunder God put it in the bowl and began sipping the indigo dye.

After sipping the first mouthful, his throat felt moist. The second mouthful brought back his strength, while the third turned his face a deep, indigo blue, and set his wings a-flapping.

Once he had gulped down the bowl of indigo dye, his whole body was bursting with energy. With a mighty shake, he knocked down the granary frame, *ka-wump!* The bowl fell with a smash. Then he toppled Bubo's house. The kids went running, crying their eyes out.

At first, Thunder God wanted to kill off all the people on the earth, but then he realized that if everybody were dead, there would be nobody to burn incense and offer him food, so he called back the kids.

Their faces all tearful, Fuyi and his sister complained, "You fooled us. You wanted to kill us. You're really mean!"

"I wouldn't ever kill you," Thunder God said. "I'll pull out one of my teeth and give it to you, to repay you for kindly saving my life. Hurry along and plant it in the ground! After a few days, there will be a great flood. Everybody will perish, but you two will survive!"

Thunder God pulled out one of his teeth and gave it to the children. Then, with his left hand, he beckoned the wind, and with his right, he summoned fire. Mounting them both, he rode back to heaven.

# » 7 «

## Venus

On his way home after he had bought salt, Bubo heard a thundering rumbling in the sky, and knew that something must have gone wrong at home, so he rushed back.

He found the whole frame of the granary broken apart, and his house in ruins. His son and daughter were bawling in each other's arms. Bubo understood just what had happened. He lowered his head and pondered just how he might deal with Thunder God.

Seeing that their father's face changed color so suddenly, Fuyi and his sister were scared they were about to be scolded and beaten. They ran to the backyard to plant the tooth given them by Thunder God. Who would have thought that, as soon as the tooth was in the ground, a plant would begin budding and sprouting? After they sprinkled it with a little water, vines began to grow from the tooth-seedling like thread coming from a spinning wheel. Overnight, the plant blossomed and bore a fruit which in three days became a gourd as big as a house. Fuyi and his sister made a hole with a knife, and scooped out the pith. Instantly, thunder rumbled and lightning flashed. The dike in heaven burst, and water began pouring down from the river and pond. Brother and sister squeezed their way through the opening in the gourd to take shelter from the rain.

Knowing that Thunder God intended to drown all the people on earth with a flood, Bubo determined to face him one more time. He opened the umbrella he carried with him, turned it upside down, making a little boat in which he could float atop the flood waters, and stepped in.

Once Thunder God breached the dike holding back the river in heaven, all the river water poured down. Dragon King was also seeking revenge against Bubo for plucking out his beard, so he released lake water, and ordered his shrimp soldiers and crab generals to push the billows about and make the waves choppy. The water rose over mountaintops and flooded as far as heaven's ceiling.

Thunder God thought that all the people on earth had been drowned, including Bubo. He opened the gates of heaven and looked down. Who would have thought that Bubo would be seen, sailing his umbrella boat right toward the gates of heaven? His chest stuck out and his sword in hand, Bubo charged Thunder God, bursting with rage.

Thunder God, his eyes shooting out flames of anger, quickly grabbed his broad ax, and flew down toward Bubo. Quick of eye and deft of hand, Bubo stamped on his umbrella boat, causing it to slip right by Thunder God's feet. Turning round as he passed, Bubo chopped off

Thunder God's feet. The latter quickly fled to the heavenly gates. Fearing that Bubo's umbrella boat would ride the tide, and force its way through the heavenly gates, Thunder God shouted again and again, "Quick, lower the water! Lower the water!"

Knowing how fierce Bubo could be, the thunder generals and thunder soldiers hastily made the water subside. Dragon King also realized that Bubo was not a man to be trifled with. He, too, helped make the water recede. The flood dropped abruptly. Bubo's umbrella dropped like something falling from the sky. When it plunged into a mountain peak, both Bubo and his umbrella were smashed to smithereens. Bubo's red heart was thrown to the ceiling of heaven, and has remained there, set in place. That is the planet Venus we see today.

## » 8 «

## Brother and Sister Marry

The water on the earth receded. The gourd with Fuyi and his sister hiding inside fell on the ground too. As the gourd was springy, it did not break. All the people on earth were dead. What could be done?

Wandering to and fro about the earth, the brother and sister came across a tortoise. The tortoise said to them, "There is nobody left on the earth now, except you two. Why don't brother and sister get married and start a new world?"

Fuyi and his sister said, "How can a brother and sister marry? We will beat you to death. If you can come back to life again, then we'll get married." Whereupon, they beat the tortoise to death. Just as they were about to leave that place, the tortoise came back to life and crawled away, laughing. Fuyi and his sister went on. Suddenly, a bamboo addressed them with a bow, kowtowing left and right. "There is no one else on the earth. Why don't you both get married and start a new world?"

"How can a brother and sister marry? We will chop you down. If you can come back to life again, then we'll get married." They cut the bamboo into sections. Just when they were about to leave, the bamboo came back to life with its sections joined together. It bowed and kowtowed as it laughed.

Unable to find any other human being, brother and sister were so distressed, they began bawling in each other's arms. Their crying startled Venus, the soul of Bubo, their father, in heaven.

Venus popped his head out of the cloud and said to them, "All the people on earth have died. Brother and sister should get married now and start a new world!"

Fuyi and his sister said, "How can a brother and sister marry?"

"Now listen to this!" Venus said. "One of you climb East Mountain and the other climb West Mountain. Each of you light a heap of firewood. If the two streams of smoke come together, it means that you two can get married."

Upon hearing his words, they separated, and one ran up East Mountain, while the other ran up West Mountain. Each lit a pile of firewood. Two columns of smoke rose up. As they reached the top of the sky, they fused with the clouds, the two columns of smoke moving together as one. Venus was so satisfied with the scene that he burst out laughing.

After the brother and sister got married, they gave birth to a fleshball. This fleshball had no eyes, mouth, hands, or feet. Not knowing whether it was a ghost or a monster, they minced it up and scattered the pieces over the mountains. These pieces became men and women. And that is how human beings began to flourish.

## » 9 «

# The End of the Tale

Bubo went up to heaven and became Venus. But what are the whereabouts of Thunder God, Dragon King, Lumeng, and Qigao?

Thunder God, who had his feet cut off by Bubo, killed a chicken and joined its claws to his legs. So from then on, Thunder God had a pair of claws for his feet. Now when he flares up with anger, he still thunders and rumbles, but he doesn't dare come back to earth and make trouble again.

After Dragon King had his beard pulled out, he ran back into the lake. Since then, his children have only two scraps of beard on their faces. You've all seen carp, haven't you? Don't they have two little beards?

Lumeng became a wandering monster living on the garbage thrown in the wilderness by men.

As for Qigao, he was detested by Thunder God because he had offended him. Moreover, he had also undermined Bubo's plan. So he ended up becoming a worm, always living under the ground. Whenever he put out his head, Thunder God would split him in two. Now when we see worms coming to the surface of the ground, we know for sure that a thunderstorm is brewing.

As for the tortoise and the bamboo, they were known to later people for their prescience, for they had matched Fuyi and his sister. That is why in later times the shamans divined fortune and misfortune by means of the tortoiseshell and bamboo roots.

## NOTES

"Thunder God Gets His Share of the Rent" (Leiwang shouzu), "Plucking the Dragon's Beard" (Ba longxu), "Pleading for Rain" (Qiu yu), "Fighting Thunder God" (Dou Leiwang), "Thunder God Gets Caught" (Qin Leiwang), "Thunder God Escapes" (Leiwang taozou), "Venus" (Qimingxing), "Brother and Sister Marry" (Xiongmei jiehun), and "The End of the Tale" (Gushi de jiewei), included in "Stories about Bubo (Bubo de gushi), from *Zhuangzu minjian gushi xuan*, vol. 1, 1982, 8–19. Collector and redactor: Lan Hongen (Han). Area of distribution: Hongshui River drainage area, Guangxi Zhuang Nationality Autonomous Region. Lan Hongen is a well-known writer and folktale expert from Guangxi Province.

**god of thunder (leiwang)**. Absent from both Han and other southwestern minority cultures, the god of thunder is a semidivine, semihuman ancestor of the Zhuang.
**Mount Bachi.** The highest mountain, according to Zhuang legend.
**douli.** A plant that grows in water and is slippery when wet.
**sha tree.** Paper-bark mulberry. Its bark becomes slippery when soaked in water.

# ANIMAL FRIENDS

## AND

# ANIMAL FOES

# Two Sisters
# and the Boa

## KUCONG TALE

Once there was an old Kucong *binbai* who had buried her husband in her youth. Her sole possessions were two daughters, the elder, nineteen years old, and the younger, seventeen. One afternoon, she returned home from working in the mountains feeling thirsty and tired, so she sat down under a mango tree to rest. This mango tree was laden with ripe, golden-yellow fruit hanging down from the branches. A breeze blew from the mountains, carrying the exquisite fragrance of ripe mangoes to her nose, making her mouth water.

Suddenly, the *binbai* heard a swishing sound, *sha-sha*, up in the mango tree, and then thin pieces of bark fell on her. The old woman thought that somebody must be up there, so without even taking a look, she called out, jokingly, "Who's the young man up in the tree whittling arrows out of mango branches? Whoever you are, if you would honor me by presenting me with a few mangoes, you can have your choice of my two daughters." Hardly had the *binbai*'s words escaped her lips, when there came the rustling of leaves, *hua-hua*, and a fully ripe mango fell *plop*, right on the ground. Feeling delighted and thankful at once, the old woman picked up the mango and began eating it, all the while looking up in the tree. Better for her had she not looked, for she was struck dumb with what she saw. Coiled all around the mango tree was a boa as thick as a bull's thigh, knocking mangoes free, its tail swishing back and forth. The *binbai* could not care less about picking up any more mangoes, and she scurried down the mountain in leaps and bounds, her bamboo basket on her back.

Wheezing and gasping for breath, the old woman entered her door. As she saw her two darling daughters coming up to meet her, she called to mind what had happened under the mango tree. She couldn't help feeling nervous and confused, as if she were stuck in a briar patch. She walked outside and was met by a strange sight. Though it was already dark, all her chickens were still circling around outside the chicken coop. She tried repeatedly to drive them inside, but they would not go. She went up to the coop and peeped in. Gosh! The very same boa which had been coiled around the mango was right there, lying in the chicken coop! As she was about to run away, the huge, long boa began to speak.

"Binbai, just now, you made a promise under the mango tree: whoever picked a mango and gave it to you to eat could have his choice of one of your two daughters. Now please, keep your promise. Give me one of your girls! If you should go back on your word, don't blame me for turning nasty!"

Seeing that boa in the chicken coop, with its brightly patterned, scaly skin, gleaming eyes, and that long, forked tongue sticking out, the binbai shivered from head to foot. She couldn't say yes, but she couldn't say no, either. So all she said was, "Now don't get mad, boa! Be patient, please. Let me talk this over with my girls, so I can tell you what they think."

The binbai went back into the house and recounted to her two daughters all that had happened. "Oh, my little darlings!" she exclaimed. "It's not that Mama doesn't love you or dote on you, but I have no choice other than to push you in the burning fire. Now you two sisters have to think it over—who is willing to marry the boa?"

No sooner had the old woman finished speaking than the older daughter started screaming, "No, no! I won't go! Who could marry such an ugly, dreadful thing?"

The younger sister thought for a while. She saw that her mother's life was threatened, while her older sister was adamant. "Mama," she said, "to prevent the boa from doing you and Sister any harm, and so you two can live in peace, I'm willing to marry the boa." And with that, she cried many a sad, sad tear.

The binbai led her second child to the gate of the chicken coop, and told the boa he could have her. That very night, the old woman took the snake into her home, and the boa and Second Daughter were married.

The next morning, when the boa was about to take her second daughter away, mother and child wept in one another's arms. How hard it was to part! Off went the boa, leading the binbai's dear child to the virgin forest, deep in the mountains, where he brought her to a cave. She groped about in the dark, dark cave, following after the boa. On and on they went, never coming to the end. So worried and afraid was Second Daughter that her teardrops fell like strings of pearls. Rounding a bend in the cave, they saw a gleam of light, and suddenly, a resplendent, magnificent palace came in view. There were endless vermilion walls and numberless yellow tiles, long verandas and tiny pavilions, tall buildings and spacious courtyards. Everywhere one could see carved beams, painted rafters, piles of gold, carved jade, and wall hangings of red and green silk. Second Daughter was simply dazzled. As she turned around, that terrifying, dreadful boa, which had been close by, had disappeared. Walking beside her now was a gorgeously dressed young man, looking ever so vigorous and handsome. "Oh!" she exclaimed, completely outdone. "How could this be?"

The young man beside her replied, "Dear miss! I am the king of the snakes of this region. Not long ago, when I went out to make an inspection tour of the snake tribes, I saw you two sisters. How I admired your wisdom and beauty! I made up my mind right then to have one of you as my wife, and that's how I thought of a way to win your mother's approval. Now, my hopes have come true. Oh, dear miss! In my palace you'll have gold and silver without end, more cloth than you can ever use, and more rice than you can ever eat. Let us love each other dearly, enjoying a glorious life, to the end of our days!"

As she listened to the snake king's words, Second Sister's heart flooded with warmth. She took hold of his hand, and, smiling sweetly, walked toward the resplendent, magnificent palace . . .

Second Sister and the snake king lived happily as newlyweds for a time. Then, one day, she took leave of her husband to go back home and visit her mother and sister. She told them all about her rich, full, married life with the king of the snakes.

Two Sisters and the Boa / KUCONG

155

How could the elder daughter not be full of regret? "Ay!" she thought. "I'm to blame for being so foolish. If I had promised to marry the boa in the first place, would not I have been the one now enjoying glory, honor, and riches in that palace, instead of my younger sister?" So she made up her mind, then and there. "Right! That's what I'll do. I'll find a way to wed a boa too!"

After the younger sister left to return to the snake king, the elder sister walked deep into the mountains, carrying a basket on her back. To find a boa, she would go only where the grass was tall or the jungles were dense. From dawn to dusk and dusk to dawn, she kept on searching until, at last, after great difficulty, she found a boa under a bush. Its eyes were shut, for the boa was enjoying a good snooze.

First Sister gingerly raked the snake into her basket and left for home in high spirits, the boa on her back. She had gone only halfway when the boa woke up. It stuck out its tongue and licked the back of her neck. Instead of being frightened by what the snake was doing, First Sister secretly felt quite delighted. "Hey!" she whispered softly. "Don't be so affectionate just yet! Wait till we get home!"

After getting back home, she laid the boa in her bed, then rushed to make the fire and do the cooking. After supper, First Sister told her mother, "Mama, I found a boa today too, and I shall marry him tonight. From now on, I can live a rich, comfortable life, just like my baby sister!" And off she went to sleep with her boa.

Not long after the mother went to bed, she heard her daughter's voice: "Mama, it's up to my thighs!"

The *binbai* did not say a word, thinking all she was hearing was a pair of newlyweds having fun playing around.

After a while, First Sister called out, her voice trembling, "Mama, it's up to my waist!"

The old woman did not understand what such words could mean, so she did not budge an inch.

Yet more time passed, until this time she heard a mournful voice from the inner room, "Mama, it's up to my neck now . . ." And then, all was silence.

The *binbai* felt something was not quite right, so she quickly rolled out of bed, lit a pine torch and went to take a look. That dreadful boa had swallowed down her elder daughter, leaving but a lock of her hair!

The old woman felt sad and nervous. She paced back and forth in the room, not knowing what to do to rescue her daughter. In the end, all she could think of doing was to pull down her dear, thatched hut, set it afire, and burn up the boa. In the raging flames a loud *bang* was heard. As the boa was being burned to death, it burst into many pieces. In a later age, these came to be countless snakes, big and little.

The next morning, the *binbai* picked out of the ashes a few of her daughter's bones that had not been consumed by the fire. She dug a hole in the ground and buried them, holding back her tears.

Afterward, she declared, "My elder daughter! This is all because of your greed!" With these words, she went off into the dense jungle, and deep into the mountains, to look for her second daughter and her son-in-law, the king of the snakes.

## NOTES

"Jiemei he she," from *Yunnan minzu minjian gushi xuan* 1982, 620–23. Storytellers: Zhage (Kucong) and Zhalai (Kucong). Translator: Yang Chengrong (Kucong). Collectors and redactors: Li Yunchang and Yu Chi (Han). Area of distribution: Jinping County, southern Yunnan near the Vietnamese border.

**binbai.** A common word in the Kucong language meaning "old woman."

# The Gold Pig

MONGOLIAN TALE

Legend has it that far, far in the distant past, a wretchedly poor, old Mongolian couple once lived on the west bank of Qilu Lake in a small thatched shed, nestled in a mountain, and facing the water.

When this couple was young, they had not only land and a house, but a son as well. In those days, like their fellow Mongolian villagers, they had built up an earthen dike and succeeded in reclaiming five mu of good rice-paddy land from the lake. By working hard at farming the year round, and spending little on food or clothing, and also taking advantage of their excellent house-building skills, they managed to build a brick house with a tile roof, with the help of other villagers. They were devoted to one another, and were thrifty and hard working. Truly, their lives were rich and fully happy.

In the course of time, it happened there was a landowner in their area who was mean and stingy, treacherous and sinister. He went about thinking of all sorts of wily, cunning ways he might bully and oppress the poor. Through robbing without restraint and playing clever tricks, he became an enormously rich man, lording over the Hexi region.

When the couple was in their thirties, the wife gave birth to a darling baby boy, a smiling, buoyantly happy, plump little thing fondly loved by everyone. Unexpectedly, before he was fully one year old, he had a serious illness, and money was sorely needed. The father and mother loved their son so dearly that, as much as they hated to do it, they went to the rich landowner and borrowed two or three ounces of silver, at an exorbitant interest rate. Before long, their son died. The loan they still owed the landlord increased as quickly as a donkey can roll over, and three ounces of silver became ten, then one hundred ounces. Before you could blink, they ran heavily in debt. The couple had lost their son and now their property, their house was occupied by the rich man, and their land was seized. Still worse, they ended up as farmhands working for him for nothing all their lives. They ate feed given to the pigs and dogs, and labored like horses and oxen. When they got old, that wretched dog of a landowner kicked them out, knowing that he could not squeeze any more blood and sweat out of them. Poverty stricken, without a roof tile to their name or a place for shelter, lacking the basic necessities and with nowhere to turn, they could not but swallow the landlord's insults meekly, and rent a small, broken-down fishing boat from him. They tried to eke out a living by catching fish and shrimp, staying in a small thatched shed they put up by Qilu Lake, and spending all of each day fishing around the lake.

At the end of one year, having paid off the rent for both boat and fish net, they bought a small, skinny pig with the little money they had saved by living frugally, and tied it with a straw rope to a dilapidated feeding trough. Every day, they fed the pig some small fish and a few shrimp they had set aside from their catch, and mixed these with tender tree leaves and greens.

Early one morning, the old man went out paddling his small boat to catch some fish. Many times he cast his net, from dawn till dusk, yet he didn't so much as glimpse a fish. Looking skyward in disgust, he sighed deeply, then carelessly tossed his net into the water one more time. After a while, he pulled it in and took a look. Still empty. In a fit of pique, he threw the net into the hold of his boat, and there came a thud. Something seemed to be rolling about, making a rattling sound, ba-dum, ba-dum. The old man spread out the fish net carefully—the source of the rattling turned out to be nothing other than a brown peach pit. Accepting his bad luck without complaint, the old man picked up this peach pit, and unconsciously tucked it in his pocket. Utterly exhausted after putting in a hard day's work, he paddled home, his empty stomach rumbling all the way. That same night, the old couple took advantage of the moonlight and buried the peach pit in the earth, beside the pig trough. After that, they manured it every day with pig's dung and urine, and irrigated and cultivated the soil.

Three winters and summers passed, followed by three springs and autumns. Despite the exhausting effort they made, working early in the morning and late at night under the moon and the stars, and taking painstakingly good care of the pig and the peach tree, for some unknown reason the skinny pig did not grow any bigger and was as lean as ever, while the tiny peach had but a couple of branches and a few sparse leaves. There was no sign of any blossom or fruit. Nevertheless, the good-hearted old couple took excellent care of them, as usual, without ever complaining.

Quite unexpectedly, one sunlit, enchanting spring morning, the small peach tree sent forth a dazzlingly beautiful pink bud. The old couple got all excited, and hurriedly loosened the earth around the tree, and watered and manured it. The next day, the flower bud dropped off, and in its place a tiny, fresh-green peach was found. The sight of this fruit on the tree delighted the old couple all the more. On the third morning, the small peach miraculously grew into a huge ripe, round, mellow fruit, bright yellow and fragrant, about the size of a small watermelon. Seeing the peach now, the old couple grinned from ear to ear. As they stood around the tree, looking closely at the ripe fruit and exclaiming over it, a puff of wind from the lake blew it off. By chance, the peach fell right into the pig trough, and the skinny little pig helped itself, gobbling down the peach in a few big mouthfuls.

Strange to say, no sooner had the pig eaten the peach than a dazzling, golden ray of light flashed all about, giving the old couple a start. Looking fixedly, they watched the lean pig give itself a good shake, then be transformed into a gleaming, gold pig. In the twinkling of an eye, the straw rope that tied the pig to the trough turned to gold, as did the broken-down trough. The old man and woman were stupefied at seeing this, feeling both startled and delighted at the same moment. Quite some time passed before they woke up to reality. Now they were afraid that if the greedy, rich landlord should learn what had happened, that would spell disaster. So they hurried to hide away the gold pig, the gold rope, and the gold trough in their thatched shed.

Just when they came out of the shed, a little yellow oriole landed on the peach tree, and sang out clearly and melodiously:

*Piggy fine,*
*piggy swell,*
*from its behind,*
*a treasure fell.*

The old couple scurried back into their shed to have a look. There they found the pig, its tail raised high, defecating one gold bar after another. They were elated. They picked up the gold ingots and gave them away to their poor fellow villagers.

Starting from that day, the pig had its usual feed of fish, shrimp, greens, and tree leaves, but every time it emptied its bowels, it pooped gold bars. Not long after, thanks to the gold pig, the Mongolian poor cleared all their debts and were freed from being exploited by the rich man any longer. One after another, they bought land and built houses, completely independently, and began to live a comfortable, affluent life.

Rich men cannot get along at all without exploiting the poor, and that's just how it was with this landlord. He was positively fuming with rage when he found that he had lost his means of making money. So, on the sly, he got his toadies to disguise themselves as poor people, so that they could go everywhere and find out just what was going on. It was not very long before one of these men learned the truth about the gold-pooping pig, and he rushed back to report to the landowner.

At first, the rich man could not believe his ears, and he rebuked his flunky for lying to him and pulling his leg. Bam! Bam! he slapped the man twice, making his ears swell. Holding his swollen face, trying to bear the pain, the toady pulled out a sparkling gold ingot for the land-lord to see, making a believer out of him. As the rich man snatched the bar from his man and put it into his vest, how his shifty eyes rolled! He couldn't wait to get the pig in his own clutches, so, right away, he ordered his lackeys to carry him in a big sedan chair at a quick trot to the thatched shed where the old couple dwelled.

When the villagers heard that the rich man was coming to seize the gold pig, they all stopped whatever they were doing and ran from every direction, completely surrounding the landlord. Seeing the size of the crowd, the cunning man did not dare act rashly. He used flowery nonsense to lie to the villagers, claiming that he would be perfectly satisfied if he could just see with his own eyes how the pig discharged gold ingots.

On hearing his lying words, the honest, sincere old couple led out the gold pig from their shed. When the landowner saw that this pig really was a gold pig, he became jealous of them. He simply had to have possession of that pig. At that very moment, he saw that the pig was slowly beginning to raise its tail straight up. Ah, yes! It was about to excrete some gold! The rich man was overjoyed. He scrambled to position himself on his stomach, with his face right beneath the pig's rump. His eyes were fixed to the spot, his toadlike mouth wide open. Now a rumbling of the bowel could be heard, *gurgle-gurgle*, and the gold pig pooped. A huge mass of dung and piss sprayed forth, covering the landlord's head, filling his mouth, nearly choking him, and leaving him breathless. "Hee-hee! Ha-ha!" Seeing how utterly ludicrous the rich man looked, the villagers all roared. The little oriole also kept singing gaily up on the branches of the peach tree, over and over again:

> *Piggy good,*
> *piggy great,*
> *dung and urine*
> *the rich man ate!*

That rich landlord was livid with rage about being so discredited, and he hastily yelled at his stooges to pull the gold pig away from him. But no matter how hard they tugged, the pig remained standing where it was, just as if it had taken root. The rich man seized his stick, ready to clobber the animal, but before he could make a move, the gold pig gave him a swift kick with its hind leg, and sent him somersaulting backward for a good distance, and left him bleeding from the blow to his head. Immediately, the gold pig jumped forward and flipped over the whole pack of toadies, tumbling them to the ground, and giving them nosebleeds and black eyes. Meanwhile, the pig ran away, taking its gold bars and pulling its gold feeding trough behind, and headed for Qilu

Lake without so much as turning its head to look back. It dove into a deep spot in the lake, and lay down quietly.

The gold pig had been forced by the rich man to run off from the poor old couple. They felt even sadder than the time they had lost their own son, for the pig was the common wealth of the Mongolian poor. That night, the old man and woman were so depressed they could not sleep. Early the next morning, when the sky was turning bright as a fish belly, the old man went out to fish in the lake, as usual. Just as his boat left the bank, he saw a big red carp swimming about leisurely in front of him. Paddling more quickly, he hoped he could catch up with the fish, but the faster he paddled, the faster the fish swam. When he slowed down, the fish also slowed down. It seemed as if the fish were teasing him on purpose, leading him to follow.

The little boat was led all the way to the deepest part of the lake, right in the center. There the big carp waved its red tail a few times, as if it were saying good-bye to the old man. Right after that, it fluttered its dorsal fin once more, and vanished without a trace, leaving a whirlpool behind.

As the old man was pondering the meaning of all this, beams of golden light suddenly projected out from beneath the whirlpool, dazzling his eyes. Now, using a punt-pole, he made a stab downward to the place from which the beams were coming, and he dragged up a golden chain. Eh! Wasn't this the gold chain he had used to tie the pig to the feeding trough? The old man was perplexed, and could not make up his mind what to do. At this point, the little oriole flew by, alighted on his shoulder, and began to sing:

> Find a link,
> cut a link,
> good old man,
> in the pink!

Following the directions of the oriole, the old man cut a link from the gold chain and went home. From that day on, he went out every day and brought back a gold link from the chain. As was his usual wont in the past, he gave away the gold chain links to the poor.

Not long after this episode, the rich man once again heard about what was going on. Rolling his shifty eyes, he thought of another treacherous plot. He disguised himself as an old man, and went down to the lake. But that one had never learned how to row a boat. As his little boat left the shore, it just sat there in the water, revolving round and round in circles. Scared out of his wits, the landlord lay on his belly in the hold of the boat, yelling for help. When his toadies came, he ordered them to put a dozen boats behind his and push him forward with punt-poles. As they came to the heart of the lake, sure enough, there in the deep water was a gleaming chain. The rich man excitedly ordered his flunkies to get out of his way. But, hard as he tried to boost his courage, he would not dare stand up in the shaky boat. He just arched his back, catlike, half sitting and half lying down at the same time. Pretending to strike up a rowing pose, the landlord made a few faint-hearted strokes, then hastily stuck his long punt-pole down to where the beams were coming from, and tried to hook something. Ha! What he dragged up was a real gold chain! He threw away his punt-pole, and with one hand gripping the gunwale tightly, he pulled the golden chain into the hold with the other. At this moment, the little oriole flew by, alighted on the bow, and sang repeatedly:

> Find a link,
> cut a link,
> rich, greedy man,
> about to sink!

How could a miserly, gluttonous man like the wealthy landlord listen to such words? He drove away the oriole and pulled the golden chain madly with both hands, deliberately lying on the deck, for he thought pulling with one hand was too slow.

The rich man saw that there was not enough room for the golden chain in the hold, yet he kept on pulling all the same, for all he was worth. His actions awoke the gold pig from a sound sleep at the bottom of the lake. It gave a sudden jerk that capsized the boat in which the man was riding. The gluttonous, treacherous, sinister, rich man sank to the bottom of the lake. The gold pig then thrashed around, causing the water to roll and surge, sending the toadies into the lake to feed the fish. The gold pig, nodding a farewell to the old couple's dwelling place at the west end of Qilu Lake, ran diagonally across the center of the water to the north, carrying its gold chain and pulling the gold feeding trough behind.

From then on, at the bottom of Qilu Lake, there has been a deep trough, running north to south, called Gold Pig Trough. It divides the vast expanse of the lake into two parts—East Lake and West Lake. It is said that the water in the former is clear and soft, and that in the latter is turbid and hard. The western part of the lake is shallow, but as boats plow across Gold Pig Trough to the eastern part, they suddenly find the water is ever so much deeper!

Legend has it that after the gold pig left Qilu Lake, it went north to the Langguang Sea, today called Star Cloud Lake, in the Jiangchuan District. There it took a short rest, then went straight north to the Chengjiang Sea, now known as Fairy Lake, in the Chengjiang District, where it lay quietly forever.

From that time on, the places where the gold pig passed by have had rich, bumper harvests, and flourishing populations. The lake regions where it stayed all are picturesque, with lovely mountains and charming streams, and are abundant in fish and shrimp. The longer the gold pig lay, the deeper the lake became. Right up to today, places around the Three Lakes District are beautiful, rich districts, with plenty of fish and rice, and the Chengjiang Sea is the deepest freshwater inland lake in Yunnan.

## NOTES

"Jin zhu," from *Yunnan minzu minjian gushi xuan* 1982, 570–75. Collectors: Yang Jinshu (Mongol) and Zhao Yinsheng (Han). Redactor: Zhao Yinsheng. Area of distribution: Xicheng, Tonghai County, ninety miles southeast of Kunming.

**mu.** Approximately 0.16 acre.
**Three Lakes District.** The three lakes, located between fifty and ninety miles southeast of Kunming, are Fuxian Hu, Qilu Hu, and Xingyun Hu.

# The Arrogant Tiger

## WA TALE

The little animals in the forest always hugely admired the coat of their dear pal the scaly anteater [pangolin], for it is made of layer after layer of scales that stones cannot break and a drenching rain cannot soak. It is both tough and durable and, when the sun shines, the coat sparkles and shimmers! The little companions around the scaly anteater all thought him really handsome in his suit of clothes, and majestic too. "Brother scaly anteater," they said, singing his praises, "we can see that this coat of yours is the source of your martial art. If anyone dares to bully you, all you have to do is bristle, and each scale becomes a sharp arrow!"

On hearing his friends' praises, the scaly anteater modestly replied, "Though I have a scaly coat to protect myself, in real fighting, something more than shining weaponry is needed. We ought to unite as one, like rattan strips twisted together. Then we could overcome ferocious enemies!"

The little animals found the scaly anteater's words quite sound. Clapping their hands in approval, they said, "Even good weapons are useless to cowards! Recently, that arrogant tiger has been trying to intimidate us all the time by taking advantage of his great physical strength. We've got to think of a way to teach him a lesson!"

The scaly anteater agreed. "Right enough! How many times in the past few days has the tiger thrown his weight around in front of us? We really have to give him a taste of his own medicine. Otherwise, he won't know whether the wild, burning hot *shuanshuanla* pepper is hot or sweet!"

The little companions were all for the scaly anteater's taking bold action. As they took leave of him, they said, "Excellent idea, Brother!

166

Well, we have to go now, as we're guests at our big brother muntjac's place. We look forward to hearing news of your victory."

After seeing off his animal friends, the scaly anteater went digging with his iron claws to make a cave-house. As soon as he started working, the arrogant tiger came a-strutting and a-swaggering along. When he caught sight of the scaly anteater, the tiger immediately sat his fanny down on a rock, and struck a fierce pose. "Hey you, small fry! I'm hungry. Get me something to eat, and be quick about it!"

The scaly anteater was not bothered a bit by the tiger. "Mr. Tiger," he responded coolly, "the rainy season here at Awa Mountain is almost upon us. Can't you see I'm busy digging a hole to make a house? Where am I going to find time to feed you? What's more, though I've worked the whole day straight, I haven't had anything to eat myself."

The tiger would have none of this. "What do I care if you die of starvation!" he roared. "Anyway, Tiger's tummy is a-growling. Small fry like you better hop and get me something to eat. Otherwise, I'll eat you instead!"

"We Wa folks have a saying: 'He who intends to eat others will be eaten by others!'"

The tiger got really mad. "Grrr! Grrr!" he roared. "I am the king of the mountain! Can there be anybody on all of Awa Mountain who would dare to harm a single hair of my head?"

The scaly anteater had come into contact with this arrogant tiger many times before. He knew well there was no use arguing with him. Just then, at the foot of the mountain slope below, he saw two men in the terraced field. They had been hoeing a dry upland area for planting. At that moment they were making a fire to cook. Suddenly, a bright idea struck the scaly anteater. He spoke to the tiger, pointing to the blue smoke at the foot of the mountain slope, "Take a look at that, Mr. Tiger! Those two men who've been working the field must have cooked rice all set by now. Since you're hungry, go help yourself!"

"I've been running about the whole day, and I'm just too tired to walk," the tiger answered, impatiently. "You go and bring the rice here for me!"

After thinking this over a bit, the scaly anteater said, "Eh! Mr. Tiger, there's no need to use your feet if you're tired. We'll simply roll down the slope. When the two men see Mr. Tiger coming, they'll be scared for sure, and will run away. Won't you eat a full meal then?"

"Hee-hee," the tiger chucked. "Ai-ya! I never thought a small fry the likes of you had a brain bigger than a pineapple. Great idea! Let's the two of us roll down the slope and see just whom the hoe folks really are afraid of."

"Men are afraid of tigers, of course!" the scaly anteater hastened to reply.

This comment made the arrogant tiger feel so full of himself, why he nearly burst with pride. "Hey! Just look at your clothes, all tattered and ragged," he said haughtily. "If I roll down the slope with you, won't the hoe folks make fun of me? You tumble down first instead, small fry!"

The anteater nodded in agreement. "Mr. Tiger, you have such pretty, decorative stripes on your fur, but deep down inside you just want to eat people! Well, I'll roll down first and see what happens. I hope those men don't want to catch me!"

The tiger felt all the more smug, and urged on the scaly anteater. "Since you know how terrible I am, why don't you get out of here and get rolling!"

Pulling in his bristling scales, the scaly anteater contracted himself into a ball and tumbled down the slope. The scales, which covered his body like an iron sheet, clinked and clanked as they banged on the rocks. On hearing the uproar, the two men below thought boulders from a landslide were tumbling down the mountain, so each kept his distance to avoid getting hurt.

When the smug tiger saw what had happened, he laughed. "Hey! Even a little scaly anteater rolling down a slope can scare people and make them give way. Obviously, the courage of human beings is smaller than a sesame seed. I'd be really surprised if those two hoe folks don't get so scared when I come rolling down that they run off and leave their tools behind!" And down rolled Mr. Tiger.

As soon as the scaly anteater saw that he had tricked the tiger, he jumped onto an elevated terrace and screamed at the top of his lungs,

"The tiger is rolling down the slope now! Quick! Come beat the tiger! Come beat the tiger!"

When he heard the anteater, the tiger roared, "Damn you, small fry! Don't you know how to talk right? You're supposed to say—'Mr. Tiger is coming down the mountain. Fetch him some well-cooked rice right now! Hurry up and . . .'"

The area farmers and the scaly anteater's little animal friends, who had been guests at the muntjac's house, didn't even wait for the tiger to finish his sentence. As soon as they heard the anteater's call, they charged up with their hoes and sticks, shouting, "Beat the tiger! Beat the tiger!" They crowded around him and let their hoes and sticks fall with a thud and a splat on his striped body, leaving him no chance to get up from the ground and escape.

The tiger, who had always proudly boasted that he was the greatest creature on Awa Mountain, was beaten to death.


## NOTES

"Jiao'ao de laohu," from Guo 1979, 37–41. Storyteller: Wang Na (Wa). Translator: Zhao Yuming (Wa). Collector and redactor: Guo Sijiu (Han). Area of distribution: Cangyuan Wa Autonomous County, southwestern Yunnan.

**pineapple-size brain.** The pineapple is said to have many "eyes" and thus is a symbol of intelligence and resourcefulness.

# The Gathering of the Birds

## YAO LEGEND

On Mount Yao in Mojiang Hani Autonomous County, Yunnan province, there is a village inhabited by the Yao people surrounded by high mountains. Every year around October, when the weather turns hazy, the village is enveloped in mist, and the autumn rain falls incessantly, partridges, in groups of three or five, can be seen whirring through the sky above Mount Yao and calling to one another: "R-rrrr, R-rrrr!" Soon the partridges are replaced by a flock of newcomers, the egrets, circling in the sky and croaking hoarsely. According to the Yao folk, the behavior of the partridges and egrets is a harbinger of the mysterious and magnificent gathering of the birds which is about to begin. At this time both the Yao and the Hani people busy themselves with ushering in this once-a-year event.

On the evening following the appearance of the egrets, the Yao folk gather piles of firewood and build scores of bonfires, big and small, on their threshing floor, and light them up. The entire mountain village is set aglow by these fires. It is then that a vast variety of birds—turtle-doves, tits, golden orioles, Chinese bulbuls, woodpeckers, long-tailed birds of paradise, whistlers, kingfishers, ring-necked pheasants, canon pheasants, silver pheasants, red pheasants, magpies, hawks, cliff swallows, white peacocks, and other, unknown birds, gorgeously plumed—make their appearance, one after another. They circle in the air, crying aloud, ascending and descending, now near, now far. With wings outspread, they sweep past the Yao bonfires and thatched houses. Half the sky of the Yao mountain village is filled with these flocks of birds, big and small, forming a surpassingly beautiful world of birds that is a complete wonder.

The most beautiful birds of all, the peacocks, will be the last to arrive, deep in the middle of the night. They fly slowly, their golden-green plumage iridescent in the sky, as though they are flaunting their sumptuous beauty. *Ai-ya, ai-ya,* sound their plaintive calls, so solemn and stirring, and in the twinkling of an eye, all the other birds appear in the air, accompanying the peacocks, circling, revolving, and crying dolefully. For the Yao people there watching this curiosity of nature, to see this gathering of the birds is like living in a fairy tale world.

How is it that this mysterious gathering of the birds should take place on Mount Yao in the autumn of every year? The Yao tell a beautiful, touching legend about the origin of this event.

It is said that in ancient times there lived in the Yao mountains a hardworking old man by the name of Zhatuoye. He was kindhearted to others and faithfully went about his work of farming and hunting. A man of moral integrity, he had never offended anybody in the village or done anything bad. But the god of heaven was always unfair to him, so that when he reached sixty, he was still childless. Because there were no children, the brows of the old man and his wife were always furrowed in despair. All day long they spoke little and never laughed. They passed their days in misery and loneliness. Glutinous rice lost its savory aroma and even sugar-water no longer tasted sweet to them.

Every year they would kill pigs and sheep to offer to the god of heaven in sacrifice, and every morning they would get up early to pray fervently to the god of heaven, beseeching him to bestow upon them a lovely child. As time went by, their wish came true. On the very evening Zhatuoye celebrated his sixtieth birthday, both of them had a dream. In their dream they saw a golden peacock, dazzlingly bright, which flew across the night sky to their side and spoke to them: "Ah! You old people are so good and honest, I am willing to be your daughter!" It was through this very dream that the old man's wife became pregnant.

From that time on, the old man's face beamed from morning to night. He became talkative and even took to singing.

After nine months passed, a baby was born, the most beautiful little girl. The old couple loved her so much that they held her in their arms all day long, hugging and kissing her again and again. They gave her a lovely, pleasant-sounding name, Azhamana, and invited all the villagers to join them in celebrating the birth of their child.

Azhamana could chuckle and laugh when she was two months old. Her chuckle was as sweet to the ear as the singing of the babbler thrush. The good old man, Zhatuoye, so delighted in her babbling that he could not fall asleep for several nights running. Azhamana knew how to walk at just six months. She was as bright and amusing as a yellow finch. Wherever the good old man went, he spoke about everything she did.

When Azhamana was one year old, her mother died of a sudden illness. The only one left in the house to look after Azhamana was her poor father, who wept and mourned night and day over the death of his wife. Azhamana comforted her father with her laughter. They depended on each other for survival, and were never apart.

At three, this pretty, clever girl learned to put sheep out to pasture. At four, she could spin, at five, weave, at six, embroider, and at seven, she knew how to cut firewood. By the time she was sixteen, Azhamana had learned all the skilled work that people know how to do.

At seventeen, beautiful Azhamana was considered the most clever girl on earth. With her quick hands she could embroider all kinds of flowers, grasses, and birds. The more she embroidered the better she got, until finally she could embroider flowers that grew and birds that flew.

When she was eighteen, she wanted to present the world with the most beautiful birds there could be, so she went and hid herself in a thatched hut and started embroidering. On the first day she embroidered a beautiful peacock which flew from the cloth and mounted up to the sky. On the second day she embroidered a lovebird, and it flew up from the cloth too. On the third day she embroidered a multicolored canon pheasant, and it also flew up into the sky. So from that time on, lovebirds and pheasants were found in the mountain forest.

Azhamana kept on working for 360 days, and 360 birds were embroidered. These birds flew off into the forest and the human world, and the forest and the human world became even more lovely.

The news that Azhamana had embroidered birds that came alive spread all across the land like a gust of wind. No one knew who told, but someone brought word to Hengluoye, the greedy headman. Hengluoye longed to have Azhamana for his concubine, so he asked a matchmaker to go to Zhatuoye's house with thirty cows and three hundred sheep as gifts, and make an offer of marriage. Despite the herds of cattle and sheep that covered the mountain, the old man's heart was not moved, and he rejected the proposal. Finally, the headman came himself bearing much gold, silver, satin, wine, and meat to seek the girl's hand. But neither gold, silver, satin, wine, nor meat could move Azhamana's heart, and Hengluoye was rejected again.

Having failed to win the beautiful Azhamana's love, though he had used every possible means, the greedy headman thought up an evil plan. He gave orders to have Azhamana tied to his horse and carried away by force.

In tears, the good old man poured out his misfortunes, telling all the Yao people. On hearing his story, they were filled with righteous indignation. With one heart and one mind, and blowing their bugles and beating their gongs, they set out bearing their longbows and crossbows to overtake Hengluoye in order to snatch beautiful Azhamana from the devil's hand.

They chased the headman to the edge of a cliff, and there the Yao men let fly a volley of arrows, hitting both the headman and his horse. Man and beast tumbled down the precipice and were smashed to bits. Poor Azhamana, who had been tied to the horse's back, was terribly crushed and nearly dead. The Yao folk tried to save her by taking her home and feeding her honey water, but she was dying. Holding his beloved daughter in his arms, the good old man cried his eyes out and mourned until his throat grew hoarse. Still, there was no hope of keeping his daughter from death. He knelt down on the earth and prayed fervently to the god of heaven, but no matter what he did, he could not save her. That evening, pretty Azhamana left the human world forever. A golden peacock flew out of the old man's arms, its plumage glittering with flashes of golden light.

The old man's bitter weeping attracted many birds, which flew around his thatched house wailing piteously. These were the birds that had been embroidered by Azhamana herself. To show that they cherished her memory, they cried plaintively in the sky above Mount Yao all through the night. From that time on, once every year on Mount Yao, there has been a lovely, mysterious gathering of the birds.

## NOTE

"Yaoshan niaohui de chuanshuo," from Huang Bocang (Han) 1982, 249–53. Collector and redactor: Liu Shu (Han). Area of distribution: Yaojia Mountain, Mojiang County, southern Yunnan. Liu Shu is director of the Simao Prefecture Cultural Center.

# Sun, Moon, and Stars

## JINGPO MYTH

When heaven and earth were first clearly divided, the world was not so bright as it is today. It was only a vast expanse of murky grey. The sun, moon, and stars did not exist. At that time, a poor woman and her three daughters lived together in the woods. The three sisters were named Hosuni, Dosuni, and Bisuni.

One day, the mother was getting ready to go out, and before she left the house, she warned her girls, "I'm going to look for something for us to eat. Keep the door locked, and stay home. Don't go out and don't open the door. I'll be back before long." And off she went.

The three daughters waited and waited inside the house for their mother to come back, but a long, long time passed, and still she had not returned.

In the forest there was a leopard-demon who had ever been scheming how to allure the daughters to leave their house so he could eat them, but he could never find a way, simply because Hosuni, Dosuni, and Bisuni were so closely guarded by their mother. That particular day, he realized the mother had been gone an awfully long while, so he passed by their door, disguised as a young man singing a folk song. At first, the three sisters were astonished to hear someone sing, and then they were scared. But the more they listened to the song, the more they liked what they heard. Surely it was a young man, after all! Convinced the leopard-demon really was a youth singing them folk songs, the three girls opened the door and walked in the direction of his voice. But once they got near and had a look, they realized that their young man was none other than a leopard-demon in disguise. Then and there, they changed direction, and ran for home. Wearing a big grin on his face, the leopard-demon gave chase, intending to catch the three sisters, but they quickly scurried up a tree. The leopard-demon tried to climb up too, but he couldn't do it.

"Hey, girls!" he said, unctuously. "I'm here on a visit to see my relatives. Rest assured I wouldn't do you any harm. Won't you please just teach me how to climb a tree? If you do, I will remember your kindness my whole, entire life long."

Hosuni and Dosuni refused to trust the leopard-demon, and wouldn't tell him a thing. But their littlest sister, Bisuni, didn't know any better, and she blurted out, unthinkingly, "Why, there's nothing at all to tree climbing! All you have to do is start with your hands, and then use your feet, back and forth, back and forth." It was much too late now for the two older sisters to shush up Bisuni. The leopard-demon climbed the tree, following the little girl's advice, alternating his front paws and back legs.

Ever since that day, leopards have known how to climb trees.

When Hosuni, Dosuni, and Bisuni saw that the leopard-demon had learned to climb, they were so nervous that they headed straight for the top of the tree. But the leopard-demon followed right behind. At that point, the three girls all bawled at the top of their lungs in a fit of despair.

Now it just so happened that a god from heaven was passing by. He was enormously sympathetic. "Little girls, now stop crying. I can save you by taking you to heaven. But there is just one problem: once you are up there, you can't come back down here. How would you feel about that?" Seeing that the leopard-demon was getting closer and closer, Hosuni, Dosuni, and Bisuni hastily agreed that they liked the idea very much. Raising his hand on high, the god took them up to heaven.

After they got to heaven, the three lived quite happily, but they missed their dear mother, and they longed to see the good earth again. So they earnestly pleaded with the god to let them return. The god said, "You may take turns. Since Hosuni is the eldest, let her go first. After that, Dosuni, then Bisuni." So, Hosuni went first. After she came back, Dosuni and Bisuni had a turn. Each of them got to visit their mother, and see the earth, the forest, and the river where they had once lived.

When their mother had returned home, and found that her daughters were missing, she had looked for them everywhere, but could not find them. She got to see them, however, when they came visiting. But now they were in heaven, while she was on the earth, and no longer could they live together.

Every day, Hosuni and her sisters would take turns seeing their mother and the earth. In the course of time, Hosuni became the sun, while Dosuni and Bisuni became the moon and the stars. From then on, there was day and night. Sometimes, Dosuni and Bisuni appear together, and at other times, the younger sister comes out all by herself. That's why, at night, sometimes the moon and the stars appear at the same time, and at other times only the stars can be seen.

## NOTE

"Taiyang, yueliang, he xingxing," from Oukunbo (Xu Kun) (Han) 1983, 16–18. Collector and redactor: Murannaodou (Jingpo). Area of distribution: Dehong Dai-Jingpo Autonomous Prefecture, western Yunnan. Oukunbo is one of Xu Kun's pen names, an acronym made from the names of three collectors and redactors of Jingpo folk literature: Duan Shengou, Xu Kun, and Zhou Xingbo. Murannaodou is the son of a Jingpo headman.

# WONDER

# AND

# MAGIC

# The Magic Shoulder Pole

## YI TALE

In the region the Yi people inhabit in the southern part of Yunnan, there is a mountain the people call Guanyin Mountain, after the goddess of mercy. On the mountain is a pond with wonderfully clear water. Herders from the villages used to let their cattle graze on the slopes nearby every day, while they themselves would have fun by the pond. When thirsty, the cattle would come down without being led to drink out of the pond, then return to grazing.

Every morning, there were, altogether, ninety-nine head of cattle that would arrive at the pond. But by noon, there would be a hundred head, and, in addition, a beautiful maiden who appeared among the herdsmen. At sunset, when the herders all went home, they would have with them ninety-nine head of cattle, as before, and the maiden would have disappeared. No one could figure out just how the cow and the maiden had left without being noticed. The herders were terribly fond of this girl, for she knew many things, and could tell many a lovely, moving story.

One day, the maiden said to the herdsmen, "Among your cattle there is a magic bull. When he moves through water, the water makes way for him. He can also walk on water. Riding this magic bull, you would have nothing to fear, even if you were to cross the East China Sea. His hide is covered with precious treasures—with just one of his hairs you could carry a load of several thousand jin, without feeling the least bit tired."

It goes without saying that the herders really wanted to know now which was the magic bull, but the maiden would not tell them. All she would say was, "Only an honest man could receive such precious treasures."

One day, while the herders had gone off to pick fruit, the whole herd of cattle ran down the slopes to a cornfield. The old man who kept watch over the cornfield could not keep away so many head, so he snatched up a flat shoulder pole that lay beside him and beat the cows one after another, until they were driven off. The pole, which he used daily, had split due to much exposure to rain and sun. When he hit the cattle hard, cracks in the pole widened, and a bit of cattle hair got jammed in the fissures. But the old man took no notice.

As the sun sloped westward, the old man tied together a big bundle of firewood to carry home, as was his wont. "Hey! How light my load is today!" he exclaimed. When he lifted the flat pole to his shoulder, he felt there was something very strange going on. Then, he added another bundle of firewood, and when he tried to carry it, it was as light as if nothing had been added at all. He did the same thing over and over again, adding more and more wood to his load, and testing how heavy it was. Now his load looked like two great mountains of firewood, with just a small opening between. The old man squeezed into this tiny space, lifted the two big bundles on his shoulder, and went merrily on his way home, his steps quick and light.

From that time on, every day the old man carried firewood to town to sell. With the money he made, he not only was able to pay for his food and wine, but each day he also had several hundred strings of cash left over. His life was getting better and better.

One day, while he was carrying his firewood to town for sale as usual, he saw a rich man walking toward him. When the rich man took in this huge load, he marveled. He looked hard at the carrier and saw that it was an old man. This made him feel the situation was stranger still. "How could this old man carry so much firewood?" he wondered. He moved closer to ask, and the old man answered, "This shoulder pole of mine is magic!" The rich man did not believe him, so he asked the old man to put down his load so he could have a try at lifting it himself. Sure enough, he felt just as though he were carrying nothing at all. Rolling his eyes evilly, the rich man said, "Let me have your pole. I'll give you five hundred liang of silver for it."

The old man was reluctant to part with his pole, but what with the rich man pressing him so hard, he could do little but accept his offer. Now the rich man became the owner of the magic pole, while the old man had a lot of silver.

When the rich man got home, he inspected his pole up and down, over and over, and was beside himself with joy. He noticed there were a few cracks which made the pole look a bit rough, so he took it himself to the shop of the most expert carpenter he knew, and had it planed all smooth and shining under his own direct supervision. He studied it again, feeling that now it was perfectly flawless. Little did he know that the hair of the magic bull, caught in the cracks, had all been planed away.

The rich man's wife thought it extremely odd that day to see her husband so ecstatic. "Last year we took in more than one thousand dan of rental grain a day, yet he was never as happy as he is today!" Knowing that he could not keep this secret from his wife, the rich man had to explain the story of his magic pole. Half believing what he said, his wife wanted to have a try at carrying a heavy load, but was afraid that she might sprain her back. So she attached to each end of the pole something weighing a mere ten jin, and bent down to lift. Ugh! How heavy it was!

"Pah! This is nothing but a shit stick! What a magic pole this is! You are simply daydreaming!"

The rich man was undaunted and remained elated about his shoulder pole. He told his wife, "How can a woman know what a treasure is? Now just look at this!" With that, he added scores of jin to each end of the pole, then bent over to lift the load. "Ai-ya! What's wrong? My magic pole has really changed."

He took up the pole and began beating his wife, all the while yelling at her, "You scum of a woman! Unlucky thing. You've driven off my pole's magic!"

# NOTES

"Bao biandan," from *Yunnan minzu minjian gushi xuan* 1982, 71–73. Collector and redactor: Pu Ying (Yi). Area of distribution: Chuxiong Yi Autonomous Prefecture,
midway between Kunming and Dali.

**jin.** About one pound.
**liang.** About 1.75 ounces.
**dan.** About 110 pounds.

# Nabulousi,
# the Life-Restoring Tree

## LAHU MYTH

Back in the very ancient past, in a village surrounded by azure hills and shaded by emerald-green bamboo, there lived a pitiful young man who had neither father nor mother. In order to get enough to eat, he had to open up a small plot of land far away in the remote mountains. This orphan was utterly devoted to his tiny plot, leaving home early every day and coming back home late at night. As the saying goes, "Where there is a will there is a way." With the rain and dew from dear heaven and his own sweat, the corn that he had sown ripened at last. How happy he was! Looking at the high rows of corn with their scarlet tassels, he felt reluctant to eat them. He touched this ear and that one, then examined another, and finally counted them all up. He returned home in high spirits, relishing the thought of how much corn he had.

That night, after he got back, he had a dream. In his dream he saw the corn, all ready for harvest, being stolen by the tribal headman. He was so worried he woke up with a start, and could not fall back asleep. He waited and waited for dawn to break, but it seemed as if it would never come. At last, burning with impatience, he ran to the distant mountain. When he reached the edge of his land, ah! his heart sank. Yesterday the cornstalks had been heavy with ears, and now not a single one was left. Everywhere the ground was littered with the leavings of corn sheaves, husks, and trampled stalks, and everywhere too were the footprints of wild boars. He turned livid with rage. His painstaking labor of an entire year, completely wasted! He actually longed to cry his heart out, but he was a man, and a man cannot shed tears easily. A man must take revenge. He decided he must make the boars pay. It was going to be his life against theirs, regardless of the danger. And so, having found a thick, strong cudgel, he proceeded to follow the tracks.

How hard he looked for them, searching on and on! At last he found them in a deep, cavernous gorge. The culprits turned out to be a whole litter of young boars, now fast asleep, their bellies stuffed from gorging themselves. Strewn about beside them were piles of discarded corn-stalks. The sow, however, was not there. Perfect! Now was the right time to take revenge! He raised his cudgel and lashed out at the young boars with all his might. Not until he had killed every last one did he feel released from his hatred. Just then, the sow came back. The young man had no time to escape. All he could do was quickly climb up a big tree nearby and hide himself.

When the sow saw that all her little ones were dead, she neither cried nor mourned, nor showed the least sign of sadness. Instead, she calmly moved over to the tree near the litter and gnawed off a piece of its bark, chewed for a while, and then fed each shoat a mouthful. Before long, all the dead boars came back to life, and the sow led her litter away.

Meanwhile, up in the tree, the orphan saw clearly all that had happened below. "Could it be that this tree that saved the lives of the boars is a *nabulousi*, a 'life-restoring tree'?" he wondered. "Maybe I should try it out myself."

He climbed down from the big *nabulousi* tree and peeled off a piece of its bark, then tucked it away in his clothes to take it home. As soon as he entered his stockaded village, he heard that a girl of a certain family was dying. He thought at once that this might be the very chance for him to test the tree, so he went straight to the young girl's home and told her parents, "Let me see if I can save her." Her parents were grieving deeply and found the young man's behavior simply shocking. But then they thought to themselves that since their daughter was dying, why not let him have a try? People around them stared at him, half believing and half disbelieving. They watched him take a piece of bark, chew it in his mouth, then put it in the mouth of the girl. After a while, she slowly came to and, before long, was able to sit up, saying she was all right now. The people were simply astonished, while the girl's parents were so ecstatic they insisted on marrying their daughter to the orphan. He could hardly resist their offer. All he could do was explain to them: "I have no parents, no relatives, not a single room, not even a plot of land or enough food to eat, let alone enough clothes to keep me warm. How can I take a wife?"

But the parents insisted: "We can be your parents and relatives. We have a house. You can marry our daughter and live with us. We guarantee that you'll have enough to eat and enough to keep you warm."

The orphan could not but accept their offer. "Wait until I get money for us to marry," he said. "I'll live with you for the time being." The parents agreed, and so the marriage was postponed. After that, the young man began practicing medicine, and never refused any patient, whether rich or poor, but helped anyone who asked. When treating his patients, he took some money from the rich, but he asked for just a cup of cold water from the poor. He became more renowned with each passing day. Villagers far and near all knew him.

One day it happened that the headman of a distant village became seriously ill. People looked everywhere for this orphan but it was not until evening that they found him. By then the headman was already dead. The orphan calmly took out his medicine and put it into the mouth of the dead man and, after a while, he came back to life. But this headman had an evil mind. He thought to himself, "If I could get hold of this medicine I would never die." But what kind of medicine was it, and where did that orphan find it? He asked his family members if they had ever seen what this medicine really looked like. They told him it seemed that the young man had in his hand a piece of tree bark. "If so," he thought, "this medicine must be from a specific kind of tree. I must get possession of it."

The headman came to the orphan bringing a little gold and silver, saying he would like to buy the tree. "That tree is everybody's tree," the young man informed him. "It would not do to let it belong to any single individual." Moreover, he would not tell the headman what kind of tree it was, or where it could be found.

The headman was incensed and ordered his caretaker to take hold of the orphan and search him, but he could not find anything at all, for the orphan never carried any medicine with him unless he was visiting patients. This was his way of guarding himself against robbers. Still, the headman would not give up. After he got home he thought of another scheme. This time he told his caretaker to find some pretext, and beat to death a poor man's child in the village. To save this child, the orphan went back to the mountain to obtain some more medicine, and when he left, the headman sent someone to follow his tracks secretly, while he himself tailed behind.

When the young man reached the nabulousi tree and began peeling its bark, the headman could not refrain from bursting out with laughter. "Get hold of him!" he shouted fanatically, and when the orphan was taken, he told him, "I nicely offered to buy the medicine, but you wouldn't sell. Now you are caught on the spot and have to give it to me for nothing!" Again he roared with laughter.

The orphan held on to the tree trunk for dear life and would not let go, but the headman ordered his lackeys to tear him away and cut down the tree. Yet, no matter how hard they pulled, they could not remove him, for it seemed as if he were glued to the tree. This made the headman even more furious. "Cut down both the tree and the man!" he cried fiercely.

No sooner did his underlings unsheath their swords and begin to chop away, than suddenly a powerful wind blew, and both earth and sky were obscured. Nothing was visible. When the gale subsided and the sky brightened again, both tree and orphan had vanished, leaving not a trace. Where the tree had once stood was only a big pit. High above, the orphan could be seen, still clinging to the tree, and flying slowly up to the moon. Ever since then, this tree has remained on the moon.

After the departure of the nabulousi tree from the earth and the subsequent murder of the Lahu hero Zhanuzhabie, by Esha, god of heaven, there has been nowhere to find the life-restoring nabulousi tree.

Later on, people wove a straw ladder that reached to heaven, and sent a white rabbit to the moon to fetch the life-restoring medicine. But Esha learned about this, and caused a gust of wind to blow the ladder away. The rabbit could not come back down to earth, but had to stay on the moon and keep the orphan company. That is why people today can still see the *nabulousi* tree, the orphan, and the white rabbit pounding medicinal herbs in a mortar on the moon.

## NOTES

"Nabulousi," from *Yunnan minzu minjian gushi xuan* 1982, 427–30. Storyteller: Zhayue (Laohu). Redactor: Zhang Rongli (Han). Area of distribution: Lancang Lahu Autonomous County, southwestern Yunnan.

**Esha.** Esha is the most powerful divinity in the Lahu pantheon, but like the mightiest gods belonging to other minorities, his power is not absolute. Divinities in minority myths often contend with and defeat a higher god.

# The Nine Brothers

YI TALE

At some unknown time, long ago, there was a couple who were approaching old age, but still had no child. The husband was most unhappy, while his wife mourned and wept all day long.

One day the woman ran to a pond intending to kill herself. At that very moment, a gray-haired old man appeared right in front of her. He asked her, calmly, "What has made you feel so sad that you should want to commit suicide?" The woman told him all about her agony. He comforted her, saying, "Don't worry! I'll give you nine special herb pellets. Take one of these every year and you will be able to give birth to one child each year. After you finish taking all nine pellets, you will have nine children." With these words, the old man disappeared.

The woman was all too eager to have children. As soon as she went back home, she took out the medicine the old man had given her. But then, she began to worry that if she took only one pellet every year, that might not be so effective, so she swallowed the whole dose of nine pellets at once.

Before long, the woman became pregnant, just as predicted. When it was time for her to deliver, she gave birth to nine babies, but no sooner were they born than they burst out crying. Now, with so many children in the house, and with nothing to feed or clothe them, the woman and her husband became very sad. Looking at their poor, miserable offspring having such a hard time made both parents feel as though a knife were being twisted in their hearts. Finding no way out, the woman dejectedly bore her babies on her back and went to the pond, prepared to cast them all into the water. But when she looked at the faces of her babies, each one smiling at her, she loved them so much she could not make the heartless decision. But if she didn't get rid of them, what could she feed them? Sooner or later, weren't they bound to starve to death? Such a dilemma! Again and again she wept bitter tears.

At this time the gray-haired old man reappeared. He asked her in the same gentle tone, "What has happened now to make you so sad?" Once again, the woman told him her troubles. He comforted her by saying, "Don't worry! Go home in peace. Your children won't be begging for food or clothing from you in the future. They will be able to grow up without your help." Then the old man selected a special name for each of the nine children: Power House, Big Belly, Never Hungry, Unbeatable, Big Foot, Fireproof, Can't Chill, Can't Chop, and Floater. Having given them names, the old man was gone.

Indeed, the nine brothers grew up on their own, without ever needing to eat.

One day it happened that one of the pillars in the imperial palace engraved with dragons collapsed. It was huge and heavy, and nobody could budge it. The emperor issued an imperial edict to the people of the world, saying, "Whoever can place this pillar back in its former position will be amply rewarded by His Highness." When this news reached the nine brothers, they talked it over and decided that Power House should go and try his luck.

That evening, Power House arrived at the palace and put the pillar back in its place without even being noticed. The next day, when the emperor saw the pillar, he was shocked. He gave an order that the man who fixed the pillar had to be found. Someone informed him that the job had been done by one of the nine brothers. The emperor could not believe this was true, so he told his servants to boil several *dou* of rice, then have the brother eat them as a test. If he could finish them off, that would prove he was the repairman who had replaced the pillar. If he couldn't eat every last *dou*, then he was a fake, and would have to be punished. When the emperor's order reached the house of the nine brothers, they decided that Big Belly should go in place of Power House.

Big Belly arrived at the palace and ate up all the rice in no time at all. He didn't even feel it was enough, and asked the emperor for more. The emperor was shocked and sent off the brother immediately.

Following that episode, the emperor could never rest easy. He thought to himself, "If I do not get rid of this man, some day he will seize my kingdom. He then thought of an evil scheme and issued a decree that the brother be caught and starved to death.

When the news came to the house of the nine brothers, they decided that Never Hungry should take Big Belly's place and try his luck.

When Never Hungry came to the palace, the emperor ordered at once that he be locked up. For seven days and seven nights, Never Hungry had nothing to eat. The emperor thought that surely the man had starved to death, but to his surprise, Never Hungry was as vigorous as he had been seven days before. The emperor could do nothing but set him free.

Sitting or sleeping, the emperor always felt uncomfortable now. He thought of another mean plan, and issued an order that the man be caught and, this time, be beaten to death. When the nine brothers heard of this, they talked it over and decided that, this time, Unbeatable should go try his luck instead of Never Hungry.

When Unbeatable came to the palace, the emperor gave orders at once that the man should be bound, then beaten to death with sticks. The palace toughs swarmed around, their sticks falling on Unbeatable's body like rain. Unbeatable shouted, "Boy, does that feel great! You're scratching me right where it itches!" Finally, the toughs broke all their sticks, without harming a single hair of Unbeatable's head. The emperor had no choice but to set the man free.

The emperor racked his brains night and day, and again thought of an evil scheme. He ordered that the man be caught and pushed over a cliff, so that he would be crushed alive. This time, Big Foot went. When the emperor's men tried to push Big Foot down the precipice, one of his feet came to rest at the foot of the cliff, while the other stood on the hilltop opposite. The emperor had failed again.

The emperor was so afraid, he could not sleep at night. All day long he was knotted up thinking bad thoughts. He pondered to himself, "Since this man never starves, and can't be beaten or crushed, why not burn him to death!" This time, Fireproof went to the palace. The emperor ordered a big heap of firewood lighted, but not a single strand of Fireproof's hair was singed. The emperor's bonfire was useless.

The emperor was really worried now. He gave orders that the man be cast on a snowy mountain and left to freeze. This time, Can't Chill went. Cold as the snow-covered mountain was, it did not do him any harm, and he came back safe and sound.

The emperor became desperate. He ordered the man caught and chopped to death. This time, Can't Chop went. The emperor's big blades fell again and again, but not only did Can't Chop not die, there wasn't a wound on his body. Instead, the swords were full of nicks and notches.

Now the emperor became furious. He decreed that the man must be caught, thrown into the river, and drowned.

Floater was cast into the river, where he swam back and forth freely, just like a fish. He was neither overcome by the waves, nor carried away by the river. Instead, he sucked up a mouthful of water and spit it at the emperor, causing the imperial family and their entire palace to roll right into the surging river, which carried them away.

The nine brothers were victorious over the emperor, and they eliminated the tyranny which had oppressed the people. From that time on, everyone lived happily, and the story of the nine brothers was ever on people's lips.

NOTES

"Jiu xiongdi," from *Yunnan minzu minjian gushi xuan* 1982, 68–70. Collector and redactor: Pu Ying (Yi). Area of distribution: Chuxiong Yi Autonomous Prefecture, midway between Kunming and Dali.

**dou.** A dry measure of rice in a square wooden tub, equivalent to 2.2 gallons.

# The Head-Baby

## LAHU MYTH

Long, long ago, in an age yet primitive, there was a village halfway up one side of a high mountain, surrounded by green bamboo, where the Lahu people lived. In this village lived a widow who had to do farm work all by herself, because she was the only person left in her family. One day, she went to the mountain to cut grass. How she chopped, on and on, so hot and tired, never pausing to rest! Looking up, she could not find even a wisp of a cloud in the endless, deep, blue sky, or a breath of air rustling the leaves. She was listless, thirsty, and soaked through with sweat. How she longed for a drink of clear, cool, spring water!

But no matter how much she wandered about the mountain, she could not find a single drop of water. She had no choice but to quickly descend to the foot of the mountain. There, she caught sight of the tracks of a huge elephant, and she followed them along until, all of a sudden, she discovered, not too far in the distance, a low-lying puddle of shimmering water. "Oh, Esha almighty! This must be water you have provided to save my life!" And she struggled on to reach the puddle. When she came near, she saw in a glance that there was a depression in the ground, made by the tramping of a giant elephant's foot, which formed a puddle into which water seeped. She lay down flat on her stomach and drank to her heart's content, not caring whether the water was clean or not. "Ah, how cool and refreshing this water is! It's sweeter than a mountain spring!" After she drank, her whole body felt refreshed and strong. But—what do you know?—she became pregnant.

Seeing the widow's belly growing bigger and bigger day by day, the people in the village began gossiping about this matter, saying that she was indecent. They thought she had disgraced the Lahu people and brought discredit to the prestige of the village, so they decided to drive her away. No matter how much she tried to explain, no one would believe her story. All she could do was leave her home in great distress, separate from her relatives and friends in the village, and live all alone in a thatched shed not far from the village.

After another two or three months went by, in the warm springtime when flowers are in full bloom, this widow gave birth to a most abnormal babe. Why, it had no body, hands, or feet, but just a head! The widow felt even more miserable. She wondered whether this might be punishment for some wrong she had done that had offended Esha. Grieved as she was, she resigned herself to there being no other way for her but to bring up this weird baby. As the bodiless babe matured year by year, he noticed his mother becoming older and feebler, and her hair turning white with each passing day. One day he said to her, "Mama! Don't worry. I can do all the work you do. I can help you clear land, plow fields, and plant crops." Casting one glance at her son—a head without a body—the mother smiled wryly. "My dear child! You cannot walk without legs. You cannot work without hands. How can you do farm work?" The head-baby replied, "Dear Mama! Take it easy! I'll show you what I can do. Please put my head in the pack you carry and hang it up on the tree by the field. Then you can go home and prepare dinner for me. After you finish cooking, come back and take me home."

The mother did not know what to do except go along with her son. She went to collect him just as the sun was setting behind the mountain. No sooner did she reach the plot of land than she cried out in amazement, "Oh, Esha! This whole stretch of uncultivated land has been cleared. Could this be my son's work?" When she asked her son how he did it, he replied, "Dear Mama! There's no need to ask so many questions. Right now, I am very hungry, so please take me home quickly and get my supper. Then bring me back here again tomorrow." The mother refrained from asking any more questions, and silently carried her son home on her back.

The next day, she again hung her son's head up on the tree by the side of the field, then returned home to fix his meal. When the sun was about to set behind the mountain, she came again to fetch him home. This time, she was even more amazed, for that large piece of land, which had been hoed only the day before, was all ploughed and ready for sowing. Although the mother felt delighted, her suspicions were aroused. But since her son was reluctant to give any explanation, she simply brought him home, without asking him a thing.

From then on, the mother carried her son to the field every day, and brought him home at sunset. In this manner, seeds were sown, seedlings shot up, and crops ripened and were harvested. Mother and son lived better and better, day by day.

One year, a war suddenly broke out between Poyayi, a god of heaven, and Poyana, a god of earth. Sand flew and rocks rolled, the sky became murky while the earth darkened. The people were frightened out of their wits. Seeing that he could not conquer Poyayi, Poyana began blowing his water buffalo horn, calling all the Lahu people on earth to assemble. "Whoever can defeat Poyayi," he proclaimed, "may choose one of my seven daughters to be his wife."

When the head-baby learned this news, he told his mother, "Mama, if Poyana meant what he said, I could overcome Poyayi, without the slightest difficulty. Please go and inform Poyana for me."

But how could this mother feel at ease about letting a son, one who had neither hands nor feet, go to war? "Forget about this," she urged. "Without hands or feet, you aren't capable of doing anything anyway. And there's no way one of Poyana's daughters would be willing to marry you. Now don't get excited. Just be patient. Mama will find you a generous, good-hearted girl to be your wife."

However, what the head-baby had said was swiftly broadcast to Poyana's waiting ears. He immediately sent his caretaker to fetch the head-baby, and proclaimed to all the Lahu people, "Today is a lucky day. Let's all accompany the bodiless babe and fight Poyayi!" Whereupon he hung the saddlebag containing the head on his saddle, then set out with himself in command of a vast and mighty contingent of foot soldiers and cavalry. The mother of the head-baby was aghast. How precious her son was to her—her very own flesh and blood! After his departure, she lost her appetite and could not sleep. How long were the nights!

WONDER AND MAGIC

How hard they were to endure! She became so worried thinking her son might be dead, she went blind.

Poyana led his troops, marching day and night at double speed, determined to fight Poyayi to the death. But just at this very time, Poyayi changed himself into an eagle, and snatched away the youngest daughter of Poyana. When Poyana learned this, it was like a bolt from the blue. He turned about and hastened back with his soldiers to save his daughter. But no matter how quickly they marched, they still had a long way to go before they reached home. Poyana feared his daughter would soon be killed, and he was burning with anxiety.

Suddenly, Poyana remembered the head. As soon as he set free the head-baby from his saddlebag, he saw a flash of lightning split the heavens, and in the twinkling of an eye, the sky turned murky, while the earth darkened. Black clouds rolled and tumbled, the wind shrieked and cranes whooped, and everyone shook and trembled with fear. This was caused by none other than the head-baby battling with the god of heaven.

Gradually, Poyayi lost his hold. The sky brightened again and the sun leapt up from behind the horizon. At the end of the fray, the head-baby destroyed Poyayi and rescued Poyana's daughter. Poyana was elated, and when he set out to receive the bodiless boy, he was greeted by the sight of his daughter hugging the head-baby in her arms She was eager to tell her father all about the brave deeds of the head-baby. With what triumph did Poyana lead his people home!

Once they were back, Poyana addressed his seven daughters. "I promised that anyone who could gain victory over our enemy, Poyayi, would be allowed to choose one of you to be his wife. Now who among you would like to be chosen?"

The six elder sisters addressed their father, earth god of the Lahu and leader of the people, "Headman Dad! All he's got is a head. How could one of us possibly spend her life with him? We all absolutely refuse to marry him!"

Suddenly, the youngest daughter, Nala, chimed in and said, "Since our father has already made this promise, he should keep his word. And since it was the head-baby who saved me, I am willing to be his wife!"

On hearing Nala's response, the six elder sisters came up to tell her just what they thought. "Silly girl! How can you live with a head? If you marry him, you'll ruin your whole life. Now stop being so idiotic."

Nala replied, "My dear sisters, please say no more. I have made up my mind, and I'll never change it again!" And so, that was how the head-baby and Nala got married. The head-baby's mother shed tears of joy when she heard the news that the youngest daughter of Poyana had really married her son, and she waited in the doorway for the return of her son and her new daughter-in-law. In came Nala, hugging head-baby in her arms. When the mother heard her son's voice, she was so elated that she stretched out her hand to stroke him.

Upon discovering that his mother had lost her eyesight, the head-baby felt crushed with grief, but he comforted her, saying, "Mama, don't be sad. You should be happy instead! Look what an ideal daughter-in-law I have brought home!" The mother said, "My son, I am happy indeed." As she spoke, she fondled the hands of her daughter-in-law. And from then on, they all lived together.

One day, Nala said to the head-baby, "You stay at home and watch the house. I'm going to market to buy a few things. I'll be right back."

The head-baby nodded in consent. But after Nala left home, he suddenly was struck with the idea of testing his wife to see whether she was faithful. He gave his head a twist, and out of it jumped a handsome young man. The handsome young man overtook his wife and walked ahead of her, keeping an eye on her. As she finished shopping, and was on her way home, he suddenly blocked her path and started flirting meanly with her, saying, "Hey there, beautiful girl! Don't you think I'm good-looking?"

Nala had no idea that the young man standing in front of her was none other than her own husband who had transformed himself. She cast her eye on him and said, "You are indeed very good-looking."

The young man asked, "Will you marry me then?"

Nala shook her head. "Thank you for your kind offer, but I am already married to another man." As she spoke, she turned her back and strode off.

The head-baby saw that his wife was faithful. He quietly returned home ahead of her, and leapt back into his head. After some time, his wife also came home. He said to her, "You're back from the market? Was it fun shopping today?"

Not understanding what he was driving at, she replied, casually, "Oh, not bad!"

The head-baby then asked her, "Did you come across anyone on your way home?"

She replied, "Yes, I did."

He pressed on. "Was he a handsome young man?"

The head-baby's wife felt something was strange, and eyed her husband. "Yes," she answered.

"Did the young man try to make love to you?"

"He did," was her answer.

"And did you agree?" he went on.

Nala glared at him. "Absolutely not!" she declared.

Then the head-baby went a step further, "You mean to say you wouldn't love such a good-looking man as he?"

This time he had made his wife angry. "What's wrong with you?" she countered. "I've already loved and married you. I will never love another man." The head-baby nodded happily, and asked no more questions.

When the next market day came around, Nala went to the market again. Head-baby tailed after her a second time to watch what she did, but still he found nothing wrong.

On the third market day, when his wife went to market again, the head-baby decided to give her one last test. He changed himself once again into a handsome young man, and followed her. Halfway to the market, he began pestering her ceaselessly. She finally got cross and said to him, "I made it clear to you before: I am already married. Why do you want to tie me in love knots?"

The young man said, "I love you, that's why."

The young wife grew impatient. "I warn you, next time you try to tie knots with me, I'll get my husband to fix you good. You'll regret it then!" With these angry words, she turned around and walked away.

Sticking out his tongue in fear, the young man quietly went back home ahead of her. But this time, he could not change back into his former self, for his blind mother, being unable to see, had accidentally swept his head into the cooking fire, and it was burned. Just at this moment, the head-baby's wife came home. When she saw the good looking young man sitting in her house, she was both angry and surprised! There was no escape, he had to tell her the truth: he was the head-baby, and he could not change back into the head again, for his mother had swept it into the fire. Hearing this, the head-baby's wife was beside herself with joy. From then on, the young couple lived a life that was happier and fuller than ever.

When the six elder sisters got word of how happy head-baby and their sister were, they all became jealous, and lacking all sense of shame, they came to see their youngest sister, saying that all of them wanted to marry the head-baby too. The little sister felt embarrassed, of course, to refuse them, but the young man was not willing to accept the idea of marrying them.

"Thank you for your good intentions," he said to the six sisters. "However, I did not like you in the past, and now I like you even less. You lack your sister's faithful love. We are living a blessed, happy life, and have no need for any help from you. Please go home!"

The six sisters were so abashed their faces fell, and with nowhere to hide their shame, they slunk away in a huff.

From then on, the young couple loved and respected each other even more. Their life was like the glorious rising sun, and the more they lived, the more beautiful and blessed it became. Both of them lived one hundred years.

## NOTES

"Dutou wawa," from Yunnan minzu minjian gushi xuan 1982, 431–36. Storyteller: Li Changfu (Lahu). Collector and redactor: Zhang Rongli (Han). Area of distribution: Not identified. (Possibly Lancang Lahu Autonomous County, southwestern Yunnan.)

**Poyayi and Poyana.** According to Lahu belief, as well as that of other minorities, there are several gods of heaven and earth. In Lahu cosmology, Poyayi
is one of the gods of heaven, among whom Esha holds the highest power,
and Poyana is one of the gods of earth. The Lahu are both polytheists and
animists.

# WISE

# AND FOOLISH

# FOLK

# Mr. Crooked
# and Mr. Straight

## JINGPO TALE

Once there were two men, one named Crooked and the other named Straight, who got into an argument one day. Mr. Straight said, "A man ought to be straight; that's best. The only good thing to do is to conduct oneself in a straight way." But Mr. Crooked disagreed. "One cannot earn a living by being straight. A man should be crooked: that's best. The only good way is to act crooked!" Each stuck to his position, so they decided to find somebody to judge.

They walked along the road until they came to the edge of a paddy field where there was a man plowing. "Big brother, which is better: to be crooked or straight, to act crooked or act straight?"

The plowman gave the question some thought, then replied. "I think it's better to be crooked. Look, the plowshare we use is crooked, the curved shoulder pole is crooked, the water buffalo's horns are crooked too. If the plowshare were straight, it would be useless for plowing!"

Mr. Crooked was elated by the plowman's words. "I told you it was better to be crooked, but you would not believe me," he said to Mr. Straight. "This time you've got to admit you were wrong!"

But Mr. Straight would not concede defeat, so they went further on until they came to a dry, upland rice field, where they saw a man clearing the land. "Big brother, please tell us which is better: to act crooked or straight?"

The man said, "This long sword of mine is straight. Of course straight is best. If the blade were crooked, it couldn't chop down trees. If this plot weren't cleared, how could it be plowed?" Mr. Straight turned to Mr. Crooked. "What do you say now? Aren't I right after all?"

But Mr. Crooked would not give in either. So they continued on their way, until they came to a river, where they saw a man fishing. "Big brother," they asked once again, "which is better: to be crooked or straight? Which is the better way to earn a living, by acting crooked, or acting straight?"

The fisherman said, "In my opinion, sometimes one needs to be a little crooked, and at other times, a little straight. It is like my fishhook. Part of it is crooked, and part of it is straight. If either part were missing, I couldn't catch a thing."

After hearing this explanation, each man felt vindicated. They walked along, quarreling away, until they came to the Mailikai River. The more they argued, the more heated they got, until finally, they came to blows. Mr. Crooked was stronger, and with one punch he knocked Mr. Straight down on the ground. Not only that, he gouged out Mr. Straight's eyes and threw them in the Mailikai River. Now Mr. Straight could not see a thing. He groped his way along, until he was able to climb up a rock by the riverside. There he sat, crying.

Old Uncle Sun God, up in heaven, holds in his hands the fates of hundreds of thousands of people. Each person has an invisible thread attached to Uncle Sun God's hand. The day of the dispute between Mr. Crooked and Mr. Straight, Uncle suddenly noticed that one of the threads felt loose. So he sent one of his attendant fairy maidens to follow the thread down to earth to investigate.

When the fairy maiden came to the Mailikai River, she saw a man crying, sitting on a rock. She went up to him and asked what was the matter. Mr. Straight told her the whole story of how he had gotten into an argument with Mr. Crooked, and how Mr. Crooked had knocked him down and gouged out his eyes. The fairy maiden went straight back to heaven to report the matter. Old Uncle said, "This affair is quite serious. I had better make a visit myself." With that, he transformed himself into an old man and went to the Mailikai River.

"Don't be sad," he told Mr. Straight. "I can help you!" Uncle Sun God dredged up Mr. Straight's eyes from the river, and put them back in their sockets. Then he asked, "Do you have some stale glutinous rice in your house that has been stored for three years?" "Yes," said Mr. Straight.

"Do you have rice wine that has been kept for three years?" Uncle continued. "Yes," answered Mr. Straight. "Go home and tell your wife to cook a whole pot of glutinous rice and put rice wine on the table. You yourself hurry and go cut bamboo. Enclose the pigsty, the chicken coop, and the cow shed. Don't sleep in your own bamboo bungalow at night. Try to stay overnight at your neighbor's instead. And no matter what sound you hear at night, absolutely do not come out to find out what it is, and don't let out a peep. Now, get along!"

Mr. Straight thanked the old man and went home. He did everything exactly as he had been told. Then he took his wife and children, and put up for the night at his neighbors. In the middle of the night, they heard pigs grunting, cows mooing, people shouting, and horses neighing. What an uproar!

The next day, when they got up and went home to see what had happened, they found the pigsty full of pigs, the chicken coop full of chickens, and the cow shed full of cows. The pot of glutinous rice they had left in their bamboo bungalow had turned into gold, while the rice wine in the big bamboo pipe had become silver. From then on, Mr. Straight's life vastly improved.

After some time, Mr. Crooked happened by Mr. Straight's house. Not only was Mr. Straight very much alive, he had recovered his eyesight and made a fortune besides. Mr. Crooked was astounded. When he asked Mr. Straight how this could be, the latter told him honestly of his encounter with the fairy maiden and the old man. Hearing his story, Mr. Crooked was overcome with envy. He got Mr. Straight to take him to the rock by the river. Then he gouged out his own eyes and threw them into the water. He too sat on the rock, crying.

He cried for some time, and as expected, a fairy maiden came along and asked why he was crying. "I have a score to settle with Mr. Straight," he told her. "He's a proud, rich man now, so he knocked me down here, gouged out my eyes, and threw them into the river!" After a while, an old man came by, asking what was the matter. Mr. Crooked repeated the same lie he had told the fairy maiden.

"Don't be sad," the old man said, "I will help you." And he dredged up Mr. Crooked's eyes and replaced them. He also told him to cook any glutinous rice he had stored over the past three years, put the rice wine on the table, have the chicken coop, pigsty, and cow shed enclosed, and stay overnight at his neighbor's. "Whatever sound you hear during the night, don't come out," the old man directed. "Just keep quiet. Now go along home!" "Yes," repeated Mr. Crooked over and over, "yes, yes, yes." In the twinkling of an eye, the old man disappeared.

Mr. Crooked rushed home and did each task, one after another. Because he wanted to get more gold and silver than Mr. Straight had, he cooked three pots of new rice that had just been harvested, and mixed his rice wine with three or four bamboo pipes of cold water. He vastly enlarged the circle of bamboo fencing around the chicken coop, pigsty, and cow shed. Then he took his wife and children to put up for the night at his neighbor's home.

At midnight, it happened, as predicted, that people cried, horses neighed, pigs grunted, and cocks crowed. Mr. Crooked thought, "This time I will surely make a huge fortune. I wonder how much greater mine will be compared to Mr. Straight's?" The more he thought, the less patient he became. He simply could not stand waiting to find out how many chickens, pigs, and cows there really were in the shed. So he sneaked out and stole a glance through the bamboo fence. When he saw that the shed was packed full, he was ecstatic, and he sneaked back to tell his wife. The two of them did not sleep a wink all night long, and as soon as day broke, they hurried back home to have a look. What should they discover as soon as they arrived but the cow shed heaped with cow droppings, the chicken coop full of chicken dung, and the pigsty full of pig shit. When they went upstairs to their living quarters, they found nothing but human crap in the cooking pot and human piss in the wine pipe.

## NOTES

"Wan he zhi," from Oukunbo (Xu Kun) (Han) 1983, 176–79. Collectors and redactors: Li Xiangqian (Jingpo) and Oukunbo. Area of distribution: Dehong Dai-Jingpo Autonomous Prefecture, western Yunnan. Li Xiangqian is the editor of a Jingpo newspaper.

**Mailikai River.** The Mali Hka in northern Burma, which flows into the Irrawaddy.

**bamboo pipe.** Thick bamboo is used to make pipes and buckets. A section capped at one end is commonly used as a wine bottle.

# Asking Permission

## HUI TALE

Once there was a farmer by the name of Haersan. He was an honest, kindly, young man, well-built and powerful, and could carry a load on his shoulder pole of several hundred jin. He lost his parents when he was yet a child, so he had to work as a hired hand at a rich man's house, where there was never enough for him to eat or clothes to keep him warm. Besides, he had to put up with the petty gripes of the rich man the year round. After a while, Haersan simply could not stand it any longer, and was ever brooding. "Whatever the weather, wind or rain, I work the four seasons of the year. And in the end, Haersan gets next to nothing for his labor, except a beating or a scolding. A tough guy like me ought to be able to take care of his basic needs." So he took off, and went to another part of the country.

The dog days of summer were in full force just then. By noon, the sun was so blasting hot that people dripped with sweat. Haersan hurried on his way, while the sun beat down like a burning fire pan, with never a cool, shady spot to rest. His face was burned black and his mouth was on fire with thirst. As he walked on and on, all of a sudden he saw a patch of dark green trees in the far distance. He hastened ahead to get a better view. Hey! A luxuriant orchard right before his eyes! The branches of the trees were so heavy with fruit that they hung down to the ground, while the ground itself was strewn with fallen fruit that had overripened. Haersan's mouth was so dry, his tongue so parched, that the mere sight of so much fruit made him grab one and gulp it down, completely forgetting proper etiquette.

After eating the fruit, he collected himself and found, right next to the orchard, a neatly dug irrigation ditch with such clear water that should a grain of wheat fall in, it could easily be visible. Haersan took off his cotton upper garment and delighted in washing his face in the ditch. At last his interminable thirst was quenched. He sat resting in this shady, cool place for a while, thinking about continuing his journey. After he put on his upper garment again, and was about to set off, he suddenly realized, "I ate somebody else's fruit for free, never asking for permission. That will never do! I can't leave until I find the owner of the orchard to ask permission." His mind made up, Haersan followed the ditch along, looking for the owner.

He had not walked far before he saw an old man with a full beard and a white cap, working away pruning fruit trees. Haersan walked slowly toward him. "Sailiangmu," he said. "Grandpa! Are you the owner of this orchard?" he asked.

The old man turned his head about and cast a quick glance at Haersan. "That's right!" he replied. "What is your business?"

Haersan began explaining how he happened to be there. "This is what happened, Grandpa! I'm just a passerby. As I had walked a long way in this hot weather, I felt so thirsty I couldn't stand it. When I came to your orchard and found fallen fruit everywhere, I could not help eating one to quench my thirst. Later, I realized I never should have tasted any fruit without asking permission. But since I already did eat one fruit, I needed to ask permission of the owner. That's why I've sought you out."

On hearing Haersan's explanation, the old man stopped his work, threw down the twigs he had pruned, and looked the young man carefully up and down. He found him to be a well-built fellow with a genuine, kind face. He knew at once that here was an honest peasant. "So you've come here to ask my permission?" he said. "That's no problem! But there is just one condition."

"Grandpa, out with it please! As long as you give me permission, I'm willing to grant any demand, no matter what!" Haersan readily promised.

"Good!" the old man carried on. "I happen to have an only daughter. The problem is, she is blind and dumb, bald too, and doesn't have any feet. If you'll agree to take her for your wife, I will give permission. Otherwise, the fruit you ate will have been taken without permission."

When Haersan heard what the old man said, he felt perplexed. "If I marry his daughter, I'll have an ugly simpleton for a wife, but if I refuse, I won't get the old man's permission." He thought for a while, and in the end, agreed to the marriage.

As soon as the decision was made, they started to make preparations for the wedding. The old man invited all his neighbors from far and near to be guests at his daughter's marriage to Haersan. The guests were all delighted to see that the bridegroom was such a fine young man, and they congratulated both the old man and Haersan profusely. But as for Haersan, he was as sad as sad can be, and scared to death of the sun going down, for then he would have to see his ugly wife.

But he had no choice.

Heaven does not accord with human wishes. Eventually, the sun set behind the mountain, and the guests gradually dispersed. Those who still hung around escorted Haersan to the nuptial chamber.

How Haersan dragged his feet, walking into that room! He noticed that his bride was beautifully dressed, and veiled with a pink gauze kerchief. He shilly-shallied for what seemed forever, then finally went up to his bride and spoke to her out of desperation, "I vow to be your husband forever." All along, as he said this, he was thinking to himself, "Since she's dumb, she won't respond." But much to his surprise, she replied immediately, "I, too, vow to be your wife forever." Her voice was so sweet that Haersan could not believe his own ears. He quickly removed her veil. Behold! There before him was a lovely girl, like a flower, like the moon, with big, bright, intelligent eyes and shining black hair. The sight of her was a complete wonder to Haersan, for the girl was totally different from the old man's description. He hurriedly asked the bride, "Say, miss! Are you the old man's daughter?"

"Yes, I am his only daughter," she replied bashfully.

"But why did your father say that you were blind and dumb, and had no hair or feet? Wasn't he lying?"

"No, my father was not lying! He only wanted to find out whether you were a man of good faith, and to this end he spoke obscurely," said the bride.

"Then what did he mean by talking like that?" asked Haersan again.

"He said I was blind," she explained, "because I had seen no evil. He said I was dumb, because I had never sown discord among people. He said I had no feet, because I had never stepped in any indecent place. He said I had no hair, meaning I have never been seen in public."

Haersan was beside himself with joy upon hearing her words. But he had one more question to ask his bride. "Since all this is true, why did your father let his beautiful daughter marry me?"

"My father has worked hard all his life to build up this orchard, and now he wants to pass it on to the most diligent, kind-hearted, faithful man in the world. He fancies you are that person."

And so, Haersan and the old man's daughter got married. From then on, he was no longer beaten and scolded by the rich, but lived a happy life with his beautiful, virtuous wife, and ran the orchard diligently and conscientiously.

## NOTES

"Yao kouhuan," from *Aiqing chuanshuo gushi xuan* 1980, 129–32. Storyteller: Zheng Xinshun (Hui). Redactor: Yuan Ding (Han). Area of distribution: Qinghai Province.

**asking permission.** The Hui, who are Moslem, stress the importance in social relations of asking permission (*yao kouhuan*) and giving permission (*gei kouhuan*).

**sailiangmu.** Common Hui greeting.

**bedroom vow.** A Hui custom whereby the bride and groom exchange a special vow in their bedroom in recognition of their marriage commitment.

# Five Tales about Ayidan

## » 1 «

## Clan-de-cline

Ayidan, who was exceptionally intelligent and witty since birth, was a tenant in the house of Lord Mu. He was often ordered about by the lord to do heavy and arduous work, yet never got enough to eat, let alone a mite of cash for his labor.

The only property to speak of in Ayidan's house was a dilapidated, treadle-operated rice-pounder. His wife depended on it to keep the family alive by husking rice and pounding *erkuai* for the neighbors. As the years went by, and the rice-pounder gradually began to break down, Ayidan got to thinking about how he might try to get his wages back from Lord Mu so as to have his rice-pounder repaired. All the while he was thinking, he was well aware that Lord Mu was a miser with a heart of stone—to squeeze even a pittance out of him would just about drive him to his death. Despite the fact that so many had toiled and sweated for him so long, did anybody ever see Lord Mu paying his numerous tenants and farm hands a single copper? It was plainly hopeless to get any wages back from him. Yet how was Ayidan to support his family if he forsook the unpaid wages? "No," he told himself. "The wages are owed me! I must try and find some means to get my money out of him!"

Now Lord Mu had a treadle-operated rice-pounder made of oak, brand new and solidly built. When it started up pounding, it sang out merrily *gu-ga-gan, gu-ga-gan, gu-ga-gan,* thumping away ever so smoothly and efficiently. "How nice it would be," thought Ayidan, "if I could take this new rice-pounder back to my house as a partial payment for my wages after so many years of hard work!"

One morning, a farmhand was pounding *erkuai* cakes with the new treadle pounder for Lord Mu's breakfast. *Gu-ga-gan, gu-ga-gan* it sang, while Lord Mu was still in his bedroom, sleeping away.

"My lord! My lord! An ominous sign! An ominous sign!" reported Ayidan, his voice uneasy, as he rushed into Lord Mu's bedroom.

"What's all this nonsense about an ominous sign?" Lord Mu called out, nearly panic-stricken, his voice tremulous, and his head halfway protruding from beneath his quilt. It seemed he had just been awakened from a sound sleep. "Get out, you! Can't you see Lord Mu is sleeping?"

"Listen, please, my lord . . . 'Mu-clan-de-cline [Mu jia bai], Mu-clan-de-cline, Mu-clan-de-cline . . .'"

"You scoundrel! *What* did you say?"

"That rice-pounder is saying something ominous! 'Mu-clan-de-cline!' You just listen, my lord."

Thrusting his head completely out of the quilt, Lord Mu listened attentively, one ear cocked toward the sound.

"Mu-clan-de-cline, clan-de-cline, clan decline! Mu clan decline!" The longer Lord Mu listened to the rice-pounder, the clearer the message!

"Don't you see, my lord? It's a bad omen indeed!" Ayidan added.

Disgruntled and wearing a frown, Lord Mu mumbled for a while, then shouted out an order: "Quick! Go and get an ax. Have the treadle pounder hacked up into kindling and burnt!"

"Now wouldn't that be a pity, my lord?"

"Well then, what? Oh, how I loathe this!" Lord Mu himself was having a rather tough time letting go of his rice-pounder that way.

"Well, the rice-pounder in my house always says something auspicious: 'Mu-clan-ex-pand [Mu jia sheng]! Clan expand! Mu clan expand!'"

"Hey now, how about swapping yours for mine?"

"If that's what would please your lordship," said Ayidan, feigning reluctance.

"I say swap, so swap we shall! No regrets! Carry mine off and bring yours back today!" ordered Lord Mu, his voice resolute, revealing at once a faint, self-satisfied smile on his greedy face.

Wearing a grin, Ayidan left immediately to carry out Lord Mu's instructions.

## » 2 «

## It's a Boy! It's a Girl!

One winter morning, when it was not quite broad daylight, Ayidan went to Lord Mu's house. A chilling breeze blew from the snow-covered mountains, numbing Ayidan's cheeks, and making him shiver. He tightened his belt, tucked both his hands deep inside his sleeves, and hugged his chest tightly, trying to keep warm. He could not stop his teeth from chattering.

"Open the door! O-pen . . . !" Before Ayidan had shouted a second time, the door opened, much to his surprise.

"How could it be that today the door is opened so quickly?" Suddenly, he felt suspicious.

"What great good fortune! Many children! Prosperity and longevity!" Lord Mu stood in the doorway, blocking the way, holding in both hands a brass ladle full of ice-cold water. Mumbling incoherently, he thrust the ladle at Ayidan's mouth. It was not until then that Ayidan understood: Lord Mu's wife had given birth last night to a child, and he, Ayidan, was the "first visitor." According to Naxi custom, the first person visiting a house following a birth has to drink cold water to protect the child from ever getting into disputes, and to ward off disasters and difficulties. Thus the child will enjoy lifelong happiness. After the cold water, the first visitor is invited to drink rice wine and eat eggs and stuffed dumplings. Since it was the Naxi custom, Ayidan could not avoid drinking down that big ladle of ice-cold water.

"Boy or girl?" Ayidan asked.

"It's a boy," Lord Mu sighed unhappily. "A young master of the house. Ai-ya!" Lord Mu was displeased because he was mindful of a Naxi belief that the first visitor determines a child's entire destiny. If the first visitor is a high official or a nobleman, the child will also become one. If the first visitor is a poor man or a slave, the child will surely suffer. Today, who should the young master of the house meet as his first visitor?—none other than Ayidan, the farmhand. Lord Mu was furious. He completely disregarded the rules of etiquette by not inviting Ayidan to drink wine or eat eggs or stuffed dumplings.

Having been so insulted by Lord Mu, Ayidan hated him to the limit, and thought up a way to take revenge. "I'm going to give you a taste of cold water!" he exclaimed under his breath.

By the end of December, New Year's was just around the corner, and the Mu clan was busy making preparations for the celebrations. But at this very time, and for several days running, Ayidan did not turn up. Many things were to be done at Lord Mu's house, but there was no one to do them. Lord Mu got very anxious, and he sent for Ayidan several times, yet Ayidan never appeared. Lord Mu had to go call Ayidan himself.

"Ayidan! Ayidan!" he shouted, pushing the door open.

"What great good fortune! A noble lord as first visitor! Many children! Great prosperity!" Ayidan came out shouting, and was all smiles as he held a big ladle full of ice-cold water in both hands, and brought it to Lord Mu's mouth.

Lord Mu had not drunk plain, cold water ever since he was old enough to know better, but now he simply had to observe the custom. He felt stuck by the awkward situation, and just managed to force himself to swallow a mouthful of water so as to be obliging. Who would have expected it, but Ayidan kept on shouting, "What great good fortune! What great good fortune!" all the while keeping the ladle close to Lord Mu's mouth. There was no escape. Lord Mu made himself drink the whole ladleful, but it wasn't easy.

"Now it's your turn to have a taste of ice-cold water!" Ayidan cursed Lord Mu inwardly, though putting on a cheerful face.

After he swallowed the water, Lord Mu began to shiver and belch, over and over again. He did not feel well at all.

"Ayidan, is it a boy or a girl?" Lord Mu assumed Ayidan's wife had given birth to a child, so he pretended to be solicitous.

"What great luck you bring me!" Ayidan replied, his face wreathed in a smile. "Male and female both, spotted four-eyed dogs!" Ayidan pointed to a corner as he spoke. Lord Mu took a look—Ayidan's dog had given birth to a litter of puppies, four or five in number. They were crawling about under their mother's belly, whimpering after her milk.

Lord Mu got so angry he wanted to grab Ayidan and beat the hell out of him, but by then Ayidan had slipped away. The only creature left behind was the bitch, baring her teeth and watching Lord Mu's every move.

## » 3 «

# Gone Fishing

It was not just once or twice that Lord Mu was tricked by Ayidan. Many was the time the lord wanted to beat him, but he never succeeded. One morning, just as Lord Mu finished his breakfast, he saw Ayidan coming to work. He said to him, "Ayidan, you are great at poking fun. If you can pull off a joke right now, you won't have to work today."

"Eh? Where would I find the time to fool around joking, my lord? I must be off." Ayidan acted as though he were in a great rush.

"Where are you going?"

"Haven't you heard, my lord? The lake water at Sandbar Flat has dried up. I'm going to catch some fish!"

"Oh! Has it? Hurry up and saddle my horse, Ayidan. I'm going too!"

"I'm so slow on foot, while you're so fast on horseback, my lord. Please get someone else to saddle your horse for you, while I get a head start." With that, Ayidan charged off, pretending he was greatly rattled.

As soon as Lord Mu heard the lake was running dry, he started to get worried. "Better be early if I want to catch the fish first," he muttered. Then he ordered that one saddle horse and two pack animals be readied for him straight away.

In a single breath he galloped the distance, more than twenty li. When he reached Sandbar Flat, all he could see was a vast expanse of gleaming

water, waves beating on waves. In the distance a few boats were bob-
bing up and down, rafts of wild ducks were quacking here and there,
flying about or flapping their wings on the water. But there wasn't a sign
of Ayidan. Lord Mu had been fooled once again.

## » 4 «

# Lord Mu Climbs the Granary

In June it was extremely sultry. The tenants and servants in Lord Mu's
house were streaming with sweat from threshing wheat. Ayidan was
sweeping out the granary, where wheat bundles had just been unloaded
around the roof posts. He was so hot he had to keep wiping away the
sweat from his brow with his sleeves.

The only person with nothing to do was Lord Mu. He sauntered over
to the threshing floor and said to Ayidan, "Say, Ayidan. You fooled me
the other day into going to Sandbar Flat. Do you think you can play
another trick on me today? Hey! If you can't, you'll end up a dead dog."
Lord Mu was joking, but his tone was menacing. He stood there panting, his left hand holding his side, and his right hand unfastening the
breast buttons of his long silk gown. Now he cast a sidelong glance at
Ayidan, his crafty eyes squinting.

"Ai-ya! My good lord! Please don't bring that up. I'll never dare to
make fun of you again." Ayidan pretended to be begging off.

"From now on, you'd better behave yourself!" Lord Mu figured that
this time he had put the fear of death in Ayidan, so he acted very cocky.

"I'm not afraid of you," said Ayidan, raising his head slightly, "and I'm
still capable of making fun of you. But . . ."

"But what?"

"My father will beat me! He said that if I keep offending you every
day, I'll get in trouble. He always has an eye on me now. If he learns
that I offended you again, he will give me a thrashing when I get home
tonight."

"Don't worry about that! I'll tell him not to beat you."

"Never mind doing that, my good lord! But how about if you climb to the top of the granary and see whether my father is at home. If he's out, I won't get caught."

Lord Mu took off his sandals and struggled up the framework of the open-air granary shed, wearing his red silk socks.

"It's OK, Ayidan! Your father is not home." Lord Mu was on the peak of the granary, his hands and feet were shaking, and he was about to fall.

Down below, Ayidan cursed Lord Mu under his breath: "Now it's your turn to find out how tough it is to climb the granary." But while cursing Lord Mu in secret, he casually remarked out loud, "That's right, my lord. My father left home early this morning to plow. He won't be back till dusk."

"Then why did you deceive me like this?" asked Lord Mu, desperately, up on the peak of the granary.

"Didn't you tell me to make fun of you once more?" Ayidan smiled, pleased with himself.

## » 5 «

## Lord Mu Eats Shit

Lord Mu always considered himself wise, but he was fooled by Ayidan over and over again. He felt extremely bad about this and intended to find some pretext whereby he could get even with Ayidan, but no matter how much he stewed, he still could not figure out what to do. At last he came up with a mean idea.

"Ayidan," he said, "I was taken in by you several times, but it's just because you were lucky. Now I want you to fool me one more time. Make me eat shit if you can. You've got three days. If you succeed in doing it, you won't have to do any hard work for one whole year. If not, ha! I'll . . ."

Ayidan didn't even wait for Lord Mu to finish his sentence. "I can do it!" he cut in. "I can. I can. And it won't take me three days either. One is all I need."

"Just as you say. One day! And no going back on your word!"

Lord Mu was delighted, for he thought that this time he was guaranteed to get one up on Ayidan. But Ayidan was as calm as ever. He kept mulling over how to make Lord Mu eat shit so as to let him know just how tough a peasant could be.

Early the next day, Lord Mu got up, washed his face, and was about to have breakfast, when Ayidan came running in, panting and shouting, "Fire! Fire! The ancestral temple is on fire. Help!" On hearing the alarm, Lord Mu's family members and servants also joined Ayidan in the shouting and ran outside.

Lord Mu was terror stricken. When he looked up toward the temple, he saw nothing but columns of thick smoke pouring from its eaves. He treasured the things inside: the shrine engraved with beautiful dragons and phoenixes; the ancestral tablet painted red, with words engraved in gold; the sacrificial utensils on the altar made of gold, silver, jade gems, and precious stones. The thought of all these treasures flashed through his mind and made him run as quickly as he could to the temple.

Just then Ayidan was at the temple struggling hard to unlock the big brass lock. As soon as Lord Mu got there, he pushed Ayidan out of the way to unlock it himself. Strangely enough, the lock seemed to be deliberately mocking Lord Mu. It refused to open. He started to get really worried. By now there was more and more dense smoke, choking people and burning their eyes. It was terrible.

Ayidan promptly made a suggestion. "It won't be hard to open the door if you would just wet the key with a little of your saliva." On hearing this idea, Lord Mu quickly pulled out the key and stuck it in his mouth a few times to get it good and wet. Ayidan burst out laughing. "Forget about the fire! What you ought to be worrying about now is you've just eaten shit!" With that, Ayidan swaggered off. Lord Mu stamped his foot in anger, but he had to hold his temper. He was too embarrassed in front of the crowd of people, and could only take this insult and humiliation in silence. He ran home, pinching his nose and spitting all the way, to rinse out his mouth with soda.

As a matter of fact, the "fire" in the Mu clan ancestral temple was set by Ayidan when he swept the temple in the morning. He took some pine needles and tree leaves and put them in a big incense burner. Then he set it on fire so that thick smoke gradually built up. After that, he stuffed the bronze lock with moist, sticky, human shit, so that Lord Mu would eat it when he panicked. And so the story of how Ayidan made Lord Mu eat shit spread among the Naxi people. Even now, grown-ups and children alike delight in hearing this story.

It is said that from then on, Lord Mu never again dared to bully Ayidan.

## NOTES

"*Clan-de-cline*" (Mujia bai), "It's a Boy! It's a Girl!" (Gong xi mu xi?), "Gone Fishing" (Nayu qu), "Lord Mu Climbs the Granary" (Mu Laoye pa liangjia), "Lord Mu Eats Shit" (Mu Laoye chi shi), included in "Five Tales about Ayidan" (Ayidan gushi wuze), from Wang Shouchun (Han) 1979, 65–74. Collector and redactor: Zhao Jingxiu (Naxi). Area of distribution: Lijiang Prefecture, Lijiang Naxi Autonomous County, in the environs of Lijiang City, northern Yunnan. Zhao Jingxiu is a well-known writer in her late seventies, a colleague of the noted author Guo Moruo, and a member of the Naxi minority from the Lijiang Special District north of Dali.

**li.** Approximately one-third of a mile.
**Mu clan.** Formerly, the sole aristocratic clan among the Naxi. Other clans were considered of low birth and often were treated as serfs or slaves.
**erkuai.** A cooked rice cake shaped with a rice pounder, from which noodles are made.
**granary shed.** A large, roofed, open-air structure, under which bundles of harvested grain are left to dry on poles.
**four-eyed dogs (siyan gou).** The eyebrows of a dog are thought to resemble eyes. A person who wears glasses may jokingly be called *siyan gou*.

# The Clever Sister

N U   T A L E

Long, long ago, there were nine sisters who were all pretty and quite grown up, but who still lived with their parents. A young man by the name of Gongzanlaoding once saw these lovely girls and wanted to have the cleverest for his wife. He thought about it endlessly, and finally came up with a way to discern which one was the brightest of all. Removing his gold ring from his finger, he hung it up on a tree branch carefully so that the ring was reflected in a well right next to the tree.

One day, the eldest sister went to the well to fetch water. As she was about to dip her bucket in, she saw a gold ring in the well, so she reached down, hoping to scoop it up with her hand. But as she dipped her hand in the water, the gold ring disappeared in the shimmering ripples. Yet, when she straightened back up again, there was that gold ring, right in the center of the well. She bent down over the edge once again, but just as soon as she moved, and the surface of the water was disturbed, the ring was no longer visible. Try as she might, over and over again, she never could succeed in picking up that ring. Finally, she returned home, toting water buckets on a shoulder pole and feeling sorely disgruntled.

The next day, it was Second Sister's turn to get water. As she approached the well and peered down inside, she glimpsed the gold ring. She stretched over the edge to grab it, but as she did so, the gold ring was gone. When she stood up tall, however, the ring reappeared. She made repeated efforts to get hold of that ring, but never could do it, so she gave up. There was nothing left for her to do but shoulder the load of water and go back.

On the third day, Third Sister went to the well. No sooner did she get there than she discovered the gold ring, and her response was no different from that of her two older sisters. She bent way down and pawed at the ring, but all she took home was two buckets of water.

From the fourth through the eighth day, Fourth Sister, Fifth Sister, Sixth Sister, Seventh Sister, and Eighth Sister all tried their luck, but their efforts were useless.

At last, on the ninth day, Ninth Sister's turn came around. She too came up to the well, saw the gold ring, and leaned over to pick it up. And when her hand went below the surface of the water, the ring was gone, as her sisters had found. She thought over the situation for a good while, and suddenly, it dawned on her! Raising her head, she looked at the tree next to the well, examining it closely. Ha! There was that gold ring, hanging from a tree branch, exactly as she had anticipated. She plucked it off the tree and merrily made her way home, bringing two buckets of water and a gold ring too.

In no time at all, the eight older sisters realized that the youngest was a success. Each of them had yearned for the gold ring, but none of them got what she wanted, and now, here was Ninth Sister holding it in her hands. The eight considered ganging up on her, but they couldn't really pull that off. They were so insanely jealous that what they did instead was to spread gossip about her in front of their parents. "Ninth Sister has got herself engaged to a beggar," they rumored, "and now she has a gold ring!"

The parents were livid when they heard this announced, for they really believed the eight were telling the truth, and they yelled for Ninth Sister. "How could you promise to marry a beggar?" they asked, madly rebuking her when she came before them. "Not only have you lost face, but you've disgraced your parents as well. Get out of this house. Go live with your beggar! We can't stand having you around any more!"

The poor girl hastily tried to explain herself. "I picked the gold ring from a tree by the well. It's not a betrothal gift from some beggar."

But no matter what Ninth Sister said, her parents refused to believe her story, and they were adamant about driving her out.

Where else could Ninth Sister go except back to the well, and pour out her heart? She wept all the way and cried her eyes out when she got to the well. An old white-haired man was sitting by the well. "Why are

you crying so hard?" he asked, amiably. Ninth Sister gave a full account
of how she had discovered the gold ring, had been stabbed in the back
by her eight sisters, and then had been thrown out of her house by her
parents. The old man was entirely sympathetic. "Now don't be so hurt,"
he urged. "Why don't you just come along with me? If you have a tough
time keeping the pace, follow the marks my golden staff leaves on the
earth." And off he went, leaning on his stick.

Ninth Sister followed right along. At first, she had no trouble staying
up with him, but after a while she slowed way down and lagged far behind. In the end, she completely lost him. Her only choice was to track
the trail left by his golden staff. On and on she went, one stretch following another, until finally she came to a small plain where there was a
young maiden herding a huge flock of sheep. Ninth Sister went right up
and asked her, "What a lot of sheep you have here! Who owns them?"

"Those that can walk and are fat belong to my house," the shepherdess replied. "The skinny ones with broken legs are your family's."

Ninth Sister was shocked. "I have no home. How could the shepherdess say those sheep belong to my family?" She walked along meditating,
and climbed over a hill, without being aware of what she had done,
until she found herself on a second small plain. Here was another young
girl, watching over a flock of horses and mules. "Who do these animals
belong to?" Ninth Sister asked.

"The plump and sturdy ones belong to my family, the underfed belong to yours."

Ninth Sister was even more amazed now. "I don't have a family," she
thought to herself. "How could it be possible for me to own so many
horses and mules? What's even more troublesome is that both of the
herders said the poorer animals are mine." Ninth Sister was so hurt she
burst into tears.

She went along following the tracks made by the golden staff, weeping as she walked. After traveling some distance, she came to a stockaded village with a lovely house near the entrance. A man was standing
in the doorway. Ninth Sister went up and asked, "Did you see an old
man leaning on a golden staff pass by this way?"

Before she had even finished her question, the man came forward.

He was young and handsome. As she looked at him closely, his features reminded her of the old man with the golden staff. He spoke to her fondly, "Come, come girl. Do come in!" Feeling his warmth and sincerity, she complied. As she walked into the house, he said, "Don't be sad. This is your home as well as mine."

Ninth Sister could not believe her ears. "What do you mean saying this is our home?" she asked.

Seeing that Ninth Sister was hesitant, and did not yet understand, the young man hastened to tell her everything. It was he who wanted the cleverest of the nine sisters for his wife, so he had hung the gold ring on the tree, and hid nearby so he could observe them. After Ninth Sister took the ring, he disguised himself as an old man and waited at the well to meet her. When Ninth Sister was driven out of her house, he had led her all the way to his. "You are the lovely, clever woman of my dreams!" he told her.

Ninth Sister listened, and felt both happy and shy at the same time. She remembered her eight jealous sisters and her parents, who had driven her out, and knew she could never return home. Then too, the young man was so earnest in his pleading that she agreed to marry him. Ninth Sister loved her husband dearly, and he loved her. They lived a peaceful, happy life.

One day, she asked her husband about the past. "On my way here I came across a shepherdess. She said that the fat, sleek sheep were hers, while the poor ones with broken legs belonged to my house. I was surprised and wounded to hear mention of my home, for I had none. Later, I walked still farther and met another girl herding horses and mules. She told me the plump, sturdy animals were hers and the weak, skinny ones belonged to my family. Hearing this kind of talk once again hurt me all the more."

The young man chuckled. "That great flock of sheep and all those horses and mules are ours."

When Ninth Sister heard that, she too laughed with delight.

# NOTE

"Congming de jiumei," from *Yunnan minzu minjian gushi xuan* 1982, 548–51. Story-teller: Liu Libai (Nu). Translator: Liu Jianwen (Nu). Collector and redactor: Chen Rongxiang. Area of distribution: Gongshan and Bijiang counties, Nujiang Lisu Autonomous Prefecture, northwestern Yunnan.

# The Guileless Man and the Trickster

Once a trickster and a guileless man went trapping together in the mountains and they caught a musk deer. Musk is a valuable source of medicine, so the trickster wanted to have the musk deer all to himself. They went into a cave located on a cliff to put up for the night, gathered some firewood, and made a fire. The trickster told the guileless man to sleep outside the cave, while he himself went to bed inside, with the fire burning between them.

"If you find it gets too hot, just back away," the trickster said. "If you are cold, move on in!" Then both of them lay down to sleep.

After a hard day of hunting, the guileless man felt exhausted. No sooner did he lay down his head than he was snoring away. The trickster got out of bed quietly and pushed the hot fire nearer to the guileless man, disturbing his sleep with the scorching heat. Inch by inch, the guileless man backed away from the fire, and farther and farther away from the cave.

Below the cave was a steep gulch. As the guileless man rolled away from the fire, suddenly he tumbled over and over, and fell down into the gulch. Luckily, there happened to be a big tree growing from the wall of the gulch, and the guileless man fell squarely on a fork of the tree, making a perfect landing, and sat up.

Under the big tree was a rocky cavern in which a tiger was sleeping. Just then, a wolf came from the valley below to report to the tiger.

"Your Majesty, the wife of a headman fell ill, and she has not recovered her health, even though *dongba* [ritual practitioners] were asked to chant scriptures. As a matter of fact, her sickness was caused by a dragon in their well. All they need do for her to get well is clean out the well and burn some incense to the dragon. But they don't know such things."

The wolf's words were accidentally overheard by the guileless man, and he kept them firmly in mind.

After a while, a leopard arrived and delivered its report to the tiger.

"Your Majesty, I know of a dry place that has no water. The people there have to walk three days to reach a river to fetch their drinking water. As a matter of fact, there is water under a great rock nearby. All those people would have to do is dig under the rock, and the water will flow. But they don't know such things."

Again, what the leopard said was overheard by the guileless man, and he made a point of remembering.

After a while, a muntjac came up and reported to the tiger.

"Your Majesty, a big tree beside the road fell down. This tree contains a priceless treasure, but none of the passersby knows it."

Once again, the muntjac's words were heard by the guileless man, and he bore them firmly in mind.

At daybreak, the guileless man climbed down from the tree and went to the headman's house.

"Has the mistress of this house taken ill?" he asked.

"Yes, we've had the dongba chant scriptures, yet she didn't get any better. Can you do anything to help?"

"Of course, I can. Otherwise, I wouldn't have come to ask about her," replied the guileless man.

"If you can cure her, you'll get whatever you desire."

The guileless man then ordered the people in the house to clean the well and burn incense beside it. Indeed, as the guileless man expected, after some time the headman's wife fully recovered, and the headman presented the guileless man with many pieces of gold and silver.

He left the headman's house and went to the place where there was no water. Coming across two girls who were just returning from the river carrying water on their backs, the guileless man went up to one, and said, "I'm thirsty. Please give me a cup of water!"

And the girl did.

After drinking one cup, he asked for another.

The girl said to him, "We've carried this water from a place three days distant. It isn't easy to get water. You've already had a cup. Why do you press us for one more?"

Listening to what she had to say, the guileless man asked, "Why do you have to walk three days to fetch water?"

One of the girls answered, "We have no water here."

"I know how to find water," the guileless man stated.

The two girls were delighted. "If you can find water, we'll give you whatever you ask."

So the guileless man went along with the two girls to the village. He pressed his ear close to a rock and listened. Hearing the gurgling sound of a stream below, he used a hoe and dug out the earth underneath the rock. With that, a clear stream gushed out. The people in the village made him a present of many pieces of silver.

The guileless man left the village and took to the road. There he found a big tree lying on the ground. He thought, "Probably this is the tree the muntjac talked about." So he began splitting it with his ax. Just as he expected, he found a priceless treasure and went back home in high spirits.

Meanwhile, the trickster had the musk deer all to himself, thinking the guileless man must have died after falling into the gulch. Who would have expected the guileless man to come back a rich man? The trickster asked him how he had made his fortune, and the guileless man told him in exact detail just what had occurred. When he heard his story, the trickster asked his companion to stay for the night in the cave again, just as they had before.

Without knowing what the trickster was up to, the guileless man followed him into the cave. This time, he was told to sleep inside the cave while the trickster slept outside, a fire burning between them. As the two men were sleeping, the trickster slowly inched farther out. When he got beyond the entrance of the cave, flop! He rolled down the cliff. It just so happened that he too fell right on the fork of the big tree and sat there.

After a while, a wolf came to the tiger and reported.

"Your Majesty, the headman's wife I told you about last time has recovered from her illness. My report must have been overheard by someone."

The tiger snorted with displeasure.

After the wolf, the leopard came to report.

"Your Majesty, last time I told you about a dry place that had no water. Now water is flowing there. What I reported to you must have been overheard by someone."

Again the tiger gave a snort of displeasure.

After the leopard came the muntjac.

"Your Majesty, the priceless treasure in the big tree I reported to you about last time has been scooped out and taken away. What I reported to you must have been overheard by someone."

The tiger was furious and wanted to find the person who had overheard these reports. He came out of his cavern, looked up, and saw a man sitting in the fork of the big tree below the cliff. He sprang on him and ate him up in one huge bite. The trickster who had been so eager to make a fortune unexpectedly became a delicious dish for the tiger.

## NOTE

"Benfen ren he jiaohua ren," from Yunnan minzu minjian gushi xuan 1982, 525–29. Storyteller: Ma Bingbo (Primi). Redactor: Li Qiao (Yi). Area of distribution: Lanping Bai-Primi Autonomous County, northwestern Yunnan; and Ninglang Yi Autonomous County, northern Yunnan.

# LOVERS

# The Girl with Tufted Eyebrows

## ACHANG TALE

In the past, we Achang people had a custom. Any girl with tufted eye-brows was regarded as a *gui tai*, a ghost-fetus—that is, the reincarnation of a ghost. She was considered to be someone who might eat people, especially her own husband. So a girl born with tufted eyebrows, no matter what family she came from, was forbidden to marry, and had to remain single to the end of her days.

What people worry about always has a way of coming true.

In the Yang clan stockaded village, there was a couple, well into their forties, who did not have any children. When a daughter finally was born to them, they were beside themselves with joy, and they named her Bao, meaning "precious." Immediately after her birth, they rushed her to the lanternlight so they could examine her closely. They were dazed out of their wits by what they saw—their dear Precious was, in fact, a girl with tufted eyebrows. But since she was the only little sprout her parents had been able to grow, how could they bear to nip her in the bud? They decided to bring her up and let her live with them while she remained single all her life.

Precious gradually got bigger, grew up, and turned out to be an ex-traordinary beauty. Why, she was even more beautiful than the big pink roses that grew alongside the Achang mountain village. When she was eighteen, her name spread to the villages far and near, like the seeds of dandelion flowers that are carried by the wind. Her virtue was like the fragrance of gardenia that fills the air in every direction. Fish rush up-stream when small rivers suddenly swell with water, and bees swarm when the flowers begin to bloom. But the young men who came to the Yangs' house to ask to marry Precious were happier than the fish, and greater in number than the bees. They came in an endless stream, hoping to pick this fresh flower. How upset were Precious's parents! They locked her up, not allowing her to meet the young suitors. Still, Precious got a good peek at each of them through a crack between the door and its frame. There wasn't a single one she loved.

Gradually, the young men who came to the house became fewer and fewer, and Precious's parents stopped locking her up. One day, a young man by the name of Kindness [Ende] came for a visit, and Precious fell in love with him at first sight. He was as straight and sturdy as hard bamboo, and as handsome as a warrior in a myth. His eyes sparkled like stars, while his voice was as pleasing to the ear as a murmuring mountain stream. Already, with their initial words together, the two of them were in love, and they vowed that from then on they would never be separated.

As the sun was setting behind the mountains, Precious's parents came back home. Kindness quickly fell to his knees before them, pleading with them to let Precious marry him. Her father resolutely turned him down, saying, "Do stand up, young man. You are well-meaning, but my daughter will never marry, for she is a girl with tufted eyebrows. Our ancestors have passed down the teaching, from generation to generation, that such a woman will cause her husband to die young. Because of her, you would not live long after marriage. If such an unfortunate marriage took place, you both would be miserable, while we all would suffer. Flowers can be found everywhere on Achang Mountain, and there are maidens within every stockaded village. Young man, go and try your luck at other households!"

Kindness went right on kneeling, refusing to get up. "In the past," he said, "old folks warned people not to go tiger hunting alone, but I have killed three fierce tigers single-handedly. Our ancestors said, 'When you hear the owl hoot, avoid going on a journey,' but I've always disregarded that taboo. I am not afraid of a thing. All I am asking is that you let me marry Precious." Seeing that Kindness was sincere, Precious's parents eventually gave their consent.

Elated, Kindness brought Precious home, only to meet with his own parents' rebuke. No matter how he argued, they would not agree to their son's marrying a girl with tufted eyebrows. Again and again, they refused his request, and Kindness had no choice but to leave his home village hand in hand with Precious, a Husa sword slung over his shoulder, and to seek a happy life somewhere else.

Having walked a long, long way, and suffered untold hardships, they finally found a village where they were granted permission to live. They told the villagers their misfortunes and won their sympathy. The old folks brought food, the young men helped them build a new house, and the young women often would come there to keep Precious company.

One day, Kindness went off by himself to cut firewood in the mountains. As it was hot and he was tired, he fell asleep, his head resting on a log.

By nightfall, Kindness still had not returned home. Precious kept going to the doorway to watch for him, but he never appeared. At last she became so upset that she woke up the young men and women of the village and got them to climb up the mountain to look for him, pine knot torches in their hands. When they discovered Kindness, he was already a stiffened corpse. Precious threw herself on him, sobbing bitterly. Then everyone helped carry Kindness home.

The next day, in accordance with the traditional Achang burial custom, they lay Kindness's body on a bamboo raft and put it in the Husa River to be carried away by the current. Precious desperately tried to climb aboard the raft, for she wanted to die with her husband, but the villagers pulled her back.

The bamboo raft floated on and on downstream, far, far away, until one day it reached a small village. Just then, it happened that two sisters were picking medicinal herbs by the river. The younger one caught sight of the bamboo raft and hastily called out, "Look, sister! What's that floating on the river?" The elder sister looked closely. "It seems there is a man sleeping on it," she said. They were drawn by this strange sight, so they pulled the raft ashore, wanting to investigate further. What they discovered was indeed a man, a handsome young man, but no matter how hard they tried, they could not awaken him.

Taking a more careful look, they realized he was dead. Oddly enough, however, his cheeks still were flushed with color. The younger sister couldn't understand, so she suggested they ask their father, a well-known herbal-medicine doctor, to come quickly. After examining the young man, the father concluded he had been bitten in the temple by a venomous snake, and was in a deep sleep, but his body was still warm and his heart was beating slightly.

The father and his two daughters hurriedly carried Kindness home and extracted the poisoned blood from his wound by means of a cupping jar. They applied herbs to his wound to eliminate the swelling and dispel the poison. Before long, Kindness regained consciousness and slowly opened his eyes. The old doctor kept giving him medicine, and the two sisters lavished him with care. It was while giving Kindness so much attention that both girls fell in love with him, and expressed their willingness to become his wives. Kindness graciously declined. Mindful of his beloved Precious, he bid the old doctor and his two daughters farewell, hurrying home even before he had fully recovered.

When Kindness had made his way back, he found that his house had been burned to the ground, and all there was left were a few smoking pillars. He cried out, "Precious, I'm home! Where are you?" All was silence in every direction. Not even so much as an echo could be heard.

When the local villagers first heard Kindness's loud cries, they wondered if it really could be he. Later, they discovered that listening to his voice was sadly moving, and finally some bold young men came out of their dwellings to go have a look. Ah! It really was Kindness who had come back after all. The entire village gathered around him and asked how he could still be alive, and how he had survived. Hearing his story, they felt worse than ever, for they had to tell him that a shaman had said that Precious, the girl with tufted eyebrows, had caused the death of her husband. She was not a human being, he claimed, but a ghost. The shaman stirred up some people who had driven her off into the dense jungle.

As soon as Kindness heard what had happened to his wife, he was overwhelmed with sorrow. With his long Husa sword slung over his shoulder, he went into the jungle to look for her in the direction the villagers indicated.

Once in the jungle, he kept calling her name as he walked, but he heard nothing but the eerie calls of wild animals and the howling of the wind in the trees. For seven days and nights he roamed, walking and calling without stopping for a moment.

On the eighth day, he was completely exhausted, and could not go on. Leaning against a big tree, he closed his eyes. Tears fell to his breast in two lines, uninterruptedly. He dreamed of a golden peacock circling above him, saying repeatedly, "Hurry and wake up, Kindness! A tiger is approaching your dear Precious. You must go quickly to rescue her."

Just as he awoke from his dream, he saw a peacock fly toward the south from the tree against which he had been leaning. Quickly, he ran in the direction of the peacock. Under a stone cliff, he found his wife, her face covered with tears. When she saw that her husband was still alive, she threw herself into his arms, and sobbed with happiness.

The wild animals stopped roaring and the soughing of the wind in the trees also ceased. The sun dispelled the dark clouds, and its golden rays penetrated the dense foliage down to the soft, wet earth.

The couple came out of the jungle, Kindness supporting Precious with his hand, and went back to the village where they had once lived together. Seeing this honest, brave young couple returning, the villagers ran beyond the stockade fence and met them joyfully. The young men helped build another new house, and the young women picked fresh flowers which they presented to them. The same day they moved in, people from far and near came to congratulate them, bringing them innumerable gifts. For fully three days and three nights, they joined in dancing and singing, feeling even more joyous than when they were newly married.

From that time on, capable Kindness often helped the villagers with their work, and the beautiful and kind-hearted Precious won ceaseless praise for her respect for the elderly and her love for the young. They had children and lived to a ripe old age, spending their days blissfully. No longer would anybody say that a girl with tufted eyebrows was the reincarnation of a ghost, or would cause her husband to die young. Nobody believed in this old superstition any more.

# NOTES

"Meijian zhangxuan de guniang," from Xu Hualong (Han) and Wu (Han) 1985, 622–25. Collector and redactor: Liu Yangwu (Han). Area of distribution: Jiuqian Township, Dehong Dai-Jingpo Autonomous Prefecture, southwestern Yunnan.

**Husa sword.** The Husa River area is famous for its Achang swords, which are bartered for by many minorities.

**cupping jar.** A cup containing heat is placed against the skin. The difference in air pressure inside and outside the cup creates suction.

# The Rainbow

DE'ANG TALE

In a De'ang family there once was a lovely, intelligent girl. Ever since she was little, she could weave sarongs with every kind of flower on them. The flowers she wove looked exactly like real flowers blooming in the mountains. As she grew up, many men came to seek her hand in marriage. The families they came from were much better off than her own, yet she refused them all. The man she preferred worked as a cow-herd for others. Her father did not like him, but though her mother did not approve of the poor boy either, she went along with her daughter's wishes, for the girl was the mother's only daughter and dearly beloved.

The young man was beside himself with joy, knowing the mother consented to the marriage. Soon a difficult problem arose, however. Although the young woman's father was destitute, he could not stand some herdboy who was even poorer than himself, so he tried every means possible to make things difficult for the couple.

According to the De'ang custom, a suitor has to offer a young woman's father all sorts of betrothal gifts—such as wine, cloth, and a horse—before he can marry her. But the young herdsman was not the least bit dismayed by this requirement. The couple talked the matter over, and decided that she would stay at home weaving sarongs, while he would go to some faraway place to work as a hired hand. When three years were up, he would be back with hard-earned gifts, and they could get married.

The maiden came to see off her lover as he was setting out on his journey. She stayed with him league after league, going over one mountain after another, until at last they came to a deep gorge where they had to separate. The girl sang this parting song:

*My love is like this valley stream,*
*and I the lotus fair.*
*As water ebbs my petals fade,*
*but roots press down full deep.*
*So when the stream flows high next year,*
*my buds will bloom, not weep.*

Thus they parted. Day after day the maiden expected her lover to come back. The agreed upon three years went by, but he had not returned. Four, then five years passed, and still there was no sign of him. She fell ill, and could neither eat nor weave sarongs. Her father wanted to look for another man for her, to be his son-in-law, but when he did find one from a rich family, this made the maiden's sickness even worse, and she wept night and day. As the time for the wedding was drawing near, she said to her mother, "I cannot do anything else but wait for the cowherd to return. If he never does, I will have no choice but to end my life. After I die, do not bury me, and do not nail up my coffin. I will wait for him still, even after I have died." Distraught and sick at heart, her mother consented to her wishes.

The day before the wedding, the maiden became sicker, and she felt sadder still. She repeated her request to her mother. "Do not bury me. I will still wait for him." With these words, she breathed her last. Her mother was profoundly upset, and would not permit anyone to bury her daughter or nail up her coffin. But the father was hard-hearted, and would have none of this nonsense. He insisted his daughter be buried at once. "I told you not to press her," the mother said, "or to interfere with her choice, but you kept putting her in a corner, until you drove her to death! If you could wait just one more day, and let the young man come to have a last look at her, she would have died without any regrets."

But the father was stubborn. He nailed the coffin shut, and ordered young men in the village to bear it away. However, when they arrived, they could not lift the coffin. Suddenly, noise was heard coming from the coffin, followed by a burst of smoke which curled up in the air, turning into a red snake. The father saw the snake, and so did all the young men of the village. Everyone was stupefied. What the mother saw, however, was not the snake in the sky, but her daughter sleeping quietly inside the coffin. Initially, her face looked sad and melancholy, but a moment later, she seemed to see her daughter smiling. Once more the mother urged her cruel husband to delay the burial one night. He had no alternative this time, but had to give in against his will.

The next day, the young man returned. Ever since learning that his beloved had taken sick, he had been trying to fight his way back, but there were all sorts of hardships along the way. He climbed innumerable high mountains, and battled tigers, leopards, and boas he encountered. He even lost his way in the jungle, and it took him three days and three nights to find his way out. When he came to the Mekong River, he found a surging torrent and not a soul or a ferryboat in sight. Felling a big tree, he pushed it into the river and jumped in after it. By clinging to the tree, he crossed the Mekong.

Rushing into the girl's house, he saw the coffin and threw himself upon it. All of a sudden, it opened, and a red snake came out and embraced him. The two were transformed into a band of smoke, a five-color rainbow that twisted up into the sky.

All the father saw, however, was a red snake. Only the mother could see her daughter and the young man embracing happily, while the villagers wept for the maiden. From that time on, De'ang parents no longer interfere with their daughters, but allow them the freedom to marry whomever they wish.

## NOTE

"Caihong," from *Aiqing chuanshuo gushi xuan* 1980, 401–3. Collector and redactor: Xu Jiarui (Han). Area of distribution: Dehong Dai-Jingpo Autonomous Prefecture, western Yunnan. The late Xu Jiarui, Xu Kun's granduncle, was chairman of the Yunnan Writers' Association.

# The Rhinoceros Hornbill

## DAI TALE

In the lush primeval jungle of Sipsong Panna there lived a hardworking and loving couple. The husband was called Yange and was known to everyone, as he was a famous hunter, while his wife, Yukan, was a celebrated beauty. No sooner would they appear at the Mekong River, carrying a red deer to dress out alongside the stream, than people would flock to watch, like moths swarming around a lantern. The young men, furtively eyeing Yukan, would interrogate her in honeyed words, pretending to ask questions about which mountain they had hunted, and so on and so forth. Everytime Yukan ran into this predicament, she would "scold the dog but point to the chicken" [zhi ji ma gou], that is, curse one thing but mean another. When she yelled at the flies that buzzed around her, she really was cursing the men: "You worthless pests!" she'd shout. "My red buck is alive. If you try to land on him and lay your eggs, you're going to die!"

Whenever Yange noticed what was going on, he would spit twice in the Mekong River, showing his contempt for these roguish young men. Then he would carry on, scraping the deer hide as if nothing had happened.

But by and by, as the days went on, as soon as Yange left his two-story bamboo bungalow, he could not help feeling anxious about his wife. The memory of those scenes dressing deer by the river would flash across his mind. He loved Yukan so dearly, every time he picked some fresh fruit he could not bear to taste them himself. Instead, he would always put them into the tongba he wore over his shoulder so that he could save them for his wife when he got home. Even if he had only one piece of fruit, they would share it together, bite by bite.

Once, in the middle of the day, Yange was running after a big bear he had wounded, when he happened to pass by the gorge near his bamboo bungalow. Quite unexpectedly, the bear's tracks disappeared along the edge of a pond. All Yange could do was return home feeling keenly disappointed. Just as he entered his home, he saw the huge footprint of a man at the edge of the huotang. Yange was devastated; it was as if a devil were gnawing his heart. His eyes were like torches flashing fire, and blue veins popped out along his neck. Bearing up, he called aloud, "Yukan, are you there? Yukan!" But there was only silence. He did not know where she had gone. All at once, several unimaginable things had occurred together and tied him in knots; already the wicked hand of jealousy crushed his heart and confused his mind. He collapsed by the cooking fire, greatly depressed.

When Yukan came back from washing clothes by the river, she saw in a glance that her husband was lying by the tang. She had no idea what had happened, but quickly lifted him up and put him to bed behind the bed curtain. Then she went and found a medicinal masangduan plant and boiled it for him to drink. After a few days, Yange fully recovered.

One morning after they had eaten their rice gruel, Yange went out hunting with his long sword hanging from his shoulder, and a crossbow in his hand. As he stepped down the bamboo stairway of his bungalow, he suddenly stopped in his tracks, feeling that some misfortune was about to happen to him again. He turned around and ran up the stairway, knelt down at his wife's feet, and said, "Oh, dear Yukan! I was going to go to the forest now by myself, but I really can't bear to leave you at home all alone. I fear those devilish rogues will come again and do you harm. I beg you, go hunting with me!"

Yukan did not realize what was behind his request. She smiled and said, "Have you forgotten that I am with child? How could I go with you chasing after wild animals? Wouldn't that cost me my life?" What she said sounded convincing to Yange. He whispered something into her ear and she nodded her head and smiled in agreement. From then on, whenever Yange went out hunting, he would remove the bamboo stairway and bar the door and windows. Yukan would always remain seated by the cooking fire embroidering her skirt, patiently waiting for Yange to bring home the game. Only after he got home was she free to come and go. In the course of time, the two of them got used to living this way.

One day at noon, Yange was relaxing in the cool shade of a pipal tree by the side of a gorge. He was dying for some water, so he descended the gorge to get a drink from the creek. As he approached the creek, he saw a dazzlingly bright, golden deer lowering its head to drink the cool water. Yange drew his bow noiselessly and shot a single arrow, striking the deer squarely in its neck. But it did not fall down. Instead, it ran desperately toward the dense forest with the arrow stuck in its neck. Yange too ran, as swift as an arrow in flight, chasing it on and on, and finally losing track of how far he had gone.

Now it was dark and he had no idea where the deer had gone. He found himself in a thick jungle that covered an unfamiliar canyon, and he lost his bearings. He ran this way and that, not knowing how to find his way home. One day followed another. He began to weep, filled with anxiety about his wife, whom he thought about endlessly. Even now he refused to eat the fruit he picked, still preferring to save it for Yukan.

After twenty days he somehow managed to find the trail home. As he passed over the mountain slope and glimpsed his own bamboo bungalow, he called out with joy, "My dear Yukan! I'm home! I'm home!" But there was no response save a long silence. Obscurely, in his mind's eye, he recalled himself discovering a man's huge footprint by the cooking fire, and he rushed to his house in a fury. He put the bamboo stairway back up and smashed open the sealed door and windows. Once inside, he found the cooking fire had died out. There was nothing stewing in the clay cooking pot on the tripod over the ashes, but just a couple of bones. He immediately ran into the bedroom. There was his wife lying still behind the black bed curtain. She had starved to death.

Realizing what had happened, Yange lost control of himself and wept bitter tears. "Suma! Suma!" he kept repeating. "Forgive me. Forgive me." With his wife now gone, he had no courage to go on living. He tore off the black curtain from the bed and the white turban wrapped around his head, and used them to bind his wife's corpse and his own body tightly together. Then he set fire to the house. Both husband and wife, together with their bamboo bungalow, turned to ashes.

After the couple died, the god of heaven noticed Yange's piteous look and his deep regret, and so had compassion on him. Instead of punishing Yange for the narrow-mindedness that caused his wife's death, the god of heaven turned them into a pair of birds—rhinoceros hornbills, which Dai people call *gekan*, after the names of the couple, Yange and Yukan. Thus, they still live on together in the jungle, flapping their wings and flying about as they like. The black and white plumage of the *gekan* is identical with the colors of the curtain and the turban the couple were wrapped together in when they were cremated. The male bird also retains a narrow-minded temperament. Whenever the female bird lays eggs and hatches them, the male bird will bring tree resin and mud in his beak to seal the tree hole, leaving only a tiny opening for fear that some misfortune will befall his mate. The male bird puts fresh fruit into the mouth of the female through this little space. When the two birds play in the jungle, the male calls to the female "*Suma! Suma!*" to show his repentance.

To this very day, these hornbills live in the jungle in pairs. They are devoted to one another. If one happens to be shot by a hunter, the other will die of grief in the forest. That is why Dai people cherish these affectionate birds greatly.

## NOTES

"Shuangjiao xiniao," from *Daizu minjian gushi* 1984, 115–19. Storyteller: Bo'aiwen (Dai). Translator and redactor: Chen Guipei (Han). Area of distribution: Sipsong Panna Dai Autonomous Prefecture, southern Yunnan.

**tongba.** A bag worn over the shoulder. It is delicately made and often is decorated with beautiful embroidery which may be a token of engagement between lovers.

**tang.** The central cooking fire or hearth, around which family members gather.

# Longsi and the Third Princess

## YAO TALE

In the past, there once lived in the land of us Yao people a man by the name of Longsi. He had been clever and intelligent ever since he was a little boy, and loved to work hard on the land. He often went out with his father, farming and hunting. By the time he was thirteen or fourteen years old, not only was he a master at constructing Yao-style houses, but he was also an expert shot.

At the end of his fifteenth year, his parents unfortunately became seriously ill, and before long, both of them died. Neither paddy field nor arable land, not even food or clothing, did his father leave him, but only a crossbow and some arrows. From then on, Longsi carried his bow and arrows wherever he went, and had to depend entirely on his hunting skills to survive. He was such a fine marksman that he never came back from the mountains empty-handed. He would exchange pheasants and rabbits he shot for provisions, and sometimes, if he got a tiger or a bear, he could trade it for a suit of new clothes.

After a few years, through long practice, his hunting skills became truly outstanding. When he encountered a tiger, he could jump on its back and pull out its whiskers. When he saw an eagle flying up in the sky, he could hit it right in the eye with a single shot. Longsi became a sharpshooter, and his name was on everybody's lips. His fame spread farther and farther, until one day, it reached the Yao king's ear.

The Yao king issued an order that, every month, Longsi must present him with twenty pheasants, twenty hares, ten muntjacs, and a tiger skin. If he should fail to procure all this game, he would be made to do hard labor in the king's mansion.

"What can I do?" Longsi wondered, exceedingly upset to receive this order. If he agreed, how could he get so much game every month?

Furthermore, if he gave it all to the king, what would he have left to live on? Should he resist, how could he prevail against the king? That would be like an arm competing against the thigh. There was no way out but to hunt day and night in the mountains. During the first few months, Longsi was barely able to keep up with the monthly quota, and as time went on, wild animals became more and more scarce. Though Longsi hunted deep in the mountains and in virgin forests, he could not kill as much game as the king ordered. Seeing this was the case, the king sent men to take Longsi and imprison him in the palace, where he was to do hard labor. From that time on, Longsi lived a miserable existence.

The Yao king had three daughters. The eldest was named Zhuoka, the second Qinka, and the third Aika. All three princesses were beauties, but the loveliest, the cleverest, and the kindest was the youngest, Aika. People who wore clothes woven by Third Princess felt cool in the summer and warm in the winter. The flowers she embroidered looked brighter in color and more pleasing to the eye than real ones. Listening to her singing, passersby would forget where they were going, and orioles would feel outdone and hide themselves in the jungle. Accordingly, the king loved her the best. But Aika had a queer disposition. She would never raise her head to look at other people, let alone let other people look at her. When the king asked her, "Why do you have to act like this?" Third Princess replied, "I do not want anyone except the man I love to look at my face."

Now the three princesses all grew up. The Yao king married the eldest to the prince of another kingdom, and the second to the son of a prominent headman, but Third Princess would not listen to her father, preferring to choose a husband by herself. The king asked her what man she intended to marry, "I'll marry the man who can make me raise my head, no matter who he is," Aika replied.

The third princess was known by all to be beautiful, clever, and kindhearted. Poor men longed to marry her, but none would dare to make an offer. As for the sons of rich families, three matchmakers a day arrived at the palace with proposals, but Third Princess would not pay attention to any of them. Hundreds of go-betweens came by, but she ignored them, and hundreds of noblemen's sons too, but she would not look up even once. These young men would loiter about in front of the palace day and night, like toads, each aspiring to win a glance from the princess. But the longer they loitered, the lower Aika dropped her head. She would pay absolutely no heed to their endless pestering.

As the saying goes, "June weather changes fast; June winds often go mad."

There came a driving rain that uprooted trees and blew off roof tiles. The rooms in the palace sprung some leaks, so the king ordered Longsi to repair them. He climbed up on top of the palace and began fixing one roof after another, starting with the side rooms along the courtyard, then the central rooms, until at last he came to the room belonging to Third Princess. When he lifted off a tile, he saw a spinning wheel down on the floor. He removed a second tile and saw a loom. Then he lifted up the third. Ha! Sitting beside a piece of dazzlingly bright, green satin was a maiden embroidering, her head bent down. Longsi knew that the third princess was the loveliest, the cleverest, and the most kind-hearted young woman in the world, and he was familiar with her wish to choose her own husband. Judging from the way this woman was dressed, he guessed she must be Third Princess. But because her head hung down, he could not see her face.

"Eh-heh, eh-heh!" Longsi pretended to clear his throat a few times, expecting to see Third Princess raise her head, but to his surprise, she went right on embroidering, as if nothing had happened. Bang! Longsi let his hand slip, dropping a tile on the floor and smashing it to smithereens. But not only did Third Princess keep her head down, she did not even cast a glance at the broken pieces. As a matter of fact, Aika had heard about the brave hunter Longsi long ago, and she knew that the person repairing the roof was he. She wanted to see whether Longsi loved her or not, so she waited to find out if he had some way to make her look up. Having already failed twice, Longsi got so upset that his head started sweating terribly. The more he worried the more he perspired. Ta-da! Two drops of his sweat fell on the tile, giving him a sudden inspiration. Remembering that Third Princess was a sensitive, kind-hearted young woman, he took up his axe and scratched his thumb slightly. Immediately blood oozed out and dripped on the princess's head. Right away, Longsi groaned deliberately, "Ai-ya! I've cut myself! Oooh! It hurts! My thumb, my thumb!"

As soon as Third Princess saw blood and heard Longsi yelling with pain, she was hurting too. She ripped off a piece of satin, *sssst*, put it on the end of a long bamboo pole, and lifted it up to Longsi. She was careful to slide her hand lower down the pole, so she could raise it higher without having to look up for even a moment. "Hey!" she called out, "take this piece of satin and wrap it around your wound!"

The pole came up to Longsi's feet, but he did not touch the piece of cloth. It reached his side; still he let it be. Even when the pole extended beyond the peak of the roof, Longsi would not take the satin. But this time he cried, "Big sister, would you please lift the pole up a little bit higher? I can't quite reach it!"

Holding on tightly to the pole, Aika mounted a chair, then a table. Most of the pole stuck out above the roof by this point, while the princess's head was practically bumping Longsi's toes. Yet he kept yelping, "Big sister, higher up, please!" The princess could not help tittering. She raised her head and saw a pair of round, bright eyes staring crazily at her. All at once, Longsi laughed gleefully, as if he were mad, "Now I see your beautiful face . . . !"

The couple poured out their hearts to one another with sweet words and honeyed phrases. Longsi asked a matchmaker to make an offer of marriage to the Yao king. Meanwhile, Aika also told her father her feelings. The king was enraged. He had never expected that his favorite daughter would fall in love with a poor man. He had Longsi brought before him. "If you can fill my mansion with so much gold and silver that it caves in with the weight, I will marry off my third daughter to you. If not, you had better get out of here fast!" Longsi understood that the king was deliberately making things difficult for him. There was nothing he could do except leave the palace, looking very depressed, and go back to hunting in the mountains as before.

One day, on his way home, Longsi came across a white-haired immortal, an old gaffer who asked him why he was so anxious. Longsi recounted what had happened from beginning to end. "Young fellow, don't worry," said the old immortal. "Go catch a pair of woodpeckers and place them on the pillars of the palace. That will take care of things." Longsi did just as he was told. As expected, once the woodpeckers stood on the palace pillars, they began pecking and hammering away, tic-tic, tock-tock-tock, dong-dong-dong, making a hollow, knocking ringing which, from afar, sounded for all the world exactly as though the palace were about to topple.

When the king heard the noise, he ran out of his room in a flurry to take a look. He saw that the mansion looked shining bright (the work of the magic woodpeckers), as if it were bursting with gold and silver. "Longsi, Longsi!" he shouted quickly, "Move out the gold and silver and don't crush my mansion with their weight! I admit defeat!"

The king's strategem had failed, but he still would not give up, and he fell upon another plan. He said to Longsi, "If you can spread satin all the way from your door to the door of my palace, I will marry my third daughter to you. If you cannot, you'd better get out of here fast!"

Again, Longsi went to the mountain to ask the old immortal for help. The immortal cut three wild banana leaves and gave them to Longsi, saying, "Take these and put one at your door, one on the road halfway to the palace, and one at the palace door. On your way back, blow a puff of air on each leaf. You will find the whole way from your door to the palace door covered with satin."

Longsi did as he was told. The road became covered with dazzling satin from his house to the palace. He hastily fetched the king. When the king saw all this satin, he was speechless.

Failing to thwart Longsi twice, the king might naturally have allowed him to marry his third daughter, yet such was not the case. He wanted to try to frustrate Longsi one last time. "How could you think of letting my third daughter live in that dilapidated, run-down house of yours?" he asked. "Hurry up and build a house as large and gorgeous as my palace. Then you can marry the third princess. If you can't do it, you'd better give up your pipe dream, the sooner the better."

When Aika heard about her father's test, she quickly sent a trusted maid to tell Longsi the way to overcome the difficulty. Longsi was elated. That same day, he took with him the longest rope he could find and went to the house of Shizong, a prominent headman, and began measuring it, raising a great hue and cry. Shizong came running and asked what was going on. "I want to marry Third Princess, but my house is too small," said Longsi. "I'm planning to build a house as big as the imperial palace. Now your house is as large as the palace. I have come to measure it so I can build one just like it."

Hearing this, Shizong burst out laughing, "You idiot! Not only do I have a house as gorgeous as the imperial palace, but also countless gold, silver, and treasure, yet my son still cannot marry the third princess. What kind of a man are you, you pipe-dreamer!"

Longsi began to shout and scream, deliberately making an uproar. "It's none of your business! Don't bother me! Let me measure!" Shizong said in disgust, "Stop measuring! If you can marry the third princess, I'll give my house to you for nothing!" At this, Longsi promptly rejoined, "You won't go back on your word, will you?" Shizong said, "No, no way!" With that, Longsi took out a long nail that he had ready at hand. "It's settled then. I'll drive the nail!" Shizong, casting a sidelong glance, said, "Go ahead!" And so, Longsi immediately drove the nail into Shizong's gate, signifying that an agreement had been made.

The next day, as Shizong was looking at the nail on his gate, he smiled. "What a joke! That poor young man wanting to marry the third princess!" As he turned around, he was shocked to see Longsi and the princess coming toward his house, talking and laughing together. He hurriedly tried to pull out the nail, but it wouldn't budge, try as he might.

At this point, both Longsi and Aika were already at the main entrance. A maid from the palace came up and said to Shizong, "Third Princess is going to marry Longsi. You have to move out quickly so they can prepare for the wedding!" All of a sudden, Shizong's face turned pale, and he dripped with sweat, yet he could not break his promise. All he could do was slip out his back door in a rush.

Now that Longsi had a house as large and as gorgeous as the imperial mansion, the Yao king could no longer find any excuse to prevent the marriage. Accordingly, Longsi and Aika were married, and lived a beautiful life in that house.

# NOTES

"Longsi yu san gongzhu," from *Aiqing chuanshuo gushi xuan* 1980, 266–71. Collectors and redactors: Wenshan Folk Literature and Folk Art Research Team. Area of distribution: Funing and Malipo counties, Wenshan Zhuang-Miao Autonomous Prefecture, southeastern Yunnan.

**drive the nail.** Longsi's act of hammering a nail into the gate does not correspond to a particular Yao custom, but is an allegorical way of marking the fact that the headman has made a strong vow.

# The Cloud That Longs
# for a Husband

## BAI LEGEND

Princess Awa, daughter of the king of Nanzhao, was fond of walking in the outskirts of the city of Dali. Every day, before having supper, to relieve her boredom she would lead the palace ladies and maidens on a walk out the west gate of the city.

One day, as she was strolling about outside the city, she met a young woodcutter face-to-face, as he was coming down from the mountain slopes, carrying two bundles of firewood on a shoulder pole. As chance would have it, the place they met was Phoenix Bridge. The woodcutter took a look at the princess, and the princess glanced furtively at the woodcutter too. He saw that she was an exquisitely beautiful young maiden, and he fell in love with her, as she did with him. Each loved the other, yet neither said a word.

After Princess Awa returned to her father's vast palace, she could not stop thinking about the woodcutter. She missed him so much during the day, she lost her appetite, while at night she lay in bed with her eyes open, never sleeping a wink.

Every day, when the woodcutter came back from chopping firewood, he would stop on Phoenix Bridge for a rest. The princess, figuring that he was about to come down from the mountains, would go and wait for him there.

When the king of Nanzhao learned that his own daughter had fallen in love with a poor beggar of a woodcutter, he was furious. Immediately, he betrothed the princess to his favorite minister, and ordered that within three days she must be married. She became distraught when she heard this news. Speaking to her father, the king, she cried,

"I've fallen in love with a woodcutter, and have decided to live with him all my life. I will not marry anyone else, not even if my life depends on it!"

But no matter how Princess Awa wept and complained, she could not touch the Nanzhao king's stony heart in the slightest way. The same day that she spoke to her father, she mounted a big high-spirited horse, and just before supper went to Phoenix Bridge to meet her woodcutter. She poured out her heart: "I don't want to marry anyone except you. I want only to live with you, all my life. But now my father has promised me to another man. Can you find some way to rescue me?"

The woodcutter was an unusually kindhearted man, and he was much moved by her deep affection. "Don't be unhappy. Since you're willing to live with me, I will carry you on my back to my home. My house is located on the other side of a mountain—a place nobody else lives, and nobody else can find."

"Are you sure you can carry me on your back?" asked the princess.

"Of course I can do it!"

With that, the woodcutter picked her up and dashed straight toward the other side of Dragon Spring Peak in the Cang mountain range west of Er Hai. As a matter of fact, the woodcutter was not an ordinary man at all, but one with fairy powers. He lived in a cave behind the Cang Mountains. He walked swift as a roaring wind with the princess on his back. After they had traveled some distance, a pair of wings suddenly grew out from under his arms, and at once they soared up into the sky. In an instant, they flew to the cave situated on Jade Mountain behind Dragon Spring Peak. They married and became a devoted couple, living in a cave, completely cut off from the outside world.

When the palace ladies and maidens realized that Princess Awa had been carried off by the woodcutter, they hurriedly reported it to the Nanzhao king. He immediately led his men and horses in pursuit, going up the Cang mountain range along three routes, starting from Dragon Spring Peak, Harmony Peak, and Jade Mountain. At that time, it was snowing heavily on the crest of the mountains, the blinding snow was nearly waist deep, and the men slipped at every step. They were simply unable to ascend, and the weather was freezing cold. How could the

Nanzhao king catch up with a man who grew wings and could fly? The king never even caught a glimpse of him. Finding themselves frustrated in their search in the mountains, the troops knocked on every door and ransacked every household on the plain below. Failing to find the woodcutter there as well, there was nothing left for them to do but return dejectedly.

The woodcutter and Princess Awa lived together in the cave. With the help of his wings, he would go all about, finding good things for her to eat. He even flew as far as Chicken Claw Mountain to steal winter melon and preserved fruit for her. But the cave was terribly cold, and Princess Awa could not stand the freezing air which pierced her to the bone. The woodcutter racked his brain to find a way to keep his wife warm, but still he could not get rid of the cold air in the cave.

"I've heard it said," he told her, "that Luo Quan, elder of the Luo Quan Temple, has in his possession a magic garment that guards his mountain. It can ward off floods and it exudes warmth. Let me go and steal it for you!"

The princess was sorely anxious. "After you go off, how can I manage by myself?"

The woodcutter comforted her, saying, "Don't worry! I'll soon be back!"

He spread his wings and, in the twinkling of an eye, flew east of Er Hai to Luo Quan Temple. Picking up the magic garment from the meditation seat of the elder of the temple, he draped it over his arm, then swiftly took off. As he was flying over Er Hai, Luo Quan chased after him carrying his staff, and hit him squarely with a blow that cast him down into a crack between two rocks in the lake beneath the temple. As soon as he fell, he turned into a stone mule, stuck inside the crack, and remained there, never able to move again.

Meanwhile, every day, Princess Awa waited anxiously for her husband to return home. She looked and looked, to the left and to the right, yet she never saw him coming. In a few days, after suffering from constant hunger and cold, she died in the cave.

Once the princess was dead, her wronged spirit would never rest. It soared straight up into the sky, and turned into a white cloud in the form of a winnowing fan flying over the top of Jade Mountain. This cloud came to be called the "cloud that longs for a husband." It is different from other clouds in that, as soon as it appears, the stone mule in Er Hai begins braying.

Local people say that this "cloud that longs for a husband" appears every year in November and December. At this time, travelers do not dare ride in a boat to visit their relatives, and fishermen do not attempt to catch yellow croakers or net edible seaweed in Er Hai, for they are afraid that the wronged spirit of Princess Awa might blow through the air, stirring up the waves and overturning their boats.

## NOTES

"Wangfu yun," from *Aiqing chuanshuo gushi xuan* 1980, 277–78. Collector and redactor: Li Xinghua (Han). Area of distribution: Dali Bai Autonomous Prefecture, western Yunnan. Li Xinghua is the daughter of Li Dazhao, one of the founders of the Chinese Communist Party. She is a specialist on Bai culture.

**Nanzhao (the Southern Kingdom).** An independent Bai state and the center of Bai culture from the eighth to the tenth century. With its capital in Dali (Great Order), on the shore of Er Hai in western Yunnan, its territory included what are now Yunnan and parts of Sichuan, Guizhou, Hunan, and Guangxi provinces, and Burma.

# The Nanxi River

## DAI LEGEND

Long, long ago, Sipsong Panna was yet a vast stretch of formidable, virgin jungle. At that time, the Dai people lived on the large, remote plain to the northeast. At one point, there was a cruel war between the Dai and people of a different race, and the entire Dai people were practically wiped out. The only Dai to survive were seven princesses who escaped and went deep into the remote, lush jungle.

The seven princesses were as beautiful as scented luxiangpai flowers. Their healthy, blooming skin gleamed like burnished gold. Their slender figures would remind one of tender willow branches when they first begin to bud. Their soft, delicate arms were similar to handsome, amber-colored wax candles, and their sparkling eyes were like stars shimmering in water at night.

They lived a lonely existence, without parent, brother, or anyone else to support them. In their solitary life, they forgot all about such things as their beauty and happiness.

One day, while they were bathing, a rooster came floating down from the upper reaches of the Nanxi River, an arrow stuck in its belly. It was a chahua rooster, the kind that is celebrated for its wonderful crowing. This one was still alive, for the snow-white arrow feather was stained with fresh, red blood.

Such a strange happening! The princesses hastily dressed in their short half-blouses and long sarong skirts, and ran pell-mell toward the upper stretches of the Nanxi River, looking for the person who had shot the chahua cock. Tree branches raveled their hair, thistles and thorns tore their skin, yet they kept moving as fast as they might. They ran with a feeling of elation—it had been so long since the seven had heard a human voice, other than their own. How they longed to hear this voice!

After running a good while, they suddenly detected voices singing. What a pleasant sound! Like the murmuring of a spring flowing from a mountain cave, or the cry of a crane in the vast, empty sky. Dodging swiftly behind a banyan tree, they peeped through an opening in the foliage, completely fascinated.

They saw seven young men, each wearing a soft, flat, yellow cap made out of the leaves of bamboo shoots, inlaid at the top with a triangular piece of white jade, tied with a golden flower. A spray of fresh flowers wrapped in green leaves was stuck in the cap. Each of them wore a long white cloak draped over his shoulders, a tight, close-fitting undergarment, and a long sarong. At their waists were long swords inlaid with ivory, gold, and silver. How handsome they were! The young men were sitting in a circle around a fire, roasting a *chahua* rooster. One of them was plucking the strings of a *bulei*, accompanying the others, who were singing enchanting melodies. They seemed to be the happiest men in the world.

The seven princesses loved them. They came out from behind the trees and stood before them, staring, utterly infatuated. The sudden appearance of the seven young women likewise took the men by complete surprise, and they too stared in blank amazement.

After a while, the seven young men stood up and walked up to the princesses, saying, "Thanks to our eyes that have let us see such beautiful maidens! There is not a flower in the world that is as delicate and charming as you! How happy and honored are we to see you! Dear maidens, we plead with you to open your lovely lips and speak your names in lovely voices!"

"We are seven princesses of the Dai people. A hateful enemy murdered our parents and our kinsmen. Only we survived and escaped to the jungle. We thought we were going to die here, soon. Never would we have dreamed that today a chance for new life would come our way through you!"

The seven young men said, "We are seven princes of the Huagou [Spotted Dog] people of Pearl-Sky [Zhutian] Mountain. Our people pride themselves in taking a solemn pledge: 'A clod of earth is less precious than gold and silver, mountain tops are higher than the jungle, and we Huagou will conquer people of other races forever!' The Huagou consider themselves to be the noblest people on earth. They hold to these rules: no intermarriage with people of other races; kill brave men of other races on the battlefield, and offer their weak ones in sacrifice to our gods on altars; make the beautiful women of other races be our slaves and serve us.

"We seven brothers could not bear to go along with these pledges and proscriptions. Our own father said we lacked the fighting spirit of the Huagou, so we were driven away from our land. How terrible we felt! But how could we marry the girls of our race? They are fierce and cruel, our own mother included. We prefer living in the malaria-infested jungle to being on the high mountain with the Huagou. We would rather live by hunting than by taking gold and silver stained with blood. We choose to dwell among tigers and leopards, rather than marry those inhuman witches. Often, we come singing and hunting in the jungles, for it lightens our spirits. We never expected to meet such lovely goddesses as you. Ah! How lovely are you maidens. Such beauty is as rare as finding seven yolks in a single turkey egg! Our hearts are skipping beats in our breasts now, like little panic-stricken deer jumping about! We cannot go home again, for that would mean our deaths. We would rather stay in the jungle forever, protecting you from wild beasts, finding you food, and guarding your house. How can we hold back our excitement! We are willing to sacrifice our lives for you." Having said these things, the seven young men made vows to the sun, and threw their caps with the badges of the Huagou race into the Nanxi River. They asked the maidens for pieces of their sarongs to make turbans.

The seven Dai princesses found the seven Huagou princes very sincere and warm-hearted; truly, they were the best young men in the world. The maidens were so moved, they wound the turbans around the heads of the young men with their own hands, leaving the surplus cloth to hang to the left. According to custom, this extra part of the turban ought to be hung on the right side, because the right hand has greater strength. But at the time, the princesses were standing facing the princes when they wound the turbans, so the surplus part was hung on the left side. Later, in memory of their ancestors, Dai people would always leave the surplus part of their turban hanging on the left.

That night, the seven princesses and the seven princes were married by the Nanxi River, and the next day, they traveled to the place where the girls lived in the jungle, showing their affection for one another all the way.

After they got married, their lives were beautiful, happy, and full. The princes built a big house with 120 banyan trees. Using thread made from the bark of the *gou* tree, they wove seven blackish-green sarongs, on which they embroidered seventy shining stars. Every day, the young women collected mangoes and litchi nuts in the jungle and made them into sweets. With the tender buds of banyans and newly sprouted banana leaves, they made pickled vegetables. They often caught *baoji* fish in the Nanxi River, and even dived to the bottom to gather moss, with which they fashioned moss-cakes. They ate well, lived comfortably, and dressed well. The women learned to laugh and sing. Today, Dai women are known as "girls who love to laugh and sing."

The princesses gave birth to many children (who, it is said, are the ancestors of today's Dai people). Having children made their lives all the happier.

One day, the seven princes went out hunting at the edge of the jungle, and they came across a large party of Huagou. These people pressed the princes to return to Pearl-Sky Mountain, but the princes refused. And so, fighting broke out. The brave princes killed many Huagou. Though their ankles were stained with blood, they went on fighting valiantly. But there were too many Huagou, and at last the princes had to retreat. To protect their wives and children, they did not retreat to their home in the jungle, but they withdrew to the Nanxi River instead. The pitiable princes were terribly wounded, their white undergarments, cloaks, and sarongs all blood-stained, while blood streamed from their cuts. Still, they fought each step of the way as they retreated. Finally, their swords broken and their blood all spilt, they were killed by their own Huagou people.

A long time went by, and yet there was no sign of the princes returning, so the seven princesses and their children left home to look for them. After ten days, they came to the edge of the jungle and found a blood-stained trail. Following this path, they discovered the bodies of the princes. Weeping bitterly, the women and children carried the corpses home and buried them that night. The seven princesses sat staring blankly through the night. By the next day, they had disappeared.

People say that the trail of blood became a flower path that night, and the blood-soaked earth grew countless flowering trees, which bloom profusely. Today, some of these flowers are as big as rice baskets, while others are as small as clothes buttons. The red ones are like red carpets, the emerald-green are the color of peacock tails, while the white remind one of silver utensils, and the scented ones smell like perfume. Among this great variety of flowers, the prettiest is a white flower dotted with red spots. It is called the *panzhi* flower, and it grows on the ceiba (silk-cotton) tree.

These flowers are said to come from the blood of the princes of the Huagou. Among the several thousand kinds of butterflies of varied colors that flutter among the flowering shrubs in the land of the Dai, there are seven species of fantastic golden butterflies. The big ones are as huge as multicolored pouches, and the small ones are as small as copper coins. These butterflies dazzle people as they flutter around their heads. The golden butterflies are said to come from the tears of the seven princesses. They are looking for their ceiba tree among the flowering shrubs. By the flower path is the river that people call the Nanxi, "Mother River." In the Nanxi there are seven big stones shaped like women. These stones are thought to be the transformations of the seven princesses after they died.

Today, the Dai people often wear white turbans as a sign of mourning for the princes and the princesses of long ago.

# NOTES

"Nanxi He," from *Yunnan minzu minjian gushi xuan* 1982, 295–99. Collector and re-dactor: Cao Ge (Han). Area of distribution: Sipsong Panna Dai Autonomous Prefecture, southern Yunnan.

**bulei.** A stringed instrument, something like a guitar or mandolin, which is plucked.

**gou tree.** Unidentified.

**baoji fish.** A large fish special to the Sipsong Panna area, known for its delicate flavor.

# Appendix

## Traditional Yunnan Ethnic Minority Cultures

### LUCIEN MILLER

Ethnic minorities in China are not objective entities, permanently defined by Chinese, Asian, or Western enthnologists. Descriptions will change—in some cases, radically—as future anthropological, historical, linguistic, literary, and folkloristic studies are completed, and will enhance our understanding of the constructed nature of the minorities. Since the myths, legends, and tales in the present volume reflect traditional, premodern minority cultures, information compiled here from several Chinese and Western sources (Lebar, Hickey, and Musgrave 1964; Ramsey 1987; Heberer 1987; Dessaint 1980; Stevens and Wehrfritz 1988; Yunnan sheng lishi yanjiu suo 1983; Mackerras 1989; Ma 1980; Zhong 1983; Shen 1989; Yunnan sheng renmin zhengfu waishiban gongsi bian [n.d.]), with supplementary information from Xu Kun, emphasizes aspects of traditional minority life.

Readers should be aware that this picture has altered considerably with the advent of modernization, industrialization, and Chinese communism. Although former ways of life and customs have often been preserved since the founding of the People's Republic of China in 1949, major changes in minority societies in Yunnan and throughout China have taken place. In the area of governance, for example, minority autonomous areas, counties, townships (xiang), towns (zhen), and villages are usually administered by locally elected members of minorities, rather than by Han Chinese, although ultimate authority rests with the Communist party secretary, who may or may not be Han (Mackerras 1989, 16). Local government in minority areas generally parallels political structures found in Han communities, with the CCP, People's Council (Renmin Daibiao Hui), and People's Government (Renmin Zhengfu) governing townships or towns with a population of at least fifteen thousand (China Daily, 2 August 1991, p. 4). Other areas of significant change were the people's communes, cooperatives, and mutual aid teams (all of which were predominant in minority as well as Han communities from the late 1950s until their dismantlement in the early 1980s), followed by the present production responsibility system, in which groups contract specific work goals. Slavery, serfdom, and polygamy have generally been eliminated, along with classes Communist authorities considered exploitive (Mackerras 1989, 29 and 64). Education of women and equality of the sexes are official policy goals, though frequently contradicted by social practice. In many minority areas, compounds of concrete high-rise apartments, ubiquitous in the whole of China, have replaced traditional forms of housing. Slash-and-burn agriculture has disappeared in many places where it once was practiced. Ethnic costume and dress often is worn only on festive occasions, or to attract Han or foreign tourists. A running suit, plastic slippers, miniskirt, or jeans may be de rigueur among urban minority youth today.

Names of ethnic minorities in this appendix are primarily Han terms in general use today, some of which are transliterations, and which are not necessarily names the non-Han peoples themselves use. The latter often vary widely, even within one minority. Alternate names (adapted after Dessaint; Lebar, Hickey, and Musgrave; and Ramsey) are given following the heading for each minority.

# Achang
## (Maingtha, Monghsa, Ngachang)

The Achang were a dominant group in the Yunlong area of western Yunnan from the fifth century A.D. through the Ming period (1368–1644). After the Ming, Han rulers forced the Achang to migrate southwest to the Dehong area. The majority of the Achang are found in Burma, while twenty thousand live among the Dai and Jingpo along Yunnan's southwestern border with Burma. Presently 90 percent are located in the Husa district of Lianghe and Longchuan counties in the Dai-Jingpo Autonomous Prefecture of Dehong, while the rest are scattered in Luxi, Ningjiang, Longling, and Tengchong counties. Well known as successful rice farmers, the Achang are also celebrated for their wood engraving and silverware. Their famed Husa swords, customarily worn and revered by Achang men, are reputed to be as flexible as a finger, and are highly prized by Tibetans, Dai, Jingpo, and Burmese. Prominent features of Achang oral culture are ballads and tales, drum and monkey dances, and musical instruments such as the bamboo flute, *sanxian* (lit., "three strings"), gourd-shaped *sheng* (common to the Dai and other minorities), and elephant-leg drum. The drum, named for its shape, is made from animal skin stretched over a wooden frame about four feet long and a few inches in width. It is hung from the shoulder or hooked to the belt, and is struck with the hands. Traditional dress for men includes a

Map 2. Prefectures (P.) and autonomous prefectures (A.P.).
Source: Yunnan sheng ditu 1990; Yang 1989; and Geelan and Twitchett 1974.

blue, white, or black, buttoned jacket. Women typically wrap their hair in blue or black cloth. Married women wear a skirt and tight-sleeved jacket. Unmarried women tie their braids on top of the head in a bun, wrap the braids with a long headcloth, and wear long pants. Achang homes are commonly constructed of wooden beams, brick, or stone. The Achang language, for which there is no written form, belongs to the Tibeto-Burman family. Achang people often speak both Chinese and Dai, and many also can read Chinese. They are culturally and religiously influenced by the Dai, thus generally being Theravada Buddhists.

# Bai

## (Ber Dser, Ber Wa Dser, LaBhu, Minchia-tzu, Pai, Pai-jen, Pai-man, Per-nu-tuu, Per-tsu, Petsen, Pe-tso, Petsu, Shua Ber Ni)

The Bai live in the Dali Bai Autonomous Prefecture in western Yunnan, which includes the lakeshore region between Er Hai and the Cang Mountains, the western part of the Yunling Mountains, and the area of the southwestern gorges of the Yunnan-Guizhou plateau through which the Salween, Mekong, and Jinsha rivers flow from north to south. The Dali area is an ancient center of civilization in what is today the southwest border region of China. New Stone Age remains have been excavated around Er Hai, as well as at Dianchi Lake near Kunming, which prefigure Bai and other minority cultures. The Han dynasty emperor Wudi set up a prefecture in the Dali region in 109 B.C. In A.D. 738, the prince of the Mengshe tribe established the Nanzhao kingdom, in which the majority of civil and military officials were Baiman people, ancestors of the Bai. In 937, the Baiman founded the Dali kingdom, which flourished until it was conquered by the Mongols in 1253.

One of the former names for the Bai, "Minjia" ("Common People" or "Families of the People"), was a term coined by Han Chinese to distinguish the indigenous people of the old Nanzhao kingdom from Han people who settled there after the Mongol conquest under Kublai Khan in 1253. Formerly non-Han territory, though incorporated nominally in the Han dynasty empire, the land "South of Yun Mountain" (Yunnan) became a Chinese province under the Yuan, or Mongol, dynasty (1206–1368), but the Bai were neither displaced by the Han nor dispersed among other groups, as was often the experience of ethnic minorities. For hundreds of years Bai have been literate in Chinese, besides developing a system whereby Han Chinese characters are read phonetically in the Bai language. Whether in ancient times the Bai had a written language is a matter of scholarly dispute. Today a system of romanization has been created by Bai linguists, and a modern Bai written language has been established.

Map 3. Counties. Source: *Yunnan sheng ditu* 1990;
Yang 1989; and *The Population Atlas of China* 1987.

The classification of the Bai language is uncertain; it contains elements that appear to be Tibeto-Burman, Mon-Khmer (Austroasiatic), Tai, and Chinese. The Dali Bai district is known for its huge holiday festivals, such as the Third Month Fair (Sanyue Jie) held in the spring, which attracts thousands of Bai and other minority nationalities from adjacent provinces. Participants gather for several days of song and dance fests, bartering, horse racing, and archery contests.

The most economically successful minority in western Yunnan, the 1,132,000 Bai (some sources estimate the population to be nearly two million) farm rice-lands and wheat fields on the fertile six-thousand-foot-high Dali plain, and follow the traditional practice of fishing Er Hai with nets and cormorants. The ancient Bai (and Yi) way of plowing with one person riding the yoke between a team of oxen while another drives them from behind is still found in Bai areas today. Dali marble is famous (the Chinese name for marble is "Dali stone"), and Bai are recognized as marble artisans, as well as architects, stone masons, wood carvers, iron smiths, carpenters, and boat builders. A cheese that Bai and other minorities make is prized by Han Chinese in Yunnan, contrary to the general Han abhorence of dairy products. Traditional dress varies according to locality. Men dress in a white jacket with buttons down the front and a white vest. Women commonly wear a colored corduroy waistcoat or vest over a white blouse with embroidered sleeves, and an embroidered sash and apron over trousers, and partially cover their hair with a patterned scarf worn in folds, or an embroidered chaplet or cap. Bai architecture in the Dali area is identified by two-storied, three-winged houses built around garden courtyards (with one wall being a decorative screen), carved wooden doors and balustrades, stone floors, and paintings of landscapes, birds, and flowers on whitewashed exterior walls of the house and patio. Walls may have arabesque patterns and pointed windows. Below the nineteen peaks of the Cang Mountains, which form a vast screen to the west of Er Hai, Buddhist pagodas and pavilions occasionally dot the lakeside landscape, evidence of the once vital presence of Buddhism during the Nanzhao and Dali kingdom periods. Many of the Buddhist temples and sculptures were decimated during the Cultural Revolution, but are undergoing restoration. Bai religious belief today includes shamanism, esoteric (ācārya [Chinese: mijiao]) Buddhism, and Daoism (Taoism), with a scattering of remnant Christians from the precommunist foreign-missionary era, while the predominant form of traditional religious practice is the cult of local or village deities (benzhu) which is celebrated at temple fairs and grand festivals.

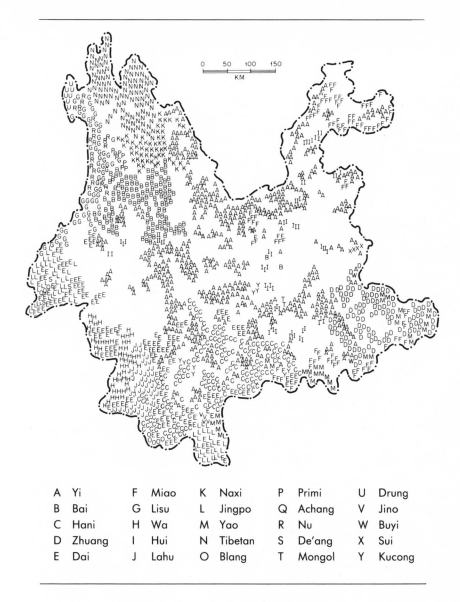

| A | Yi     | F | Miao | K | Naxi     | P | Primi  | U | Drung  |
|---|--------|---|------|---|----------|---|--------|---|--------|
| B | Bai    | G | Lisu | L | Jingpo   | Q | Achang | V | Jino   |
| C | Hani   | H | Wa   | M | Yao      | R | Nu     | W | Buyi   |
| D | Zhuang | I | Hui  | N | Tibetan  | S | De'ang | X | Sui    |
| E | Dai    | J | Lahu | O | Blang    | T | Mongol | Y | Kucong |

Map 4. Distribution of ethnic minorities. Source: Lebar, Hickey, and Musgrave 1964; U.S. Central Intelligence Agency 1971; *The Population Atlas of China* 1987; and *Zhongguo shaoshu minzu diqu huaji congkan* 1986.

# Blang

## (Bulang, Da-ang, Humai, Kunloi, Palaung, Rumai)

The Blang are a Mon-Khmer minority in the most southwestern section of Yunnan, and are strongly influenced by Dai (Shan) and Burmese cultures. Most Blang live outside of China, especially in Burma. Their population in China is approximately fifty-nine thousand. The Blang in Yunnan dwell along both sides of the lower reaches of the Mekong River, in areas where there are mountain ridges and narrow, deep valleys. Their main locations are the mountain districts of Blang Mountain, and Bada, Xiding, Mengman, and Daluo, which lie within Menghai County in the Dai Autonomous Prefecture of Sipsong Panna. Other Blang are dispersed through twenty-one other counties in Yunnan, and live among various ethnic minorities. The Blang, like the De'ang and the Wa, are considered to be descendants of an older ethnic stratum in the northern regions of Southeast Asia known in Chinese historical records as the Pu people, whose ancestors were among the earliest inhabitants of the Mekong and Salween river valleys. Living in the region between the Mekong River and Simao, the Blang were influenced by Han culture, and became partially assimilated into other ethnic groups, but eventually developed their own ethnic identity. Primarily tea growers and basket weavers, the Blang are one of the producers of Pu'er tea, famous in China and abroad. Villages, sometimes stockaded, are located on mountainsides and ridges.

The Blang are both polytheistic and Buddhist in their beliefs. They worship more than ninety human, dragon, animal, and plant spirits, as well as water and valley spirits, to whom they offer sacrifices before any agricultural activity. Each year many Blang hold a festival to worship the bamboo rat, which represents the souls of parents. Living in close proximity to the Dai, the Blang universally speak Dai, sing Dai hymns, and dwell in Dai-style two-story bamboo houses. Blang dress is similar to that of the Dai. Traditionally, men wear a collarless jacket, loose black trousers, and a black or white sarong. Tattooing is common. Women dress in a striped or black sarong and a close-fitting collarless jacket, with their hair worn in a bun covered by layers of cloth. Dai influence has also led to the practice of Theravada Buddhism. Every Blang village has a Buddhist temple where boys study the Dai script, Dai literature, and the Buddhist sutras written in Dai. Through this educational process, some Dai oral literary works are circulated among the Blang, significantly influencing Blang folk literature.

# Buyi
## (Bouyei)

The Buyi language belongs to the Zhuang-Dai branch of the Tai family of languages and, like Zhuang and Dai, is closely related to Thai and Lao. The 2,120,000 Buyi live mainly in southern Guizhou province. Those found in the Guangxi Zhuang Autonomous Region are called "Zhuang." In fact, Buyi and Zhuang really are not different. In Yunnan there are more than twenty thousand Buyi, numbers of whom are to be found in Luoping, Fuyuan, and Shizong counties in eastern Yunnan, with scattered pockets in Maguan and Hekou counties in southeastern Yunnan. They are hard to differentiate from the Han, as they generally speak Chinese and wear Chinese clothes, being sinicized, as are the Zhuang. In some areas, men wear a head scarf and short buttoned jacket, while ceremonial dress for women may include a head scarf, silver jewelry, a long robe, and a pleated skirt. Originating in central China, the Buyi began migrating to Southwest China in the thirteenth century to avoid the Mongol invasion. Valley dwellers, paddy-rice growers, and adept batik artisans, they live in bungalows or large two-story homes constructed on piles, whose style is sometimes imitated by other ethnic minorities. Most of the Buyi in Yunnan migrated from Pu'an and Zunyi counties in Guizhou, retaining aspects of Buyi culture and traditional customs, such as the Flower Dance Festival, marked by horses wearing brass bells and lines of dancing youths playing drums, vertical bamboo flutes, and moon-shaped guitars. Their widely esteemed love songs depicting the stages of love of courting couples (called "Langxiao songs" in Chinese—a transliteration of a Buyi word meaning "sweet-talk") are the focal point of festivals and social gatherings.

# Dai
## (Baiyi, Che, Chinese Shans, Eastern Shans, Khe, Lu, Lue, Nua, Pai-i, Shan Tayok, Shui, Tayok)

"Tai" is the name of both a language family and the largest group of non-Han Chinese in South China. "Dai" is the name of a distinctly identifiable minority nationality in western and southern Yunnan; Han-Chinese records of the Dai go back to the first century B.C. "Dai" is also a collective term for the different languages belonging to the Tai language family, spoken in western and southern Yunnan. Culturally speaking, the Dai are Southeast Asian and quite similar to the Thai of Thailand. The 840,000 Dai are distributed along the Mekong River in Sipsong Panna Dai Autonomous Prefecture, elsewhere in southern Yunnan, and in the drainage area of the Salween and the Ruili rivers in the Dehong Dai-Jingpo Autonomous Prefecture, in western Yunnan. In both western and southern Yunnan, the Dai are valley dwelling paddy-rice growers. The Dai were under the control of the Nanzhao and Dali kingdoms from the eighth through the twelfth centuries. In their relation to China, the Dai were vassals, sending tribute to the Chinese court, and subject to the latter's appointment of Dai head-men, but the Dai were never part of China until the Republican era (1911–1949). In the twelfth century, the Jinglong kingdom was established by a Dai chieftain. Han Chinese ethnographers commonly claim that the western and southern Dai are basically similar in terms of religion, culture, and language, but the Dai themselves disagree. Their languages, for example, are not mutually intelligible, and scripts are different. Although Sipsong Panna has been heavily logged (less than 30 percent of the land is tropical forest, which in 1950 covered 60 percent of the region), it retains some dense jungle forest, a rich variety of flora and fauna, and its celebrated subtropical beauty.

Traditional Dai homes are located on flat, level embankments, facing rivers or lakes, and are built of bamboo on stilts, with hinged walls, and a trap door and ladder leading below. Traditional dress for women is an ankle-length sarong, worn in a variety of colors, a close-fitting narrow-sleeved tunic, and a sash. Long hair is tied in a bun. Men wear a collarless jacket with tight sleeves, dark loose-fitting pants, and a black or white turban. In traditional Dai society, tattooing is popular among men. The mid-April Water-Splashing Festival, marked by the firing of rockets, dragon boat races, and games to discern a romantic mate, is celebrated with the belief that disaster and illness can be warded off by people splashing one another with water. Most Dai are Theravada Buddhists, and Buddhism plays a central role in their culture. In the Sipsong Panna area, every village has a temple, and young men normally spend a period of their youth as monks living in the temples and studying the Buddhist sutras. The Dai have several different scripts. Their most important literary form is the long poem (rare in Han-Chinese literary history), of which there are some 550 collections, note-worthy for lively metaphors and meticulous characterizations. Amateur folk singers maintain the continuity of folk literature, narrating Dai myths, legends, and tales at village festivals. The peacock is a central symbol of grace and well-being in Dai myth, and is celebrated in the popular Peacock Dance, in which performers imitate the preening and strutting of the elegant, proud bird.

# De'ang
## (Benglong)

The De'ang are one of three Mon-Khmer minorities found in China, the other two being the Blang and the Wa. Their small population of 12,300 is located along both sides of the Chinese-Burmese border, the majority being located in Burma. Those found in Yunnan are distributed on mountain ridges in Luxi County in Dehong Dai-Jingpo Autonomous Prefecture and other parts of western Yunnan, as well as in Sipsong Panna in southern Yunnan. Because they have long been scattered among the Dai, Jingpo, and Han (as well as among the Wa and Lisu), many De'ang speak Dai, Jingpo, and Han Chinese, and are able to write in Dai. Thought to be descendants of the ancient Pu people of southwestern Yunnan, the De'ang, as well as other ethnic groups, were subjugated by Dai rulers in the fourteenth century and became vassals and tenant farmers of the Dai tusi (local chief or village head). The De'ang are largely farmers, growing paddy and upland rice and other grains, tea, and tropical fruits. They are devout Theravada Buddhists, and most De'ang villages have a Buddhist temple. The influence of Dai and Jingpo literature is significant, and the content of De'ang oral art is a mixture of Dai and Jingpo sources, though some long narrative poems exhibit the particular character of the De'ang people. Like the Dai, the De'ang celebrate the Water-Splashing Festival. A popular event at weddings is the Water-Drum Dance, which requires hollowed drums filled with water. The dance originates in the legendary story of a man who rescued his beloved from a crab monster. De'ang houses are square, two-story bamboo and wood structures raised on stilts, with woven straw roofs. Living quarters, kitchen, and storeroom are upstairs, while animals are kept in sheds below. Women wear a dark- or light-colored blouse-jacket and striped or black skirt, along with colored rattan or bamboo hoops around the hips, and silver necklaces and earrings. In some areas, they dress in black leggings and attach yarnballs to the upper sleeves of blouses. Men wear turbans, and are also fond of silver ornaments. Tattoos of animals, flowers, and plants may be worn on the legs, arms, or chest.

# Drung
## (Dulong)

The five thousand Drung live in the extreme northwest of Yunnan, mainly in the Drung River valley, which is separated from the Salween River gorge by a high mountain range, and which is located in Gongshan Drung-Nu Autonomous County. Their Tibeto-Burman language has affinities with the languages of both the Jingpo and Nu, the latter of whom are their immediate neighbors. The ninety-five-mile-long Drung River valley, formed by waters originating in the eastern part of Tibet, is flanked by the 16,400-foot-high Gaoligong Mountains to the east, and the 13,000-foot-high Dandaglika Mountains to the west. The Drung call themselves "Drungchang," while Han Chinese historical records identify them as "Qiu," "Qiuzi," or "Qu." Elderly Drung say the Drung "came from the place of the sun," which may indicate the east, corresponding with research suggesting that they migrated west from the Lijiang-Jianchuan-Lanping area. Under the jurisdiction of the Nanzhao and Dali kingdoms between the ninth and twelfth centuries, the Drung were generally ruled by Naxi headmen who, until the end of the Qing dynasty in 1911, were chosen by the Chinese court. At the end of the nineteenth century, the Drung began to engage in primitive agriculture, with gathering, hunting, and fishing remaining important. Traditional village longhouses are made of logs or bamboo, with individual families belonging to a clan living in separate rooms. Animal skulls from hunting expeditions are hung from roof beams. Women and men dress in a long, striped, ornamental cloth woven from hemp, which is wrapped around the body and tied at one shoulder with straw or bamboo needles. Women wear shoulder-length hair, covering the forehead, hanging down straight, or ending in two braids. Animists in belief, the Drung hold that prosperity and disaster are determined by the workings of spirits. Traditionally, Drung women believed that facial scarification was beautiful, and many still practice the custom today, considering it a sign that they were members of the Drung clan, and a way to ward off evil. An important yearly festival is Kaquewa, during which bulls are sacrificed and their meat eaten. Bull sacrifice is found among a number of ethnic minorities in Southwest China.

# Hani

## (Aini, Akha, Ekaw, Haoni, Honi, Huni, Kaw, Kha Ko, Ko, Koni, Woni)

Like the terms "Dai," "Yao," and "Miao," "Hani" is an umbrella designation for a large number of groups. The estimated 1,060,000 Hani are located in the most southern reaches of Yunnan, mainly along both banks of the Yuan and the Mekong rivers, between the Ailao and Mengle mountains. Counties where Hani dwell are Honghe, Yuanyang, Luchun, Jianshui, and Jinping in Honghe Hani-Yi Autonomous Prefecture; Mojiang, Jiangcheng, Pu'er, Lancang, Jingdong, Jinggu, and Zhenyuan in Simao Prefecture; Menghai, Jinghong, and Mengla in Sipsong Panna; and Yuanjiang, Eshan, and Xinping in Yuxi Prefecture. Hani villages are interspersed among those of Han, Yi, Dai, Lahu, Miao, and Yao people, in a network that facilitates economic and cultural interchange between groups. The Hani speak a variety of dialects belonging to the Tibeto-Burman language group. Hani clothing is commonly made from homespun dark blue cloth. Both men and women wear silver ornaments and leggings. Men's dress is a coat with front or side buttons, trousers, and a white or black turban. Women wear a collarless blouse with laced cuffs, and either pants with laced cuffs, a long pleated or narrow skirt, or dark shorts with an embroidered sash. Women adorn themselves with silver chains, coin necklaces, earrings, and caps or headdresses studded with coins. Unmarried women may be identified by a braided knot worn on the top of the head. Teeth are often darkly stained from betel-nut chewing. The impressively terraced rice paddies of the Hani rise many hundreds of feet up steep mountain slopes. On Nannuo Mountain in Sipsong Panna they grow a special variety of upland rice needing little irrigation, as well as varieties of tea, including Pu'er. Villages of two- or three-story houses are often located on hillsides. Houses are traditionally built on wooden supports and are constructed from a variety of materials such as bamboo, mud, wood, and stone, and in some areas have mud walls and thatched roofs. Hani oral art is highly developed and varied, ranging from creation and flood myths to ballads and riddles. The Hand Clapping and Fan dances are performed widely. In the special Hani tradition of spontaneous song, tunes and melodies are never repeated by the same person in the same location. Music for large gatherings of people at sacrifices, festivals, weddings, and funerals may be performed only by shamans and old people. Hani traditionally practice ancestor worship and are polytheists.

# Hui

## (Ho, Hui-tze, Hwei, Pang-hse, Panthe, Pathee)

The 7,300,000 Hui are Muslims, and are found throughout China. Uighurs, Kazakhs, and others who follow Islam are distinguished by a variety of features, such as linguistic group, but the Hui, whose language is basically Han Chinese, are identified as a minority nationality in China solely on the basis of religion. Muslims came to China by land in the tenth century, perhaps earlier by sea, and as mercenary soldiers sent by Kublai Khan in the thirteenth century. Some Hui are assimilated descendents of these Muslim ancestors from Persia, Arabia, and Central Asia, but the majority are Han Chinese who converted to Islam. In Chinese cities, the Hui presence is marked by separate enclaves, such as mosques, and by special restaurants and markets that adhere to the Muslim prohibition against eating pork. The largest number of Hui are located in Ningxia and Gansu in northwest China. In Yunnan, there are around 380,000 Hui. They live in nearly all of the 128 municipalities and counties, as well as many townships. Although scattered about the province, the Hui maintain an intense ethnic consciousness and a devout faith.

# Jingpo
## (Chingpaw, Jinghpaw, Kachin, Kakhieng, Singhpo, Theinbaw)

The majority of Jingpo live in northern Burma, but some ninety-three thousand of these hill dwellers are found in the westernmost section of Yunnan, in Dehong Dai-Jingpo Autonomous Prefecture, where the Ruili, Daying, and Longchuan rivers form a valley basin that projects into Burma, directly southwest of Myitkyina. Some Jingpo live in Nujiang Lisu Autonomous Prefecture in northwestern Yunnan. They are a strong cultural presence, and their language, which belongs to the Tibeto-Burman family, is used by various ethnic groups on both sides of the border. Houses are raised, rectangular structures, made of wood and bamboo, often with grass roofs. Livelihood is mainly through slash-and-burn agriculture, whereby each spring trees and brush are cleared, dried, and burned to ashes before crops are planted by people dropping seeds into holes in the ground made by sticks. Men clear land and plant, while women maintain crops and do the harvesting. Hunting, gathering, and animal husbandry supplement farming. Men wear a black or white turban decorated with small colored balls, short trousers, and a dark jacket buttoned in front, and carry a long knife at the waist and an embroidered bag. Common dress for women is a collarless black velvet jacket, with buttons down the front; a mid-calf-length knit wool sarong with patterned stripes in various colors; rattan hoops or sashes at the waist, neck, wrist, and ankles; and jewelry made from silver, glass beads, and shells. On formal occasions a woman's bodice is covered with silver ornaments and baubles sewn into the clothes or hung around the neck and breast. The supernatural world contains major deities common to all Jingpo, and minor ones who are usually immediate ancestors, all of whom are believed to affect the well-being of the community, and contact with whom is practiced through shamans, diviners, and priests. According to popular legend, the Jingpo originated in the Jade Stone Mint region of the Kunlun Mountains of north China, and in the seventh century A.D. migrated from the southern part of the Qinghai-Tibetan plateau to Yunnan. Traditionally, in Jingpo culture the singer of tales plays a key role. When a boy comes of age, he carries a "bamboo scarf" (a kind of neckerchief), a long knife, grain rations, and liquor, and goes about searching for teachers to study singing. Outstanding singers master an extensive repertoire, and are capable of reciting poems several thousand lines in length. Harvest songfests and circle dances draw tens of thousands of participants.

# Jino
## (Jinuo, Juno)

The Jino are a small Tibeto-Burman ethnic minority with a population estimated to be twelve thousand. They are hill farmers living in some forty villages near the Mekong River in the southern tip of Yunnan, in the Jinuoloke or Youle Mountains (Youle Shan, a Chinese transliteration of the Jino name meaning "the place the Han cannot find"), southeast of Mengyang, in Jinghong County, Sipsong Panna Dai Autonomous Prefecture. Youle, one of Yunnan's six major tea-producing mountain regions, is famous for its Pu'er tea. Formerly the Jino were mainly slash-and-burn farmers and hunter-gatherers. Culturally similar to the Hani, who live in the same area, and sharing linguistic affinities with the Yi and Burmese, the Jino were classified as Yi in China until 1979. The traditional clan longhouse is no longer common. The Jino social organization is the village head system, which is based on the patriarchal family. Every hamlet has a Village Father and Village Mother, the eldest members of the community, who administer it. Their job is to promote religious activities and to determine the date of the New Year and appropriate seasons for farming. The Jino are animists and ancestor worshippers. Both men and women wear bracelets and earrings or large wooden earplugs. Women dress in a short, red-bordered black skirt; a collarless colored jacket with embroidered bands; leggings; and a peaked, white flax bonnet. Hair is coiled above the forehead. Men wear a white collarless jacket and blue or white cotton pants. Traditionally, men's hair is divided into three topknots.

# Kucong
## (K'ou-ts'ong-jen, Kutsung, K'uts'ung, Woni)

The three thousand Kucong live between the Yuan River and the Black River (Chinese: Lixian Jiang), in the border region between southern Yunnan and northern Vietnam. They have not yet been designated as an official ethnic nationality in China. Some sources suggest that the Kucong are one of the Hani (Woni) tribes who speak an Yi dialect, while others put them in the Lahu group. One branch of the Kucong located around Yuxi and Simao practices paddy-rice cultivation, due to the influence of other ethnic groups in the area.

Another more primitive branch, living along the mountain ridges bordering Jinping County in Honghe Hani-Yi Autonomous Prefecture, was virtually sealed off from the modern world until the mid-twentieth century.

# Lahu
## (Lohei, Muhso, Musso, Mussuh)

The Lahu are a Tibeto-Burman group of seminomadic hillfolk, found in mountain villages between the Salween and Mekong rivers in southwestern Yunnan and northern Southeast Asia, along the Yunnan-Burma border, and in northern Burma, Thailand, and Laos. The three hundred thousand Lahu in southwestern Yunnan are mainly concentrated in Lancang Lahu Autonomous County in Simao Prefecture, southern Lincang Prefecture, and Menghai County in Sipsong Panna, while some are interspersed elsewhere among the Han and the Dai, Wa, Hani, Blang, and Yi minorities. The Lahu may be of Tibetan or Yi ancestry, or may have originated in nomadic tribes living in the Er Hai region of western Yunnan who migrated south during the Nanzhao era. Formerly celebrated for their legendary ability to hunt tigers, the Lahu are skilled hunters, using crossbow and poison-tipped arrows as well as firearms. Linguistically they are close to the Hani and Yi in the Tibeto-Burman language family. Formerly without a written language, the Lahu use an alphabetic script developed by Catholic missionaries and modified by Chinese linguists. They differentiate themselves as Black, Yellow, and Red Lahu. Typically, as at Nannuo Mountain, west of Jinghong in Sipsong Panna, their villages are located on flat ridges at elevations above four thousand feet, higher than the Hani hamlets. A Lahu house, similar in style to that of the Dai, is a raised bamboo structure built on stilts, with the upper story for human habitation and space below for animals. Food is supplied through slash-and-burn agriculture and hunting. Outside of China, opium is produced as a cash crop. Lahu women traditionally have waist-length hair, or wrap the hair in a single dark cloth more than ten feet in length, with colorful tassels hanging at the side of the head. They may wear a long robe with slits cut along both sides, or black pants and jacket trimmed with striped sleeves, laces, or geometric patterns. Silver or beaded earrings and bracelets are worn, as well as silver ornaments on the clothes and headdress. Men wear a black turban, loose-fitting long pants, and a collarless jacket. In traditional Lahu culture, the village chief is the main authority, along with the priest-shaman and warrior. In religion, there is some influence of Mahayana Buddhism as well as Tibetan Lamaism, but the principal belief of the Lahu is in good and evil spirits as sources of well-being or sickness. The Lahu say that their god Esha (G'uisha) is the creator of and supreme being over all creation. Every village hamlet reveres Esha as its guardian spirit, and each household displays an altar table. Poles carved with geometric designs are traditionally used in religious rites. During religious festivals the Pawku (shaman) presides over rites and sacrifices. A skilled singer of epics, the Pawku enjoys considerable social prestige in this oral culture and is asked to chant marriage songs, exorcise spirits causing illness, call the souls of the dying, and sing funeral dirges.

# Lisu
## (Li-hsaw, Li-shaw, Lisaw, Liso, Lu-tzu,
## Yaoyen, Yaw-yen, Yawyin, Yeh-jen)

The majority of the 480,000 Lisu in China dwell near the tops of high mountain ranges in Bijiang, Fugong, Gongshan, and Lushui counties, in the Salween-Mekong watershed area in northwestern Yunnan; and in Nujiang Lisu Autonomous Prefecture, with some dispersed about western Yunnan and others living along the Sichuan border north of Yunnan. Outside of China, Lisu are found across the Burmese border west of the Nmai Hka River, as well as in Thailand and Northeast India. Northern Lisu are known for their fierce independence; in former years they would attack Han caravans as well as one another. In the Bijiang-Gongshan counties area, vestiges of a slavery system existed until the mid-twentieth century. Southern Lisu tend to be acculturated to Han ways. They raise paddy rice, often marry Han Chinese, and are bilingual. Linguistically and culturally, the Lisu are related to the Yi. Lisu men often know several languages. One writing system, a syllabary of symbols reputed to be the invention of a Lisu, Wang Renbo, with approximately five hundred writing signs, has been employed in a few counties around Weixi in northwestern Yunnan. Two other alphabetic Lisu scripts used early in the twentieth century were the work of Protestant missionaries. Moving north to south, and distinguishing differences in dress, Han commentators once classified Lisu as "black" ("northwest" or "wild"), "tame" ("southern" or "flowery"—refering to variegated, multilayered clothing worn by women), or "white," terms seldom used today. Women dress in an ankle-length gunny skirt, long-sleeved blouse, and dark vest or jacket. They may wear a folded scarf on the head or a beaded headdress, and red and white beads, coral chains, or strings of agate, seashells, and silver coins around the neck and head. Easily defended villages at elevations of between five thousand and nine thousand feet are surrounded with thickets of fir and bamboo. Houses are either boxlike, planked-roof structures built on the ground and made from timber, or raised, thatched-roof, split-level bamboo and wood houses constructed on piles. The Lisu raise paddy rice in the valleys, and higher up they engage in hunting, slash-and-burn agriculture, gathering, and animal husbandry. They believe in animism, totemism, and Christianity. Traditional clans in the Salween River valley take totems such as Tiger, Mouse, Bee, Buckwheat, and Frost for their clan names. A feature of the traditional Lisu New Rice Festival is that people are not allowed to eat until the dogs are fed. According to an ancient legend, the king of heaven once took all of the people's rice, but a dog stole back three grains, from which the paddy rice of today is descended.

# Miao
## (Hmong, Hmu, Hmung, Meo)

The 5,300,000 Miao belong to the Miao-Yao language family and, along with the Yao, are one of the most widely dispersed ethnic minorities. An ancient oral tradition claims that the Miao migrated from Central Asia to the Arctic before moving south. The Miao ancestors may have originated in western Hunan and eastern Guizhou. Today Miao are also found in Vietnam, Laos, and Thailand, as well as in the United States, Canada, and Europe. In Yunnan, the Miao are scattered about eighty-seven counties and municipalities, with around 60 percent in Wenshan Zhuang-Miao Autonomous Prefecture and Honghe Hani-Yi Autonomous Prefecture, both in southern Yunnan. Their dispersion was influenced by their practice of slash-and-burn agriculture, which led them to move along mountain ranges, by the Mongol invasion during the Yuan dynasty, and by government suppression of Miao rebellions in the eighteenth and early nineteenth centuries in Guizhou, during which the Flowery Miao (Hua Miao) migrated to Yunnan. Because of dispersion, Miao differ widely in language, clothing, folk arts, and festivals. Many Miao today are paddy rice farmers working terraced hillsides. Miao can be found in remote cultural islands amidst valleys and hills, or dispersed among other ethnic groups, creating aggregate cultures. One form of traditional house, a rectangular structure, is built on the ground and has walls made of bamboo, mud, stone, or wood, a central hearth fire, and a thatched, fir bark, tiled, or stone-slab roof. Another type is the thatched hut with walls of branches plastered with mud. Homes raised on piles, with animals below and living quarters above, reflect the influence of other ethnic minorities. Miao are known for their batiks. Women are fond of elaborate headdresses and jewelry. Christian missionaries were a strong presence among the Miao in the late nineteenth and early twentieth centuries, and developed a writing system that has been superseded by a romanization system established by the Chinese government. The Reed Pipe Dance, in which young men and women accompany their collective dancing by playing reed pipes, typifies the use of dance for wooing and courting among the Miao and other Yunnan minorities.

# Mongol
## (Menggu)

In China there are some 3,500,000 speakers of Mongolian proper, an Altaic language that belongs to the Mongolian family of languages and ranges from eastern Manchuria through Inner Mongolia to Xinjiang in the west, and to Yunnan in the southwest. The Mongols have a written language and a well-developed tradition of written literature, which includes literary classics written in the Mongol script, such as *The Secret History of the Mongols* (*Mongolyn nuuts tovchoo*, 13th cent.), *The Jeweled Summary* (*Erdeniin tovch*, 17th cent.), and *The Hall of Red Weeping* (*Ulaana ukhilakh*, a 19th-cent. imitation of the 18th cent. Chinese novel *Dream of the Red Chamber* [*Honglou meng*]). In the area of folk literature, heroic epics written in alternating prose and poetry, such as *Geser Khan* (a Mongol version of the Tibetan *Gesar of Ling*), are used for oral instruction among Mongolians, and are sung by folk artists who play the "horse-head" guitar, a bowed stringed instrument with a scroll carved in the shape of a horse's head.

In Yunnan, the Mongol population is small, numbering approximately 6,200. They are the descendents of troops who came to Yunnan in the thirteenth century with Kublai Khan (grandson of Genghis Khan) at the beginning of the Yuan dynasty, during the expansion of the Mongol empire. After the Yuan was overthrown by the Ming, these Mongols settled in central Yunnan on the banks of Qilu Lake in Tonghai County, south of Kunming, and made their living farming and fishing. As a result of this settlement, they gradually lost their special identity as nomadic herders. Over the past several hundred years, they have intermarried with Han, Yi, and Hui people, and have become distant from the traditional culture of the northern Mongols in language, customs, and dress. In many places they have become much closer to the local Yi; their speech, for example, is largely an adaptation of Yi. The Mongols' celebration of the Torch Festival, honored by many ethnic groups in Yunnan, shows the influence of other nationalities, an influence that can be seen in their folk literature.

# Naxi

## (Luhsi, Lukhi, Moso, Mosuo,
## Nachri, Nahsi, Nakhi, Nashi, Nazo, Wuman)

The 250,000 Naxi—*na* means 'black,' and *xi* means 'person'—are thought to originally have been a pastoral people, possibly from northeastern Tibet or Qinghai-Gansu, and of Qiang descent, as are the Yi, who migrated south and founded a once-prosperous kingdom in the alpine meadows of the southern part of China's Tibetan highland plateau. Naxi are located in Yunnan, Sichuan, and Tibet. Their cultural and religious affinity with Tibetans may be seen in buttered-tea, yak raising, Lamaism, and Bon religion (Tibetan shamanism). Villages surrounded by terraced fields and rock walls range between six thousand and ten thousand feet in elevation. Naxi is a designation that incorporates two groups in Yunnan: the Lijiang Naxi and the Yongning Naxi. The former, the greater population of Yunnanese Naxi, are located mainly in Lijiang Naxi Autonomous County, Lijiang Prefecture, which averages nine thousand feet in elevation and lies in the great north-south loop of the Jinsha River, north of Er Hai. (Elsewhere in Yunnan, Naxi are found in Weixi, Zhongdian, Ninglang, Deqin, Yongsheng, Heqing, Jianchuan, and Lanping counties.) Lijiang Naxi are patrilineal, believe in a religion practiced by specialists called *ntomba* or *dongba*, show influence of the Red (Nyingmapa) school of Tibetan Buddhism, as well as Chinese Daoism, and have a pictographic script. Yongning Naxi (who call themselves "Nari" in their own language, or "Mosuo" when speaking Chinese), live in northern Ninglang County in the area of the town of Yongning and Lugu Lake. Their society is erroneously termed matriarchal in various sources, but is in fact matrilineal in clan and family organization, whereby genealogy is determined along maternal lines and inheritance is matrilineal. The Mosuo are heavily influenced by the orthodox or Yellow (Gelugpa) sect of Tibetan Buddhism, and do not have a pictographic script. A traditional form of relationship between the sexes is the *azhu*, or temporary companion marriage. The Lugu Lake and Yongning region, described in Marco Polo's *Travels*, may be the "land of women" alluded to in Chinese history books.

Two-story, three-wing houses in the Lijiang area have brick or earthen walls, tiled roofs with gables, and interior courtyards. Rural houses have earthen floors; stone, log, or mud brick walls; and wood-plank roofs. Mosuo houses are made almost entirely of timber. Most Naxi make their livelihood through herding and farming, supplemented by local trading and hunting. Naxi men are known for their love of horses and music. They garden and care for children. Women have considerable freedom and economic independence, and do much of the work, except for plowing and hunting. Naxi women typically wear a wide-sleeved, loose fitting tunic, a vest or long-sleeved jacket, and long pants, with a decorated sash or belt. A special feature of their dress is the T-shaped sheepskin cape, embroidered with sun and moon designs, and seven circles symbolizing the stars. In Ninglang County, Mosuo women dress in a long multi-folded skirt, silver earrings, and a dark cotton turban.

Naxi is one of the few Tibeto-Burman languages in Yunnan that has a written script, combining rebus-type pictographic and syllabic features, in which a rich literary tradition of legends and rituals is preserved. The texts are used by the *dongba* or *ntomba* (Bon priest or ritual practitioner) as mnemonic aids for story telling when conducting services. Active *dongba* are no longer numerous, but a *dongba* cultural research institute is working to preserve their culture. Over six hundred volumes of Naxi texts (totaling more than seven million characters), the *Ntomba Classics* (*Dongba Classics*), have been collated. They are divided into twelve types and deal with sacrifices to the wind and dragon king, funeral rites, and warding off disaster. A number of oral literary works depicting the creation of the world, the survival of floods and famines, and wars between the Black and White Naxi have been collected and preserved. Most Naxi worship their ancestors. Among important Naxi festivals is the Mule Fair, during which people trade their animals for goods brought by traveling merchants.

# Nu

## (Anu, Lutze, Lutzu, Noutze, Noutzu, Nusu, Nutsu, Nutzu)

The Nu are located in southeastern Tibet and extreme northwestern Yunnan, along both sides of the Salween (Nu) River, after which they are named (some linguists believe their name is instead a variant of nu, "black"). The Salween River originates in the Tanggula Mountains in eastern Tibet, and pummels its way between the towering precipices of Biluoxue Mountain and the Gaoligong range in northwestern Yunnan. In Yunnan, the population of approximately twenty-three thousand Nu is distributed in the counties of Bijiang, Fugong, Gongshan, and Lanping, within Nujiang Lisu Autonomous Prefecture. Legends refer to two different sources of the Nu, one saying that they stem from the Nuosu, a branch of the ancient Lulu People, the other claiming that the Nu come from the region of the Gong Mountains on the west side of the Salween River, and from an ancient people who called themselves the Along or Long clan. The Nu of the Gong Mountain area speak a Tibeto-Burman language related to Drung, while the Bijiang Nu language is quite similar to Yi. Bijiang Nu preserve a clan structure and totem worship that are identical to those found among the Black Yi of the Daliang (Greater Cool) and Xiaoliang (Lesser Cool) mountains in Sichuan province. Two-room village houses, constructed from bamboo or pine logs, have plank walls and roofs of large stone shingles. Sources of livelihood include slash-and-burn farming, fishing, hunting, herding, and raising domestic animals. The Nu religion combines Lamaism and animism. One form of traditional dress for women is a length of woven linen wrapped about the body, or a striped skirt over trousers. The hair may be covered with a cloth scarf, and both hair and neck decorated with shell and silver ornaments. The ears are adorned with shoulder-length copper earrings or bamboo tubes. Rattan bracelets, anklets, and belts are also common. Men wear a linen gown cinched at the waist and linen shorts, and carry a bow and ax. Each clan is differentiated from others according to the land, trees, and stones that it takes as its objects of worship, which are the symbols around which village society is organized. The Nu have a number of dances, most of which symbolize animal behavior.

# Primi
## (Pumi)

The Primi, numbering approximately twenty-four thousand, are distributed in the northwestern Yunnan counties of Lanping, Weixi, Ninglang, Lijiang, and Yongsheng. Their main settlements are on Lanping County's Laojun Mountain (Old Noble Mountain) and Ninglang County's Maoniu Mountain (Yak Mountain). Primi territory is known for its wooded landscape covered with pine and larch trees and bamboo, natural pastureland, rare birds and animals, and medicinal herbs. The Primi are thought to have once dwelled in the Qinghai (Koko Nor)–Gansu region. As a nomadic, herding tribe, they lived by following water and grazing land, and in the middle of the thirteenth century migrated to northwestern Yunnan, where they became hill farmers. Houses generally are made of logs or boards, with two floors. Men dress in a linen or sleeveless sheepskin jacket and loose-fitting long pants, and carry a sword. Women wear a long pleated skirt, or trousers, a brightly colored sash about the waist, a long-sleeved jacket under a jacket vest, a sheepskin draped over the back, and silver jewelry. A special feature of Primi women's dress in Ninglang and Yongsheng counties is long hair plaited with yak tail and silk, with the head wrapped in long scarves. The Primi especially revere ancestors. When someone dies, the shaman is invited to hold a Sheep Guide (Gei Yangzi Yishi) rite whereby a sheep leads the wandering spirit of the deceased to the land of the ancestors. Primi is a Tibeto-Burman language very similar to the language of the Qiang minority, to whom the Primi people are related. The Primi have no written language.

# Sui
## (Shui)

The 290,000 Sui are concentrated in southern Guizhou Province, along the banks of the Long and Duliu rivers, and in Sandu Sui Autonomous County, with small numbers in the northwestern part of Guangxi Zhuang Autonomous Region and in eastern Yunnan. The Sui people in Yunnan migrated from Guizhou, number less than ten thousand, and are distributed in Fuyuan and Shizong counties in eastern Yunnan. The Sui language belongs to the Kam-Sui branch of the Tai family of language (in China the Tai family is called the Zhuang-Dong family). The Kam-Sui, the northernmost Tai speakers, are possibly aboriginal remnants never assimilated by the Han. The Sui have a simple writing system of symbols and pictographs used for divination. Polytheistic animists, they worship wells, large stones, and trees. They believe that all negative events are the work of ghosts and spirits, and that when one occurs, a shamanness or spirit-master must be asked to make a sacrifice and to divine so as to drive off the ghosts. Sui women wear silver jewelry, long dark pants or a skirt, an embroidered apron, and a collarless blouse. Hair is normally worn in a bun. Men dress in a turban and a black or blue long gown. The Sui live mainly in river basin areas, where there are interlocking streams. They grow two crops per year and supplement their income with fish farming. An important feature of their culture is the bronze drum, which is hung below flying buttresses and double-eaved roofs of the temple and played during seasonal festivals and dances.

# Tibetan
## (Bo, Boba, Bod, Guzi, Guzong, Weiba, Zang, Zangba)

There are nearly six million speakers of Tibetan, located in Tibet, Nepal, Bhutan, Sikkim, Qinghai, southern Gansu, northwestern Sichuan, and northwestern Yunnan, including large numbers of refugees who have fled Chinese rule to live in India and Western countries. Those in Yunnan number more than eighty-nine thousand, and are mainly distributed in Zhongdian, Weixi, and Deqin counties, with some found in Lijiang, Gongshan, and Yongsheng counties. These districts represent the southern section of the Qinghai-Tibetan plateau, which averages over nine thousand feet in elevation. Tibetan stone houses are simple in structure, with flat roofs and several windows, and often face south to facilitate exposure to the sun. Tent dwellings are used in pastoral work. Both men and women wear fur or felt hats, jewelry, and woolen or leather boots. Women prefer skirts, wear jackets that fasten on the right, and decorate their braids with ornaments. Men wear trousers with a long waistband. The sixteen Tibeto-Burman languages now recognized by the Chinese government (others under study may be added in the future) are divided by the Han Chinese into four branches: Tibetan, Yi, Jingpo, and Qiang. The Tibetan branch includes Tibetan and Monpa. Tibetans have a long documented history and a highly developed culture known for its architecture, lamaseries, Buddhist sculpture, mystical and philosophical literature, dancing, and music. Their writing system, based on Indic models, was created in the seventh century. A rich literary tradition of texts includes translations of the Mahayana Buddhist canon, as well as texts about medicine and grammar. By the tenth century Tibet's flourishing literary tradition had produced many distinguished writings, such as *Tibetan Chronicle* by the Fifth Dalai Lama, Ngadbang Lobzang Gyamtso; the *Biography of Milarepa*, attributed to Rechung-pa; Sankya Pandita's *A Treasury of Precious Sayings*; and *The Love Songs of Tsangyang Gyamtso*, by the unorthodox Sixth Dalai Lama, Lobzang Rindzin Tsangyang Gyamtso. The widely celebrated heroic poem *Gesar of Ling*, nearly eighty volumes in length in its Tibetan and Mongolian versions, as well as in Chinese translation, is perhaps the longest epic poem in world literature, vying with India's *Mahabharata*.

# Wa

## (Hai, Hkun Loi, K'a-la, Kawa, K'a-wa,
## Khawa, La Lawa, Loila, Nyo, Tai Loi, Va, Vu, Wu)

The largest population of Wa are located in northern Burma. The three hundred thousand Wa in southwestern Yunnan are thought to be one of the area's oldest indigenous peoples, descendants of the ancient Pu people, as are the De'ang and Blang. Those who are called "tame" Wa by the Dai (Shan) are nominally Buddhist, while the "wild" Wa are not. Formerly the latter were well known as headhunters. Skull possession was believed to ward off sickness and ensure successful crops. The Wa are found on high mountain slopes running north-south along the Chinese-Burmese border, in Cangyuan, Ximeng, Menglian, Lancang, Gengma, Shuangjiang, Zhenkang, and Yongde counties, between the Salween and Mekong rivers; they are also located in the Sipsong Panna area and in Dehong Dai-Jingpo Autonomous Prefecture. The Wa consider Cangyuan Mountain and the western side of Mengwa Mountain (6,000 feet above sea level) their central location, calling it Awa Mountain District. Wa make their living mainly through growing paddy rice and through slash-and-burn agriculture, the latter frequently the cause of denuded hillsides. Rice liquor is kept in bamboo containers. Larger Wa villages are surrounded by earthen ramparts or walls covered by thickets, and are entered through long tunnels. Wooden roofs are decorated with carved designs, and animal skulls are hung on outside walls. Dress differs widely according to area. Men commonly wear colored tassels in pierced ears, a red or black turban, wide-legged pants, collarless jackets, and bamboo or rattan shin coverings for ornamentation. Women wear a plain, dark-colored scant blouse, a woven skirt or sarong with several folds, rattan hoops around the hips and calves, large circle-shaped or tube earrings, and rattan or silver bands or cloth scarves about the head. The Wa language is related to the Mon-Khmer language family. Wa folk literature is richly varied, including distinctive animal tales and myths, as well as long narrative poems, epics, folk songs, folk rhymes, and riddles. The largest collection of primitive painting in Yunnan, the Wa Lancang Cliff Paintings, depicts life in Neolithic times.

# Yao
## (Kim Mien, Kim Mun, Mien, Myen, Mun, Yu Mien)

Like the Miao, with whom they are commonly confused, the Yao are one of the most widely scattered of the minorities in south China, living in distant mountain hamlets quite separated from other communities. Their principal location is Guangxi Zhuang Autonomous Region. Of the 1,411,000 Yao, less than half speak Myen (the native name for the Yao language, which belongs to the Sino-Tibetan language family), while nearly a third speak Punu, which is a variety of Miao. Others speak Tai or Dong. In Yunnan, their population of more than 140,000 is greatly scattered about, with small concentrations found interspersed among other minorities in southeastern Yunnan; in Funing, Guangnan, Malipo, and Maguan counties within Wenshan Zhuang-Miao Autonomous Prefecture; and in Hekou, Yuanyang, and Jinping counties in Honghe Hani-Yi Autonomous Prefecture. Possibly early settlers along the South China coast, the Yao were dispersed south of Hunan Province from the twelfth through the nineteenth centuries. Partly as a result of this long-term dispersion and fragmentation, ethnic identification is uncertain, as many groups known as "Yao" do not share the same cultural characteristics, while often those who do call themselves by other names. Depending on the area, Yao practice dry-field, slash-and-burn, or paddy-rice agriculture. Bee keeping, kitchen gardens, and indigo dying, as well as some animal husbandry, are economies followed by different Yao. Single-story, rectangular village houses are built on the ground, on mountain slopes, with bark or tile shingles and air-dried brick. Houses on pilings are also found. The Yao believe in exorcism, ancestor worship, and various gods and demons, and tell in myths of a dog ancestor. Yao clothing varies widely. One form of dress for men is a belted buttoned jacket and pants that reach the instep, or else knee breeches, in blue, black, or white, and a cloth headwrapping. In some areas, a hairbun is worn by men. Women wear a silver or ribbon headdress; silver jewelry; short or long slacks or a skirt; and a jacket. Jacket lapels, sleeves, skirts, and pant legs are embroidered. Married women are identified by hair dressed in a single cone on top of the head, which is covered by a red scarf. The Hourglass Drum Dance, named for an hourglass-shaped drum held in the middle with one hand and struck with the other, is dedicated in connection with work activities such as harvest or house building to a Yao god.

# Yi

## (A-hsi, Asi, Hei-I, Hei Ku T'ou, I, I-chia, Kolo, Ko-pu, Kouo-lo, Laka, Laulau, Leisu, Lo-kuei, Lolo, Lou-lou, Man-chia, Man-tzu, Mosu, Neisu, Nesu, Ngosu, No, Norsu, Nosu, Pei-I, Pei Ku T'ou, Pula, Shani, T'ou-jen, Tsuan-man, Wu-man, Y-jin)

Yi is a collective term for a large Tibeto-Burman group, replacing the former pejorative name, Lolo. Interestingly, some Yi still call themselves Lolo, though none call themselves Yi except when speaking Chinese. Their origins go back to the ancient Qiang tribal groups, peoples who were located mainly in the mountainous regions of large river systems. As early as the second century B.C., there existed cultural and economic interchange between the Yi and the central government of the Han Chinese. The largest minority nationality in Southwest China, the 5,500,000 Yi live in distant mountainous regions in Yunnan, Sichuan, and Guizhou. Their primary area in Sichuan is the Daliang Mountains. Dispersion has given rise to several Yi dialects. In Yunnan Yi are found from the valley of the Jinsha River in the north to the Yuan River valley in the south. Over three million Yi live in Huaping, Ninglang, and Yongsheng counties along the Yunnan border northeast of Lijiang; Chuxiong Yi Autonomous Prefecture between Dali and Kunming; Honghe Hani-Yi Autonomous Prefecture in southwestern Yunnan; and the Xiaoliang Mountains in the northeast.

Formerly a slave-owning society, and long resistant to Han domination, the Yi of the Daliang Mountains in Sichuan and the Xiaoliang Mountains in Yunnan were a remote and feared minority for hundreds of years, down through much of the first half of the twentieth century. Ancestors of the Yi are thought to have been the court royalty and military leaders of the Nanzhao kingdom. Two twentieth-century Yunnan warlords were Yi. Of the two castes of Yi in the Cool Mountains region, Black Yi or Black Bones (Nosu or Nuosu) were formerly the aristocracy who captured Han Chinese and made them slaves, while White Yi or White Bones (Qunuo), descendants of Han slaves, were either commoners who did the farming and were serfs of Black Yi, or were slaves mainly serving White Yi commoners. A typical Yi village in southern Yunnan is identified by two-story adobe houses with flat roofs. Traditional dress varies widely. Among Yi men and women in the Cool Mountains area of Sichuan, it includes felt capes, with men wearing large turbans. Hair may be dressed in a chignon. In Honghe Hani-yi Autonomous Prefecture, Yi women favor cockscomb-shaped hats. Sani Yi women in the Stone Forest region southeast of Kunming wear a knee-length white or light-blue linen smock, long black pants, an apron, and a headband, cloth helmet, or headscarf. In many Yi regions, shoulder bags, vests, head helmets, and waistbands are highly embroidered and decorated with silver ornaments, beads, and shells in elaborate patterns. Another well-known Yi handicraft is exquisitely worked paper cutting. Traditional Yi writing is a syllabary used for divination and magic by the literate *bimo* (*beima* or *pimu*), the shaman-historian-doctor of a village. Some two thousand works of Yi written literature, often recorded in the form of poems with five or seven syllables to a line, have been collected. Among these works are sacrificial rites, divinations, funeral chants, histories, calendars, ethical guidelines, legends, tales, and mytho-poetic epics. Traditional religion in Yi villages in Weishan County south of Dali and in the Ailao Mountains southwest of Chuxiong includes the worship of local gods who were the successive kings of the Nanzhao kingdom. Depending on the locality, during the traditional Torch Festival celebrated by Yi, Bai, and other minorities, bullfights and wrestling contests are held, torch towers are burned in village squares, and people walk the fields bearing torches to ward off harmful influences, such as snakes and evil spirits. Festivals are also occasions when Yi people go to the mountains to pick medicinal herbs. The Leaping Palace Dance, named after the dance site made to look like a palace, and performed over a three-day period, commemorates a battle in which the Yi defeated Tang dynasty (618–907) soldiers in Yunnan. In some areas, during special dance festivals, *bimo* may oversee dancing and singing activities that center around a bamboo pole erected in the center of the marketplace.

## Zhuang
### (Chuang, Tho, T'u, T'u-jen)

The 13,400,000 Zhuang are sinicized, bilingual Tai, China's largest minority. They are found mainly in Guangxi Zhuang Autonomous Region, but also in the provinces of Hunan, Guangdong, Guizhou, and Yunnan. The 820,000 Zhuang in Yunnan are located to the southeast in Wenshan Zhuang-Miao Autonomous Prefecture, in the prefectures of Zhaotong in the northeast and Qujing in the east, and in the autonomous prefectures of Honghe in the south and Dali in the west. The Zhuang language belongs to the Tai family, along with Dong, Sui, Dai, and Buyi. Zhuang is one of five major minority languages given special status by the Chinese government, the others being Tibetan, Mongolian, Uighur, and Korean. Books, films, and radio and television broadcasts are produced in Zhuang. Paddy-rice farmers living on the plains, or on steep hillsides noteworthy for their well-terraced paddies, the Zhuang are often so assimilated that in life-style and appearance they are basically the same as the Han among whom they live. In the countryside, women may wear a headdress and a dark-colored tunic that fastens under the arm. Traditional Zhuang homes are split-level wooden houses, with animals on the first floor and living quarters above. The Zhuang are related culturally and linguistically to the Dai, whose influence is more visible among the southern Zhuang in Vietnam, evidenced in betel chewing, tattooing, and pile buildings. The antiquity of Zhuang culture is attested to by copper drums produced during the Han dynasty (206 B.C.–A.D. 219) and by cliff paintings near Hua Mountain and the You River in Guangxi that date from the Qin dynasty (221–207 B.C.). Large-scale Zhuang song fairs which today draw thousands of people are described in Song (A.D. 960–1279) and Yuan dynasty historical records. In Zhuang folk literature, the sister myths of the Zhuang gods Buluotuo and Bubo are disseminated in numerous versions.

# Glossary

Achang minority 阿昌族

Aduma 阿堵麻

Ahli 阿里

Aika 爱卡

Ailao Mountains 哀牢山

Ailuobuwo 艾洛卜我

*Aiqing chuanshuo gushi xuan* 爱情传说故事选

akajiema 阿卡解麻

alima 阿里麻

Along (clan) 阿龙

Amoyaobu 阿摩遥补

Apierer (Api'e'e) 阿匹额额

Apo 阿颇

Atilaba 阿提拉八

Awa (princess) 阿娃

Awa Mountain 阿佤山

Ayidan 阿一旦

"Ayidan gushi wuze" 阿一旦故事五则

Azhamana 阿扎玛娜

*azhu* 阿注

"Ba longxu" 拔龙须

*baba* 粑粑

Bachi, Mount 芭赤山

Bada 巴达

Bai minority 白族

*baihua* 白话

Baiman 白蛮

Bangao 板告

Bao 宝

"Bao biandan" 宝扁担

"Baodeng" 宝灯

bawu 把乌

Bazhen 巴珍

Beipan River 北盘江

"Benfen ren he jiaohua ren" 本份人和狡猾人

Benglong minority 崩龙族

benzhu 本主

"Bianfu" 蝙蝠

Bi'enmuxi 比恩木西

Biluoxue Mountain 碧罗雪山

bimo 毕摩

binbai 宾摆

Bing Xin 冰心

Bisuni 毕苏妮

blang (bulan, spirit) 布兰

Blang (Bulang) minority 布朗族

Blang (Bulang) Mountain 布郎山

Bo'aiwen 波岩温

Bojie 柏节

Bu Song 卜松

Bubo 布伯

"Bubo de gushi" 布伯的故事

bulan. See blang (spirit)

Bulang minority. See Blang minority

"Bulang shaonian" 布郎少年

bulei 不垒

Buluotuo 布洛陀

Buyi minority 布依族

"Caihong" 彩虹

Cang Mountains 苍山

Cangyuan Mountain 沧源山

Cao Ge 曹格

Cen Laoliang 岑老梁

Cen Yuqing 岑玉清

*chahua* 茶花

Chen Guipei 陈贵培

Chen Lufan 陈吕范

Chen Rongxiang 陈荣祥

Chengdu 成都

Chengjiang Sea 澄江海

*chi xingu shuo jiuhua* 吃新谷说旧话

Chiang Yee 蒋怡

Chicken Claw Mountain 鸡足山

Chongzibian 冲子边

"Chuangshi shenhua liuze" 创世神话六则

*chuanshuo* 传说

Chuncheng 春城

Chuxiong 楚雄

"Congming de jiumei" 聪明的九妹


Dai minority 傣族

*Daizu minjian gushi* 傣族民间故事

Dali 大理

"Dali shi" 大理石

Daliang Mountains 大凉山

Daluo 打洛

"Damayi ba tiandi fenkai" 大蚂蚁把天地分开

*dan* 石

Dangse.Ding 当色·顶

De'ang minority 德昂族

Dehong 德宏

Dianchi Lake 滇池

Dong language 侗语

*dongba* 东巴

Dosha'apo 多沙阿波

Dosuni 朵苏妮

dou 斗

"Dou Leiwang" 斗雷王

douli 豆藜

Dragon Spring Peak 龙泉峰

Drung (Dulong) minority 独龙族

Drung River Valley 独龙河谷

Du Chaoxuan 杜朝选

Du Huirong 杜惠荣

Du Wenxiu 杜文秀

Duan Qicheng 段其诚

Duan Shengou 段胜鸥

Duliu Jiang 都柳江

Dulong minority. *See* Drung minority

"Dutou wawa" 独头娃娃


East China Sea 东洋大海

Ende 恩德

Er Hai 洱海

erkuai 饵块

ertong wenxue 儿童文学

Esha 厄沙


Fairy Lake 抚仙湖

Fei Xiaotong 费孝通

Fuliang River 妇良江

Fuxi 优曦

Fuxian Hu 抚仙湖

Fuyi 优依


Gajin Pool 嘎金湾

Gamupeng 嘎姆朋

Gaoligong Mountains 高黎贡山

gekan 歌坎

Geluofeng. *See* Ko-lo-feng

Gong Mountains 贡山

"Gong xi mu xi?" 公喜母喜

Gongzanlaoding 贡咱劳丁

*gou* tree 构树

Gu Jiegang 顾颉刚

Guanyin Mountain 观音山

*guanyu shenghuo hen xianshi de gushi* 观于生活很现实的故事

*gui tai* 鬼胎

Guiyang 贵阳

Guizhou 贵州

Gumishafeima 顾米莎菲玛

"Gumiya" 顾米亚

Guo Moruo 郭沫若

Guo Sijiu 郭思九

Guo Xu 郭旭

"Gushi de jiewei" 故事的结尾


Haersan 哈儿三

Haimei 海妹

Han 汉

Hani minority 哈尼族

Harmony Peak 中和峰

He Quan 和诠

Heng Zhabeng 恒乍绷

Hengluoye 亨洛爷

Hexi 河西

Hong He 红河

*Honglou meng* 红楼梦

"Hongshui fanlan" 洪水泛滥

Hongshui River 红水河

Horse Ear Mountain 马耳山

Hosuni 荷苏妮

Hsieh Jiann (Xie Jian) 谢剑

Hu Gui 胡贵

Hua Miao 花苗

Huagou 花狗

Huang Bocang 黄泊沧

Huaxi 花溪

Hui minority 回族

Hunan 湖南

hunluan 混乱

"Huoba jie" 火把节

"Huoshao songming lou" 火烧松明楼

huotang 火塘

Husa 户撒


Jade Mountain 玉局峰

Jia Zhi 贾芝

Jianchuan 剑川

jiang gushi 进故事

Jiao Haimei 绞海妹

"Jiao'ao de laohu" 骄傲的老虎

Jiao'ao de laohu: Wazu dongwu gushi 骄傲的老虎：佤族动物故事

Jiaqing 嘉靖

"Jiemei he she" 姐妹和蛇

Jieri de chuanshuo 节日的传说

jilu 记录

jin 斤

"Jin zhu" 金猪

Jinghong 景洪

Jinglong kingdom 景龙金殿国

Jingpo minority 景颇族

Jingpozu minjian gushi 景颇族民间故事

"Jingxian zuxian de laili" 敬献祖先的来历

Jino minority 基诺族

Jinsha River 金沙江

Jinuoloke Mountains 基诺洛克山

"Jiu xiongdi" 九兄弟

Jiuqian Cooperative 九阡公社

Jiuqian Township 九阡乡

"Jiuxiang quan" 酒香泉

Kammu (Kemu) 克木
Kaquewa 卡雀哇
Kemu. *See* Kammu
Keqin 克钦
*kexue ben* 科学本
Ko-lo-feng (Geluofeng) 阁罗凤
Kong Meijin 孔美金
Konge 控格
Kucong minority 苦聪族
Kunlun Mountains 昆仑山
Kunming 昆明

Lahu minority 拉祜族
Lan Hongen 蓝鸿恩
Lancang (Mekong) River 澜沧江
Langguang Sea 浪广海
Lanping 兰坪
Lao She 老舍
Laojun Mountain 老君山
*leiwang* 雷王
"Leiwang shouzu" 雷王收租
"Leiwang taozou" 雷王逃走
li (measure) 里
li (mythical animal) 立
Li Changfu 李长福
Li Chengming 李承明
Li Dazhao 李大钊
Li Qiao 李乔
Li Rongguang 李荣光
Li Weihan 李维汉
Li Xiangqian 李向前
Li Xinghua 李星华
Li Yunchang 李云长

Li Zixian 李子贤

*liang* 兩

Liang Shoude 梁守德

Li'en 利恩

"Lieren she taiyang" 猎人射太阳

Lin Yutang 林语堂

Lisu minority 傈僳族

*Lisuzu minjian gushi xuan* 傈僳族民间故事选

Liu Derong 刘德荣

Liu Fu 刘福

Liu Huihao 刘辉豪

Liu Jianwen 刘建文

Liu Libai 刘利白

Liu Shu 刘曙

Liu Yangwu 刘扬武

Liuliu 六六

"Liuyue liu de laili" 六月六的来历

Lixian Jiang 李仙江

Lizhemuzhe 力者木者

Lolo (Luoluo) 罗罗

Long River 龙江

Longsi 隆斯

"Longsi yu san gongzhu" 隆斯与三公主

Lu Xun 鲁迅

Lugu Lake 泸沽湖

"Lujiao zhuang" 铲角桩

Lula.Ding 鲁腊·顶

Lumeng 陆盟

Luo Quan 罗荃

Luo Shiyuan 罗世元

"Luomu'azhi gushi size" 罗木阿支故事四则

Luoyu He 落雨河

*luxiangpai* 绿香排


Ma Bingbo 马兵波

Ma Weiliang 马维良

Ma Yin 马寅

Mahei 麻黑

Mailikai (Mali Hka) River 迈立开江

Maiyinzipo Mountain 埋银子坡

Mali Hka River. *See* Mailikai River

Maniu 麻妞

Manyuanpo 漫远坡

Mao Dun 茅盾

Mao Zedong 毛泽东

Maoniu Mountain 牦牛山

*maqie* 吗怯

*masangduan* 麻桑端

"Meijian zhangxuan de guniang" 眉间长旋的姑娘

Meng Guocai 孟国才

Mengbanaxi 孟巴纳西

Menggu minority. *See* Mongol minority

Mengman 猛满

Mengshe (tribe) 蒙舍

Mengyang 猛养

Miao minority 苗族

"Mihou yuhai" 猕猴育孩

*mijiao* 密教

Minjia 民家

*minjian gushi* 民间故事

*minzu* 民族

Mixi 密西

Mojiang 墨江

Mongol (Menggu) minority 蒙古族

Moon Mountain 月亮山

Mosuo 摩梭

Mu, Lord 木老爷

*mu* (measure) 亩

*Mu jia bai* 木家败

*Mu jia sheng* 木家胜

"Mu laoye chishi" 木老爷吃屎

"Mu laoye pa liangjia" 木老爷爬粮架

Mubengge 木崩格

Mubo 姆伯

Mubupa 木布帕

"Mubupa niedi" 木布帕捏地

Mukemudamu 姆克姆大木

Mumeiji 木美姬

Murannaodou 木然脑都

"Nabulousi" 纳布娄斯

Nala 娜拉

Nanning 南宁

Nannuo Mountain 南糯山

Nanpan River 南盘江

"Nanxi He" 难夕河

Nanzhao 南诏

Naxi minority 纳西族

"Nayu qu" 拿鱼去

"Niaodiao Shan" 鸟吊山

Niwadi 尼瓦帝

Nu minority 怒族

Nu River 怒江

"Nuli de nü'er" 奴隶的女儿

Nuosu 诺苏 or 纳苏

Nüwa 女娲

Oukunbo 鸥鹍勃

Pan Gu 盘古

Pan Zhifa 潘志发

panzhi hua 攀枝花

Payaman 怕亚曼

Payatian 怕亚田

Pazhao 帕召

Peng 朋

Peng Yingming 彭英明

Penggenpeng 彭根朋

"Penggenpeng shangtian qu xifu—Tianshen gei wugu zhongzi, shengchu" 彭根朋上天娶媳妇—天神给五谷种子、牲畜

Pineapple Village 菠萝庄

Pingtan 平坦

"Poshui jie" 泼水节

Poyana 帕雅纳

Poyayi 帕雅依

Primi (Pumi) minority 普米族

Pu people 蒲人 or 蒲蛮

Pu Yang 普阳

Pu Ying 普英

Pu'er tea 普洱茶

Pumi minority. See Primi minority

Pusa 菩萨


Qiang minority 羌族

Qigao 契高

Qilu Lake 杞麓湖

"Qimingxing" 启明星

"Qin Leiwang" 擒雷王

Qing Ming 清明

Qinghai 青海

Qinka 琴卡

"Qisi huo Yanwang 气死活阎王

"Qiu yu" 求雨

"Qixing pijian de laili" 七星披肩的来历

Qu Minzhou 瞿民周

Qu Nuo 曲诺


Ransu 然苏

"Raosanling de laili" 绕三灵的来历

"Ren yu bulan zhengdou" 人与布兰争斗

Renmin Daibiao Hui 人民代表会

Renmin Zhengfu 人民政府

"Renzu Li'en" 人祖利恩

Ruey Yih-fu (Rui Yifu) 芮逸夫

Ruili River 瑞丽江


*sailiangmu* 赛俩目

Sanhezhai 三合寨

Sani 撒尼

*sanxian* 三弦

Sanyue Jie 三月节

Sha Che 沙车

*sha* tree 纱树

Sha Yi Po 沙衣坡

*Shan cha* 山茶

Shang Zhonghao 尚仲豪

Shangguan 上关

"She ri yue" 射日月

Shen Congwen 沈从文

"Shen di" 神笛

*sheng* 笙

*shenhua* 神话

Shi jing 诗经

Shizong 石宗

"Shuangjiao xiniao" 双角犀鸟

*shuanshuanla jiao* 涮涮辣椒

Shui minority. *See* Sui minority

Shuilong 水龙

"Shuizu weishenme zhu mulou" 水族为什么住木楼

Sipsong Panna (Xishuangbanna) 西双板纳

Sireabi 斯热阿比

*siyan gou* 四眼狗

Song Zhe 宋哲

Star Cloud Lake 星云湖

Sui (Shui) minority 水族

Sun Mountain 太阳山

"Taiyang yueliang he xingxing" 太阳月亮和星星
tang 塘
Tang Qitian 唐奇甜
Tanggula Mountains 唐古拉山
Tao Yonghua 陶永华
"Tian di ren de youlai" 天地人的由来
Tian Wang 天王
Tian Zheng 田政
tongba 通巴
tonghua 童话
tusi 土司

Wa minority 佤族
Wai Weng Pool 外翁湾
"Wan he zhi" 弯和直
Wang Na 王娜
Wang Shouchun 王寿椿
Wang Yujian 王予见
"Wangfu yun" 望夫云
Wei Yurong 韦玉容
wenxue ben 文学本
Wu Jufen 吴菊芬

Xi River 西江
Xiaguan 下关
Xiang (surname) 祥
xiang (township) 乡
Xiaoliang Mountains 小凉山
Xicheng 西城
Xingyun Hu 星云湖
xinima 西尼麻
"Xiongmei jiehun" 兄妹结婚
Xishuangbanna. *See* Sipsong Panna

Xu Hualong 徐华龙

Xu Jiarui 徐家瑞

Xu Kun 徐

Ya 牙

Yama (Yan Wang) 阎王

Yan Wang. *See* Yama

"Yanchihai" 雁池海

Yang 杨

Yang Chengrong 杨成荣

Yang Jinshu 杨进书

Yang Luta 杨路塔

Yang Yuke 杨玉科

Yange 岩歌

"Yangque zao riyue" 阳雀造日月

Yansang 岩桑

Yao, Mount (Yaojia Mountain) 瑶山（瑶家山）

"Yao kouhuan" 要口还

Yao minority 瑶族

"Yaoshan niaohui de chuanshuo" 瑶山鸟会的传说

Ye Shengtao 叶圣陶

Yi minority 彝族

Yibin 宜宾

Yijimiguli 亦鸡咪咕哩

Yongning Town 永宁镇

Yongxi 庸西

You River 右江

You Zhong 尤中

Youle Mountains 友乐山

Yu Chi 禺尺

"Yu guniang" 鱼姑娘

Yuan Ding 袁丁

Yuan River 元江

*yuefu* 乐府

Yukan 玉坎

Yulong Xueshan 玉龙雪山

*yun* 云

Yunlong 云龙

Yunnan 云南

*Yunnan minjian gushi wushi pian* 云南民间故事五十篇

*Yunnan minzu minjian gushi xuan* 云南民族民间故事选


Zang (Tibetan) minority 藏族

*zanha* 赞哈

"Zanha de shizu" 赞哈的始祖

Zewangrenzeng 泽汪仁增

Zhage 扎哥

*zhaizi* 寨子

Zhalai 扎来

*zhang* 丈

Zhang Fusan 张福三

Zhang Gongjin 张公谨

Zhang Lianhua 张联华

Zhang Rongli 张容立

Zhang Shijie 张士杰

Zhang Tianyi 张天翼

Zhang Wenchen 张文臣

Zhanuzhabie (Zanuzabie) 扎努扎别

Zhao Jingxiu 赵静修

Zhao Yinsheng 赵寅生

Zhao Yuming 赵玉明

Zhatuoye 扎妥耶

Zhayue 扎约

*zhen* 镇

Zheng He 郑和

Zheng Xinshun 郑新舜

*zhengli* 整理

"Zhepoma he Zhemima" 遮帕麻和遮米麻

*zhi ji ma gou* 指鸡骂狗

Zhong Xiu 钟秀

*Zhongguo minjian fengsu chuanshuo* 中国民间风俗传说

Zhou Enlai 周恩来

Zhou Xingbo 周兴勃

Zhou Zuoren 周作人

Zhoutan 周覃

Zhu Faqing 祝发清

Zhu Jialu 朱嘉禄

"Zhuang jin" 壮锦

Zhuang minority 壮族

Zhuang-Dong language family 壮侗语族

*Zhuangzu minjian gushi xuan* 壮族民间故事选

Zhuoka 卓卡

Zhutian Mountain 珠天山

"Zongshu he guishu" 棕树和桂树

Zuo Yutang 左玉堂

# Bibliography

Aarne, Antti. Translated by Stith Thompson. *The Types of the Folktale: A Classification and Bibliography*. 2d rev. ed. Folklore Fellows Communications, no. 184. Helsinki: Academia Scientarum Fennica, 1961.

*Aiqing chuanshuo gushi xuan* [Anthology of romantic legends and tales]. Kunming: Yunnan renmin chuban she, 1980.

Barth, F., ed. *Ethnic Groups and Boundaries: The Social Organization of Culture Difference*. Boston: Little, Brown and Co., 1969.

Bassnett-McGuire, Susan. *Translation Studies*. New York: Methuen, 1980.

Beauclair, Inez de. *Tribal Cultures of Southwest China*. Asian Folklore and Social Life Monographs, no. 2. Taipei: Orient Cultural Service, 1970.

Ben-Amos, Dan, ed. *Folklore Genres*. Austin and London: University of Texas Press, 1976.

Birch, Cyril. *Chinese Myths and Fantasies*. London: Oxford University Press, 1962.

Boas, Franz. *The Mind of Primitive Man*. New York: Macmillan, 1922.

Bottigheimer, Ruth B. Conference report. "Secondes journées d'étude en littérature orale, Paris, 23–26 March 1987." *Merveilles & Contes* 1:1 (May 1987), 68–69.

Burne, Charlotte S. *The Handbook of Folklore*. 1914. Reprint. Liechtenstein: C. B. Hendeln, 1967.

Bynum, David E. *The Daemon in the Wood: A Study of Oral Narrative Patterns*. Publications of the Milman Parry Collection, Monograph Series, no. 1, Harvard University. Cambridge, Mass.: Center for the Study of Oral Literature, 1978.

Chafe, Wallace L. "Integration and Involvement in Speaking, Writing, and Oral Literature." In *Spoken and Written Language: Exploring Orality and Literacy*, edited by Deborah Tannen. Norwood, N.J.: Ablex, 1982.

———, ed. *The Pear Stories: Cultural, Cognitive and Linguistic Aspects of Narrative Production*. Norwood, N.J.: Ablex, 1982.

Champagne, Roland A. "A Grammar of the Language of Culture: Literary Theory and Yury M. Lotman's Semiotics." *New Literary History* 9 (1977–78): 205–10.

Chang, Chi-jen. *The Minority Groups of Yunnan and Chinese Political Expansion into Southeast Asia*. Ann Arbor: University of Michigan Press, 1956.

Chen, Lufan. *Whence Came the Thai Race? An Inquiry.* Text in Chinese and English. Kunming: Guoji Wenhua Publishing Company, 1990.

Chen, Shou-jung. *Southwest China.* Palo Alto: Stanford University Press, 1956.

Christie, Anthony. *Chinese Mythology.* Middlesex, England: Hamlyn Publishing Group Ltd., 1968.

Clarke, Samuel R. *Among the Tribes in Southwest China.* London: Morgan and Scott, 1911.

Cohen, Joan Lebold. *Yunnan School: A Renaissance in Chinese Painting.* Minneapolis: Fingerhut Group Publishers, 1988.

Cook-Gumperz, Jenny, and John Cook-Gumperz. "From Oral to Written Culture: The Transition to Literacy." In *Variation in Writing,* edited by Marcia Farr Whitehead. Hillsdale, N.J.: Lawrence Erlbaum Associates, 1978.

Credner, William. *Cultural and Geographical Observations Made in the Tali (Yunnan) Region with Special Regard to the Nan-chao Problem.* Translated by E. Seidenfaden. Bangkok: Siam Society, 1934.

*Daizu minjian gushi* [Dai folktales]. Kunming: Yunnan renmin chuban she, 1984.

Davies, Henry Rodolph. *Yunnan: The Link Between India and the Yangtze.* Cambridge, England: Cambridge University Press, 1909.

Deal, D. M. "Policy Towards Ethnic Minorities in Southwest China, 1927–1965." *Journal of Asian Affairs* 1, no. 1 (1976), 31–38.

DeFrancis, John. "National and Minority Policy." *Annals of the American Academy of Political and Social Sciences,* no. 277 (1951), 146–155.

Dennys, N. B. *The Folklore of China and Its Affinities with That of the Aryan and Semitic Races.* London: Trubner and Company, 1876.

Dessaint, Alain Y. *Minorities of Southwest China: An Introduction to the Yi (Lolo) and Related Peoples and an Annotated Bibliography.* New Haven: Human Relations Area Files Press, 1980.

DeVos, George, and Lola Romanucci-Ross, eds. *Ethnic Identity: Cultural Identity and Change.* Palo Alto: Mayfield, 1975.

Doré, Henri. *Recherches sur les superstitions en Chine.* Variétiés Sinologiques. 18 vols. Shanghai: Imprimerie de la Mission Catholique, 1911–38.

Dreyer, June Teufel. *China's Forty Millions.* Cambridge, Mass.: Harvard University Press, 1976.

Duggan, J. Joseph, ed. *Oral Literature.* New York: Barnes and Noble, 1975.

Eberhard, Wolfram. *Typen chinesischer Volksmärchen.* Folklore Fellows Communications, no. 120. Helsinki: Suomalainen Tiedeakatemia, Academia Scientiarum Fennica, 1937.

——— . *Chinese Fairy Tales and Folk Tales.* Translated by Desmond Parsons. London: Kegan Paul, 1938.

——— . *Volksmarchen aud Südost-China, Sammlun Ts'ao Sung-yeh.* Folklore Fellows

Communications, no. 128. Helsinki: Suomalainen Tiedeakatemia, Academia Scientiarum Fennica, 1941.

―――. "Kultur und Siedlung der Randvölkers Chinas." T'oung Pao 38 (1942), supplement.

―――. Lokalkulturen im alten China. 2 vols. Leiden and Peking: E. J. Brill, 1942.

―――. Folktales of China. Foreword by Richard M. Dorson. Chicago: University of Chicago Press, 1965.

―――. "Notes on Chinese Story Tellers." Fabula 11 (1970), 1–31.

―――. Chinese Fables and Parables. Asian Folklore and Social Life Publications, no. 15. Taipei: Orient Cultural Service, 1971.

―――. China's Minorities: Yesterday and Today. Belmont, Calif.: Wadsworth, 1982.

―――. "Epic Poetry Among the Minorities of South China." In Life and Thought of Ordinary Chinese, 205–26, 228–30. Taipei: Orient Cultural Service, 1982.

Edwards, E. D. Festivals and Songs of Ancient China. London: George Routledge, 1932.

Eoyang, Eugene. "A Taste for Apricots: Approaches to Chinese Fiction." In Chinese Narrative: Critical and Theoretical Essays, edited by Andrew H. Plaks, 53–69. Princeton, N.J.: Princeton University Press, 1977.

Fei, Xiaotong (Hsiao-tung Fei). On the Social Transformation of China's Minority Nationalities. Tokyo: The United Nations University, Sub-project on Endogenous Intellectual Creativity (EIC), 1979.

―――. "Ethnic Identification in China." Social Sciences in China, no. 1 (1980), 94–107.

―――. Minzu yu shehui [Nationality and society]. Beijing: People's Press, 1981.

―――. Toward a People's Anthropology. Beijing: New World Press, 1981.

―――, and Chih-i Chang. Earthbound China: A Study of Rural Economy in Yunnan. Chicago: University of Chicago Press, 1945.

Finnegan, Ruth. Oral Poetry: Its Nature, Significance, and Social Structure. Cambridge, England: Cambridge University Press, 1977.

Fitzgerald, Charles P. The Tower of Five Glories: A Study of the Minchia of Tali, Yunnan. London: The Cresset Press, 1941.

―――. The Southern Expansion of the Chinese People. London: Barrie and Jenkins, 1972.

Foley, John Miles. "Oral Literature: Premises and Problems." Choice 18 (1980), 487–96.

―――, ed. Oral Traditional Literature: A Festschrift for Albert Bates Lord. Columbus, Ohio: Slavica Press, 1981.

Fortune, Reo, ed. "Yao Society: A Study of a Group of Primitives in China." Lingnan Science Journal 18 (1939), 341–455.

Fujisawa, Yoshimi. The Historical Studies of the Tribes in South-west China: Historial Studies of the Nan-chao Kingdom. Tokyo: Daian, 1969.

Geeland, P. J. M., and D. C. Twitchett, eds., *The Times Atlas of China*. London: Times Books, 1974.

Ghosh, Stanley. *Embers in Cathay*. Garden City, N.Y.: Doubleday, 1961.

Gill, Lunda Hoyle, and Colin Mackerras. *Portraits of China*. Honolulu: University of Hawaii Press, 1990.

Goody, Jack, ed. *Literacy in Traditional Societies*. Cambridge, England: Cambridge University Press, 1968.

Goullart, Peter. *Forgotten Kingdom*. London: John Murray, 1957.

Graham, David C. *Songs and Stories of the Ch'uan Miao*. Smithsonian Miscellaneous Collection 123, no. 1. Washington, D.C.: Smithsonian Institution, 1954.

Granet, Marcel. *Danses et légendes de la Chine ancienne*. Paris: Felix Alcan, 1926.

Grantham, A. E. *Hills of Blue*. London: Methuen & Co., Ltd., 1927.

Grunfeld, A. Tom. "In Search of Equality: Relations Between China's Ethnic Minorities and the Majority Han." *Bulletin of Concerned Asian Scholars* 17, no. 1 (1985), 54–67.

Gumperz, John J., Hannah Kaltmann, and Catherine O'Connor. "The Transition to Literacy." In *Coherence in Spoken and Written Discourse*, edited by Deborah Tannen. Norwood, N.J.: Ablex, 1984.

Guo Sijiu, ed. *Jiao'ao de laohu: Wazu dongwu gushi* [The arrogant tiger: Wa animal tales]. Kunming: Yunnan renmin chuban she, 1979.

Guojia minwei [State Commission for Nationalities Affairs], ed. *Minzu zhengce jianghua* [Talks on the policy toward nationalities]. Beijing: Minzu chuban she, 1979.

——— . *Zhongguo shaoshu minzu* [China's minority nationalities]. Beijing: Minzu chuban she, 1981.

Guowuyuan renkou pucha bangongshi [Census Office of the State Council], and Guojia tongjiju renkou tongjise [Department of Population Statistics, National Statistics Bureau], eds. *Zhongguo 1982 nian renkou pucha 10% chouyang ziliao zhuyao shuzi* [Ten percent sampling tabulation on the 1982 population census of (the People's Republic of) China]. Beijing: Zhongguo tongji chuban she, 1983.

Hall, Daniel George Edward. *Burma*. London: Hutchinson's University Library, 1950.

Handelman, D. "The Organization of Ethnicity." *Ethnic Groups* 1 (1977), 187–200.

He, Liyi. *The Spring of Butterflies and Other Chinese Folk Tales of China's Minority Peoples*. London: Collins, 1985.

Headland, Isaac Taylor. *Chinese Mother Goose Rhymes*. New York: Fleming H. Revell, 1900.

Heberer, Thomas, ed. *Ethnic Minorities in China: Tradition and Transformation*. Papers of the 2d Interdisciplinary Congress on Sinology/Ethnology, St. Augustin, Germany (26 June–1 July 1984). Aachen, Germany: Rader Verlag, 1987.

———. *China and Its National Minorities: Autonomy or Assimilation?* Armonk, N.Y.: M. E. Sharp, 1989.

Holloman, R. E. "The Study of Ethnicity: An Overview." In *Perspective on Ethnicity*, edited by R. E. Holloman and S. A. Arutiunov. The Hague: Mouton, 1981.

Honko, Lauri. "Wooden Bells Ringing." *Nordic Institute of Folklore Newsletter* 14, nos. 2–3 (October 1986), 3–16.

Hrdlickova, Vera. "The Professional Training of Chinese Storytellers and the Storytellers' Guilds." *Archiv Orientalni* 33:2 (1965), 225–48.

Hsieh, Jiann [Xie Jian]. "China's Policy Toward the Minority Nationalities in an Anthropological Perspective." Alumni Working Paper Series, no. 1. Honolulu: East-West Center, 1984.

———. "Population Structure and Family Pattern Under Directed Socio-Cultural Change: the Samei Case in Yunnan, People's Republic of China." *International Review of Modern Sociology* 14, no. 1 (1984), 1–22.

———. "China's Nationalities Policy: Its Development and Problems." *Anthropos* 81 (1986), 1–22.

———. "The CCP's Concept of Nationality and the Work of Ethnic Identification Amongst China's Minorities." Centre for Contemporary Asian Studies, Institute of Social Studies, Chinese University of Hong Kong, Occasional Papers, General Series, no. 6 (September 1987), 1–36.

———. *Yunnan de Samei zu* [The Samei nationality of Yunnan]. Hong Kong: The Chinese University Press, in press.

Hsieh, Winston. *Chinese Historiography on the Revolution of 1911: A Critical Survey and a Selected Bibliography*. Stanford: Stanford University Press, 1975.

Huang Bocang, ed. *Jieri de chuanshuo* [Festival tales]. Changsha: Hunan renmin chuban she, 1982.

Huang Fenglan, ed. *Zhong-Fen minjian wenxue souji baoguan xueshu yantao hui wenji* [Proceedings of the Sino-Finnish Seminar on Collecting and Archiving Folk Literature]. Beijing: Zhongguo minjian wenyi chuban she, 1986.

Hung, Chang-tai. *Going to the People: Chinese Intellectuals and Folk Literature, 1918–1937*. Cambridge, Mass.: Harvard University Press, 1985.

Iser, Wolfgang. *The Implied Reader*. Baltimore: Johns Hopkins University Press, 1974.

———. *The Act of Reading: A Theory of Aesthetic Response*. Baltimore: Johns Hopkins University Press, 1985.

Izikowitz, Karl Gustav. "Lamet: Hill Peasants in French Indochina." *Etnologiska Studier*, no. 17. Göteborg: Etnografiska Museet, 1951.

Jagendorf, M. A., and Virginia Weng. *The Magic Boat and Other Chinese Folk Tales.* New York: Vanguard Press, 1980.

Jia, Zhi. "On Collection and Collation of Chinese Folk Literature." *Nordic Institute of Folklore Newsletter* 14, nos. 2–3 (October 1986), 17–30.

Jiang Yongxing. "Cong Guizhou minzu shibie gongzuo tanqi" [Discussion on the basis of Guizhou's ethnic identification work]. *Minzu yanjiu jikan* 2 (1985), 303–16.

Jousse, Marcel. *Le Style oral rythmique et mnémotechnique chez les Verbo-moteurs.* Paris: G. Beauchesnes, 1925.

———. *Le Parlant, la parole, et le souffle.* Vol. 3 of L'Anthropologie du geste. Preface by Maurice Houis. Ecole Pratique des Hautes Etudes. Paris: Gallimard, 1978.

Karlgren, Bernard. "Legends and Cults in Ancient China." *Bulletin of the Museum of Far Eastern Antiquities* 18 (1946), 199–365.

Keyes, Charles F. *The Golden Peninsula: Culture and Adaption in Mainland Southeast Asia.* New York: Macmillan, 1977.

King, Ben, and E. C. Dickinson. *A Field Guide to the Birds of South-East Asia.* London: Collins, 1975.

Kinkley, Jeffrey C. *The Odyssey of Shen Congwen.* Stanford: Stanford University Press, 1987.

Kroeber, A. L., and C. Kluckholn. *Culture: A Critical Review of Concepts and Definitions.* Peabody Museum Papers 47, no. 1. Cambridge, Mass.: The Museum Papers of the Peabody Museum of American Archaeology and Ethnology, Harvard University, 1952.

Kunstadter, Peter, ed. *Southeast Asian Tribes, Minorities, and Nations.* Princeton: Princeton University Press, 1967.

Lang, Andrew. *Blue Fairy Book.* Rev. ed. Hasmondsworth, England: Kestrel Books, 1975.

Lebar, Frank M., Gerald C. Hickey, and John K. Musgrave. *Ethnic Groups of Mainland Southeast Asia.* New Haven: Human Relations Area Files Press, 1964.

Lévi-Strauss, Claude. *Totemism.* Translated by Rodney Needham. Boston: Beacon Press, 1963.

———. *The Savage Mind.* Chicago: University of Chicago Press, 1966.

———. *The Raw and the Cooked.* Translated by John and Doreen Weightman. New York: Harper and Row, 1970.

———. *Myth and Meaning.* The 1977 Massey Lectures, Ideas series, CBS radio. New York: Schocken Books, 1979.

Li Weihan. *Guanyu minzu lilun he minzu zhengce de ruogan wenti* [A few problems concerning the theory and policy on nationalities]. Beijing: Renmin chuban she, 1980.

———. *Tongyi zhanxian wenti yu minzu wenti* [The problem of united front and the problem of nationality]. Beijing: Renmin chuban she, 1981.

Liang Shoude. "Lun Liening guanyu shehuizhuyi zhidu xia de minzu zijuequan yuanze" [On Lenin's principle of national self-determination under the socialist system]. *Minzu yanjiu* [Nationality studies], no. 6 (1980), 2–14.

Lin, Yueh-hwa [Lin Yuehua]. "Social Life of the Aboriginal Groups in and Around Yunnan." *Journal of the West China Border Research Society* 15 (1944), 47–56.

———. *Liangshan Yijia.* Shanghai: Commercial Press, 1947. Translated by Ju-shu Pan and edited by Wu-chi Liu under the title *The Lolo of Liang Shan.* New Haven: Human Relations Area Files, 1961.

Lindell, Kristina, Håkan Lundström, Jan-Olof Svantesson and Damrong Tayanin. *The Kammu Year: Its Lore and Music.* Studies on Asian Topics, no. 4. Scandinavian Institute of Asian Studies. London and Malmö: Curzon Press, 1982.

Lindell, Kristina, Jan-Öjvind Swahn, and Damrong Tayanin. "The Flood: Three Northern Kammu Versions of the Story of the Creation." *Acta Orientalia* 37 (1976), 183–200.

———. *A Kammu Story-Listener's Tales.* Scandinavian Institute of Asian Studies Monograph Series, no. 33. London and Malmö: Curzon Press, 1977.

———. *Folk Tales from Kammu II: A Story-Teller's Tales.* Scandinavian Institute of Asian Studies Monograph Series, no. 40. London and Malmö: Curzon Press, 1978.

———. *Folk Tales from Kammu III: Pearls of Kammu Literature.* Scandinavian Institute of Asian Studies Monograph Series, no. 51. London and Malmö: Curzon Press, 1984.

Liu E. "Quyu zizhi shi woguo jiejue minzu wenti de jiben zhengce" [Regional autonomy is my country's (China's) basic policy to solve the problem of nationalities]. In *Minzu wenti yu minzu zhengce* [The nationalities problem and the nationalities policy], edited by Bianji weiyuan hui [The editing group]. Chengdu: Sichuan minzu chuban she, 1980.

Llata, Richard, and Mario Barrera. "The Chinese National Minorities Policy." *Aztlan: International Journal of Chicano Studies* 6, no. 3 (Fall 1975), 379–408.

Lord, Albert B. *The Singer of Tales.* Harvard Studies in Comparative Literature 24. Cambridge, Mass.: Harvard University Press, 1960.

Lou, Cukuang [Lou Tsu-k'uang], ed. *Folklore and Folk Literature.* Beijing: Beijing University Press, 1970.

Luria, Aleksandr Romanovich. *Cognitive Development: Its Cultural and Social Foundations.* Translated by Martin Lopez-Morillas and Lynn Solataroff; edited by Michael Cole. Cambridge, Mass.: Harvard University Press, 1976.

Ma Weiliang. "Minzu wenti yu jieji douzheng de guanxi" [The relationship between the problem of nationalities and class struggle]. *Minzu yanjiu* [Nationality studies], no. 3 (1980), 1–6, 11.

Ma, Yin, ed. *China's Minority Nationalities*. Beijing: Foreign Languages Press, 1989.

Mabuchi, Toichi. "Tales Concerning the Origin of Grains in the Insular Areas of Eastern and Southeastern Asia." *Asian Folklore Studies* 23, no. 1 (1964), 1–92.

Mackerras, Colin. "Folksongs and Dances of China's Minority Nationalities." *Modern China* 10, no. 2 (April 1984), 187–226.

————. "Introduction." In *Portraits of China*, by Linda Hoyle Gill and Colin Mackerras, 1–67. Honolulu: University of Hawaii Press, 1989.

Maranda, Pierre, and Elli Kongas Maranda, eds. *Structural Analysis of Oral Tradition*. Philadelphia: University of Pennsylvania Press, 1971.

Miller, Lucien. "Children's Literature East and West." *Alumni Paper Series*, no. 9. Honolulu: East-West Center Association, 1987.

Minford, John. *Favourite Folktales of China*. Beijing: New World Press, 1982.

Moseley, George. "China's Fresh Approach to the National Minority Question." *China Quarterly* 24 (October–December 1965), 19–22.

————. *The Consolidation of the South China Frontier*. Berkeley: University of California Press, 1973.

Mote, Frederick W. "The Rural 'Haw' of Northern Thailand." In *Southeast Asian Tribes, Minorities, and Nations*, edited by Peter Kunstadter. Princeton: Princeton University Press, 1967. vol. 2, 487–524.

Nida, Eugene A. *Toward a Science of Translating*. Leiden: E. J. Brill, 1964.

————, and Charles R. Taber. *The Theory and Practice of Translation*. Leiden: E. J. Brill, 1969.

————, and Jin Di. *On Translation: With Special Reference to Chinese and English*. Beijing: Zhongguo duiwai fanyi chuban she, 1984.

Niehoff, A. H. *A Case Book of Social Change*. Chicago: Aldine, 1966.

Ogden, Michael K., and David Y. H. Wu. *National Policy and Minority Cultures in Asia and the Pacific: A Partially Annotated Bibliography*. Honolulu: Institute of Culture and Communications, East-West Center, 1985.

Okpewho, Isidore. *The Epic in Africa: Toward a Poetics of the Oral Performance*. New York: Columbia University Press, 1979.

Oliver, Robert T. *Communication and Culture in Ancient India and China*. Syracuse, N.Y.: Syracuse University Press, 1979.

Olson, David R. "From Utterance to Text: The Bias of Language in Speech and Writing." *Harvard Educational Review* 47 (1977), 257–81.

Ong, Walter J. *The Presence of the Word*. New Haven: Yale University Press, 1967.

————. *Orality and Literacy*. New York: Menthuen, 1982.

Osgood, Cornelius. *Village Life in Old China: A Community Study of Kao Yao, Yunnan*. New York: Ronald Press, 1963.

Oukunbo [Xu Kun], ed. *Jingpozu minjian gushi* [Jingpo tales]. Kunming: Yunnan renmin chuban she, 1983.

Peabody, Berkley. *The Winged Word: A Study in the Technique of Ancient Greek Oral Composition as Seen Principally Through Hesiod's Works and Days*. Albany, N.Y.: State University of New York Press, 1975.

Peng Yingmin and Tang Qitian. "Minzu wenti ji qi shizhi qianlun" [A preliminary discussion of the problem of nationalities and its essence]. *Minzu yanjiu* [Nationality studies], no. 1 (1981), 7–14.

Plaks, Andrew H., ed. *Chinese Narrative: Critical and Theoretical Essays*. Princeton: Princeton University Press, 1977.

Plenge, V. *The Sun, the Moon, and Rahu—and Other Tai Tales and Stories Recorded in Northern Thailand*. In *Lampang Reports*, edited by Søren Egerod and Per Sørensen. The Scandanavian Institute of Asian Studies Special Publication, no. 5. Copenhagen: The Scandinavian Institute of Asian Studies, 1976.

Polard, Samuel. *In Unknown China*. Philadelphia: J. B. Lippincott, 1921.

Polo, Marco. Trans. by Aldo Ricci. *The Travels of Marco Polo*. New York: Viking Press, 1931.

*The Population Atlas of China*. Compiled and edited by the Population Census Office of the State Council of the People's Republic of China, Institute of Geography, Chinese Academy of Sciences. Hong Kong and Oxford: Oxford University Press, 1987.

Pratt, Mary Louise. *Toward a Speech Act Theory of Literary Discourse*. Bloomington: Indiana University Press, 1977.

Propp, Vladimir. *Morphology of the Folktale*. Translated by Laurence Scott. 2d ed. Published for the American Folklore Society and Indiana University Research Center for the Language Sciences. Austin: University of Texas Press, 1968.

Purcell, Victor. *The Chinese in Southeast Asia*. New York: Oxford University Press, 1951.

Ramsey, S. Robert. "The Minorities of South China." In *The Languages of China*. 230–91. Princeton: Princeton University Press, 1987.

Reitlinger, Gerald. *South of the Clouds*. London: Faber and Faber, 1939.

Renmin wenxue chuban she [People's Literature Press], ed. *Yunnan ge minzu minjian gushi xuan* [Selection of folktales from each ethnic group in Yunnan]. Beijing: Renmin wenxue chuban she, 1962.

Roberts, Moss. *Chinese Fairy Tales and Fantasies*. New York: Pantheon, 1979.

Rock, Joseph F. *The Ancient Na-Khi Kingdom of Southwest China*. Harvard-Yenching Institute Monograph Series, vols. 8–9. Cambridge, Mass.: Harvard University Press, 1947.

Rosenberg, Bruce A. "The Genres of Oral Narrative." In *Theories of Literary Genre*.

Yearbook of Comparative Criticism, no. 8. University Park, Penn.: Pennsylvania State University Press, 1978.

Ruey, Yih-fu [Rui Yifu]. *Zhongguo minzu ji qi wenhua lungao* [A treatise on Chinese nationalities and their cultures]. Taipei: Yiwen chuban she, 1972.

Sadler, Catherine Edwards. *Treasure Mountain: Folktales from Southern China*. New York: Antheneum, 1982.

Salahuddin, M. "China: Islam Behind the Bamboo Curtain." *Arabia* 1 (1981), 34–41.

Schwarz, Henry G. "Communist Language Policies Towards China's Ethnic Minorities." *The China Quarterly* 12 (1962), 170–82.

——. *Chinese Policies towards Minorities*. Occasional Papers, no. 2. Program in Asian Studies. Bellingham, Wash.: Western Washington State College, 1971.

Scott, Dorothea Hayward. *Chinese Popular Literature and the Child*. Chicago: American Library Association, 1980.

*Shancha* [Camelia]. No. 5. Kunming: Yunnan renmin chuban she, 1982.

Shen, Che. *Life among the Minority Nationalities of Northwest Yunnan*. Beijing: Foreign Languages Press, 1989.

Shibutani, Tamotsu, and K. M. Kwang. *Ethnic Stratification*. London: Macmillan, 1965.

Sichuan minzu chuban she [Sichuan Nationality Press], ed. *Minzu wenti yu minzu zhengce* [The nationality problem and nationality policy]. Chengdu: Sichuan minzu chuban she, 1980.

Solinger, Dorothy J. "Minority Nationalities in China's Yunnan Province: Assimilation, Power and Policy in a Socialist State. *World Politics* 30, no. 1 (October 1977), 1–23.

Song Zhe. *Yunnan minjian gushi* [Folktales from Yunnan]. 2 vols. Hong Kong: Hongye shuju, 1961.

Stevens, K. Mark, and George E. Wehrfritz. *Southwest China: Off the Beaten Track*. Chicago: Passport Books, 1988.

Tan Hongkai and Zhang Xiaogang. "The Rise and Rise of the Township Government." *China Daily*, August 2, 1991, p. 4.

Tannen, Deborah. "Implications of the Oral/Literate Continuum for Cross-Cultural Communication." In *Georgetown University Roundtable on Languages and Linguistics 1980: Current Issues in Bilingual Education*, edited by James E. Alatis. Washington, D.C.: Georgetown University Press, 1980.

——. *Coherence in Spoken and Written Discourse*. Norwood, N.J.: Ablex, 1984.

——, ed. *Georgetown University Roundtable on Languages and Linguistics 1981: Analyzing Discourse—Text and Talk*. Washington, D.C.: Georgetown University Press, 1982.

Thompson, Stith. *The Folktale*. New York: Holt, Rinehart and Winston, 1964.

———. *Motif-Index of Folk Literature*. 6 vols. Rev. ed. Bloomington: Indiana University Press, 1955–58.

Ting, N. T. *A Type Index of Chinese Folktales in the Oral Tradition and Major Works of Non-Religious Classical Literature*. Folklore Fellows Communications, no. 223. Helsinki: Suomalainen Tiedeakatemia, Academia Scientiarum Fennica, 1979.

Ting, N. T., and Lee-hsia Hsu Ting. *Chinese Folk Narratives: A Bibliographic Guide*. San Francisco: Chinese Materials Center, 1975.

U.S. Central Intelligence Agency. *People's Republic of China Atlas*. Washington, D.C.: Government Printing Office, 1971.

Vitale, Baron Guido Amedeo. *Pekinese Rhymes*. 1896. Reprint. Hong Kong: Vetch and Lee, 1972.

———. *Chinese Merry Tales*. Beijing: Pei-t'ang Press, 1901.

Wang Shouchun, ed. *Yunnan minjian gushi wushi pian* [Fifty Yunnan folktales]. Kunming: Yunnan renmin chuban she, 1979.

Werner, E. T. C. *Myths and Legends of China*. London: George Harrap, 1922.

Wibulswasdi, Pismai. "Hmong and Chinese Interaction with Thais in Thailand." In *Ethnicity and Interpersonal Interaction: A Cross Cultural Study*, edited by David Y. H. Wu, 85–108. Singapore: Maruzen Asia, 1982.

Wiens, Harold J. *Han Chinese Expansion in South China*. New Haven: The Shoe String Press, 1967. (Originally published as *China's March Toward the Tropics*, 1954.)

Wingate, A. M. S. "Recent Journey from Shanghai to Bhamo Through Hunan." *Geographical Journal* 14, no. 6 (December 1899).

Winnington, Alan. *The Slaves of the Cool Mountains*. London: Lawrence and Wishart, 1959.

Winters, Clyde-Ahmad. *Mao or Muhammad: Islam in the People's Republic of China*. Hong Kong: Asian Research Service, 1979.

Wu, David Y. H., ed. *Ethnicity and Interpersonal Interaction: A Cross-Cultural Study*. Singapore: Maruzen Asia, 1982.

Xie Jian. *See* Hsieh, Jiann

Xu Hualong and Wu Jufen, eds. *Zhongguo minjian fengsu chuanshuo* [Chinese folk customs and legends]. Kunming: Yunnan renmin chuban she, 1985.

Xu Kun. "Zhongguo ge minzu minjian wenxue de jiaoliu he xianghu yinxiang" [Mutual interchange and influence among Chinese national minority folk literatures]. Translated by Lucien Miller. Unpublished interview (Amherst, May 1986).

Xu Kun. *See also* Oukunbo

Yang, Lixiang, and the Cartographic Section, Department of Geography, Australian National University, eds., for Thai-Yunnan Project. *Map of Yunnan Province*. Canberra, 1989.

Yin, Ming. *United and Equal: The Progress of China's Minority Nationalities*. Beijing: Foreign Languages Press, 1977.

You Zhong, ed. *Zhongguo xinan de gudai minzu* [Ancient minority nationalities of Southwest China]. Kunming: Renmin chuban she, 1979.

Young, O. Gordon. *The Hill Tribes of Northern Thailand*. 2d ed. 1982. Reprint. New York: AMS Press, 1982.

*Yunnan minzu minjian gushi xuan* [Anthology of Yunnan minority folktales]. Kunming: Yunnan renmin chuban she, 1982.

*Yunnan sheng ditu* [Map of Yunnan Province]. Beijing: Zhongguo ditu chuban she, 1990.

Yunnan sheng lishi yanjiu suo [Historical Research Institute of Hunan Province], ed. *Yunnan shaoshu minzu* [The minority nationalities of Yunnan]. Rev. ed. Kunming: Renmin chuban she, 1983.

Yunnan sheng renmin zhengfu waishiban gongshi bian [Foreign Affairs Office of Yunnan Provincial People's Government], ed. *Highlights of National Minorities in Yunnan*. Kunming: Yunnan sheng renmin zhengfu waishiban gongshi

Zhang, Zhi-yi. *The Party and the National Question in China*. Translated by George Moseley. Cambridge, Mass.: M.I.T. Press, 1966.

Zhong, Xiu. *Yunnan Travelogue: 100 Days in Southwest China*. Beijing: New World Press, 1983.

*Zhongguo shaoshu minzu diqu huaji congkan: Yunnan* [Illustrated series on ethnic minority regions in China: Yunnan]. Vol. 4 of *Zhongguo shaoshu minzu diqu huaji congkan*. Beijing: Minzu chuban she, 1986.

Zhou Enlai. *Guanyu wo guo minzu zhengce de jige wenti* [On some problems of my country's (China's) nationalities policy]. Beijing: Renmin chuban she, 1957.

Zhou Zheng. "Yunnan: A Multinational Frontier Province." *Beijing Review* 29 (18 July 1983), 23.

Zhu Faqing, Zuo Yutang, and Shang Zhonghao, eds. *Lisuzu minjian gushi xuan* [Anthology of Lisu folktales]. Shanghai: Shanghai wenyi chuban she, 1985.

*Zhuangzu minjian gushi xuan* [Anthology of Zhuang folktales]. Vol. 1. Nanning: Guangxi renmin chuban she, 1982.

Zipes, Jack. "Critical Observations on Recent Psychoanalytical Approaches to the Tales of the Brothers Grimm." *Merveilles & Contes* 1, no. 1 (May 1987), 19–30.

# Index

This index includes references to the General Introduction, the Introduction to Yunnan National Minority Folk Literature, the notes to the stories, and the Appendix. The stories themselves are not indexed.

Achang people, 240, 266, 268; tales of, 43; language of, 268
Action in oral literature, 28
Agonistic tone in oral literature, 29–30
Agriculture, 266–89 passim
"Ailuobuwo," 44–45
Along clan, 285
Amoyaobu, 67, 73
"The Ancestor of Humankind, Li'en," 43
Ancestor worship, 277, 278, 279, 285, 286, 289
"The Ancestors of Dai Singers," 31
Animal sacrifice, 276
Animals, 31, 45, 49
Animism, 201, 276, 279, 282, 286, 287
Apierer, 36
Architecture, 268–92 passim
"The Arrogant Tiger," 30, 34
"Asking Permission," 28, 29, 31, 34, 37
Autonomous minority areas, 8
Awa Mountain District, 288
Azhu marriage, 284

Bai people, 5, 22, 46, 258, 268, 270; tales of, 46, 47, 48, 50–51; language of, 268
Baiman people, 268
Baiyi people. See Dai people
Baoji fish, 264
"The Bat," 49–50

Batik, 282
Beipan River, 3
Benglong people. See De'ang people
Binbai, 157
Bing Xin, 11
"Bird-Perch Mountain," 47
Black River, 279
Blang (spirit), 66
Blang people, 94, 272, 288; tales of, 44
"A Blang Youth," 31, 32
Bo'aiwen, 103, 247
Bon religion, 284
The Book of Songs, 12, 17–18
Bubo, 292
Buddhism, 115, 270, 288; Theravada, 268, 272, 274, 275; esoteric, 270; Mahayana, 280, 288; Tibetan, 284, 288; literature of, 288
Bulang people. See Blang people
Bulei, 264
Buluotuo, 292
Burma, 5
Burma Road, 5
Burne, Charlotte, 13
"The Burning Tower," 46
Buyi people, 273
Bynum, David E., 36

Cang Mountains, 5, 47, 270
Cangyuan Mountain, 288
"Cart-Rumble Village," 47
Cen Laoliang, 101

Characters in oral literature, 29

Chen Guipei, 21, 103, 247

Chiang Yee, 11

Children: literature, 10–12, 38–39, 48–49; education of, 38–39, 48–49

Chinese government, 287, 290, 291

Christianity, 270, 282. See also Missionaries

Clan structure. See Social organization

"The Clever Sister," 33, 34

Clothing, 266–92 passim

"The Cloud That Longs for a Husband," 27–28, 32, 34, 47

Communism, 265

Creation tales, 33, 34, 43–44, 94, 285

Cultural Revolution, 14, 20, 270

Culture, 7

Customs, 46, 47

Dai people, 4, 37, 273–74, 275, 288, 292; tales of, 27, 44; language of, 273

Dali, 4, 5, 258, 268

Dali kingdom, 5, 268, 274, 276

"Dali Marble," 47

Dan, 184

Dance, 274, 275, 277, 282–83, 286, 290, 291, 279

Dandaglika Mountains, 276

Dangse. Ding, 66

Daoism, 270, 284

"Daughter of a Slave," 31, 32, 37

De'ang people, 275, 288; tales of, 44

Deforestation, 5–6

Devils, 48

Dianchi Lake, 4, 268

"The Divine Flute," 48

Dong language, 289

Dongba, 284, 285

Dorson, Richard M., 19–20, 21

Dosha'apo, 46

Dou, 193

Douli, 150

Dragon king, 84

Dragons, 49, 84

Drung people, 66–67, 275–76, 285; tales of, 44; language of, 275

Drung River valley, 275–76

Drungchang people. See Drung people

Du Chaoxuan, 46

Du Wenxiu, 22, 46

Duality in oral culture, 36

Duan Qicheng, 46

Duan Shengou, 177

Dulong people. See Drung people

Ear Lake. See Er Hai

Earth, gods of, 201

Eberhard, Wolfram, 19, 21

Endings of tales, 33, 34

Episodic structure, 34

Epithets, 32–33

Er Hai, 5, 47, 258, 268

Erkuai, 222

Esha, 189, 201, 280–81

Ethnic change, 6, 265–66

Ethnic identity, 6–10, 39–40

Ethnic minorities, 6–10; population of, 8; unity of, 22; description of, 265; relations with Chinese government, 274, 287, 290, 291

Evil, 49, 84

Fairies, 49

Fairy tales, 48–49

Famine, 285

Fan Dance, 277

Fei Xiaotong, 7

Festivals: Water-Splashing, 4, 37, 274, 275; Torch, 46, 283, 291; Kaquewa, 67, 276; Pure Brightness (Qing Ming), 106; Third Month Fair, 270; Blang, 272; Flower Dance, 273; New Rice, 282; Mule Fair, 285

Feudal society, ethical code of, 51

"The Fish Maiden," 9

"Five Tales about Ayidan," 28, 30, 31, 32, 34, 50

"The Formation of Heaven, Earth, and Humankind," 33

"Four Tales about Luomu'azhi," 50

Floods, 44, 285

Flower Dance Festival, 273

Folk literature: collection of, 12–14, 18–20, 51–52, 54, in Yunnan, 14; critics of, 13–14; folkloristic research and texts, 15–16, 19, 22; translation of, 15, 16, 23–26, 53–54; authenticity of texts, 16–20, 39–40; used by modern writers, 17–18; evolution of research, 18–23; collections, 19; as propaganda, 19–20, 21–22; Chinese concept of, 21; moral didacticism in, 21; origin tales in, 21, 43; collation of, 22–23; literary texts, 22; redaction of, 22–23, 38, 54–55; animals in, 31, 49; epithets in, 32–33; mnemonic devices, proverbs, and sayings in, 32–33; creation tales, 33, 34, 43–44, 94, 285; structure of, 33–34; writerly texts of, 35; landscapes in, 47; folktales, 48–52; recording of, 52–54; Blang, 272; Dai, 272, 274; Hani, 277; Naxi, 285; Wa, 289; Zhuang, 292. See also Oral literature; Songs

Folk singers, 274

Folklorists, 15–16

Folktales, 48–52. See also Folk literature; Oral literature

Forests, 5–6

Frazer, James G., 13

French, influence of, 4

Froebel, Friedrich, 11

Fuliang River. See Yuan River

Fuxi, 73

Fuxian Hu (Lake), 165

Gaoligong Mountains, 276

"The Gathering of the Birds," 32, 47

Geluofeng. See Ko-lo-feng

"The Girl with Tufted Eyebrows," 29, 32, 34, 37

Gods: Thunder God, 29, 150; blang, 66; of heaven, 67, 73, 84, 201; power of, 189; of earth, 201; worship of, 290, 291; in literature, 292

"The Gold Pig," 28, 29, 32, 35

Golden Sand River. See Jinsha River

Great Leap Forward, 5

Great Proletarian Cultural Revolution. See Cultural Revolution

Grimm brothers, 17, 18, 23

Gu Jiegang, 13, 19

Guangxi Zhuang Autonomous Region, 4

"The Guileless Man and the Trickster," 31, 33, 37

G'uisha. See Esha

Guizhou, 4

Guo Moruo, 11

Guo Xu, x-xi, 23–25

Hn people: relations with minorities, 8; language of, 9, 268; migration of, 9–10; mythology of, 73, 84; festivals of, 106

Hand Clapping Dance, 277

Hani people, 46, 276–77, 279; language of, 277

Hanoi-Kunming railroad, 4

"The Head-Baby," 32, 35, 36, 48

Headhunting, 288

Headland, Isaac Taylor, 13

Heaven, gods of, 67, 73, 84, 201

Heng Zhabeng, 46

Herding, 283, 286

Heroism, 46–47

Historical events, persons, and sites, 46, 47

Hmong people. See Miao people

Homer, 32

Hong He. *See* Red River
Honko, Lauri, 20–21, 23
Hourglass Drum Dance, 290
Hsieh, Winston, 17
Hui people, 22, 46, 213, 277–78
Hunting, 280
Husa swords, 240, 266

Incest, 33, 44, 73
Industrialization, 265
Irrawaddy River, 3
Islam, 213, 277–78

Jade Dragon Snow Mountain, 3
Jameson, Raymond, 18
Jia Zhi, 22
Jin, 184
Jinglong kingdom, 274
Jingpo people, 278–79; tales of, 48,
    49–50; songs of, 53–54; language of,
    276, 278, 288
Jino people, 32, 73, 279; tales of, 44;
    language of, 279
Jinsha River, 3

Kammu people, 15. *See also* Kemu
    people
Kam-Sui people, 287
Kaquewa Festival, 67, 276
Kazakh people, 277
Kemu people, 7, 15
Kingston, Maxine Hong, ix
Kinkley, Jeffrey C., 18
Ko-lo-feng, 5
Kong Meijin, 66
Korean language, 292
Kublai Khan, 5, 277, 283
Kucong people, 7, 15, 279–80; lan-
    guage of, 279
Kunming, 4
Kunming-Chengdu railroad, 4

Lahu people, 189, 201, 280–81; tales
    of, 45, 48; language of, 279, 280
Lamaism, 280, 284, 286
Lan Hongen, 21, 150
Lancang River. *See* Mekong River
Landscapes, 47
Lang, Andrew, 11, 13
Language: Han, 9, 268; folk, 14; de-
    scriptive, 28; Achang, 268; Bai, 268;
    written, 268, 270, 272, 274, 280, 281,
    282, 283, 284, 285, 287, 291; Dai,
    273; Tai family, 273, 287; Drung,
    275; Jingpo, 276, 278, 288; Nu, 276;
    Hani, 277; Burmese, 279; Jino, 279;
    Kucong, 279; Yi, 279, 283, 285, 288;
    Lahu, 279, 280; Miao, 282; Altaic,
    283; Mongolian family, 283, 292;
    Naxi, 285; Tibeto-Burman, 285, 288;
    Primi, 286; Qiang, 286, 288; Kam-
    sui, 287; Sui, 287; Zhuang-Dong
    family, 287; Monpa, 288; Tibetan,
    288, 292; Dong, 289; Myen, 289,
    Punu, 289; Tai, 289; Wa, 289; Yao,
    289; Korean, 292; Uighur, 292;
    Zhuang, 292
Lao She, 11
Lao-tzu (Laozi), 9
Leaping Palace Dance, 291
Legends, 46–47; Lisu, 282
Li (animal), 94
Li (measure), 222
Li Changfu, 200
Li Dazhao, 13
Li Qiao, 21, 115
Li Xiangqian, 208
Li Xinghua, 258
*Liang*, 184
Lin Yutang, 11
Lindell, Kristina, 15
Ling, Deidre, ix
Lisu people, 46, 84, 281–82
Literary tales, 16
Literate culture, 26–27

Literature: vernacular, 12; Dai, 272, 274; Buddhist, 288; Tibetan, 288. *See also* Folk literature; Myths; Oral literature; Poetry; Written literature
Liu Fu, 13
Liu Libai, 227
Liu Shu, 21, 174
Lixian River. *See* Black River
Lizhemuzhe, 67
Lolo people. *See* Yi people
Long clan, 285
"Longsi and the Third Princess," 30, 31, 33, 36
Love stories, 50–51
Lu Xun, 11
Lugu Lake, 284
Lula. Ding, 66
Lulu people, 285
Luo Shiyuan, 101

Ma Bingbo, 231
Magic, 49
"The Magic Shoulder-Pole," 25–26, 29, 37, 48
Mailikai River. *See* Mali Kha River
Maiyinzipo, 94
Mali Hka River, 3, 209
Manchu people, 8
Mandalay, 5
Mao Dun, 11
Mao Zedong, 20
Marble, 270
Marco Polo, 5
Marriage: brother-sister, 33, 44, 73; human-animal, 45; and love, 51; Hui, 213; *azhu*, 284
Matriliny, 284
May Fourth movement, 10, 11, 12, 13, 39
Mekong River, 3
Memory, 35–36
Mengbanaxi, 103

Menggu people. *See* Mongol people
Mengshe people, 268
Mengwa Mountain, 288
Miao people, 18, 87, 282–83; tales of, 44; language of, 282
Migration, 9–10
Miller, Lucien, x–xi, 23–26
Minjia people. *See* Bai people
Minorities. *See* Ethnic minorities
*Minzu. See* Ethnic minorities
Missionaries, Christian, 280, 281, 282
Mnai Hka River, 3
Mnemonic devices, 32–33
Modernization, 265
Mon-Khmer people, 272, 275
Mongol invasion, 5, 268, 273, 277, 282, 283
Mongol people, 8, 283
Monpa language, 288
Monsters, 48
Moon, 44
Morality, 21, 38
Mosuo people. *See* Naxi people
Mount Bachi, 150
"Mr. Crooked and Mr. Straight," 30, 36–37
Mu, 165
Mu clan, 222
Mubengge, 67
Mubupa, 84
Mukemudamu, 66
Mule Fair, 285
Muntjacs, 94
Music, 277. *See also* Musical instruments; Songs
Musical instruments, 264, 266, 273, 282–83, 287, 292
Muslim people. *See* Islam
Myen language, 289
Myths, 33, 34, 42–45
"Myths Concerning the Creation of the World," 33

"Nabulousi, the Life-Restoring Tree,"
32, 34–35, 37
Nanpan River, 3
"The Nanxi River," 27, 28, 34
Nanzhao kingdom, 4, 5, 258, 268, 274,
276, 280, 290, 291
Nari people. See Naxi people
Nationalities. See Ethnic minorities
Nature, 44–45
Naxi people, 222, 276, 284–85; tales of,
43, 47; Lijiang, 284; Yongning, 284;
language of, 285
New Rice Festival, 282
Nida, Eugene A., 24
"The Nine Brothers," 28, 34
Niwadi, 84
Nomads, 283, 286
Ntomba, 284, 285
Nu people, 285–86; language of, 276
Nu River. See Salween River
Numbers, 33
Nuosu people, 285
Nüwa, 73

Ong, Walter J., 26, 29, 32
Oral culture, 26–27, 41–42; sound
and speech in, 30–32; tradition
and memory in, 35–36; duality in,
36–37. See also Oral literature
Oral literature, 26–37; intellectual
view of, 14; compared to written,
15, 16; relation between storyteller
and audience, 16, 17; agonistic tone
in, 29; characters in, 29; schizoid
behavior in, 30; endings in, 33, 34–
35; numbers in, 33; repetition in,
33; structure of, 33–34; tests in, 33;
ways of beginning tales, 33–34; inconsistencies in, 35. See also Folk
literature; Oral culture; Songs
"The Origin of Making Offerings to
the Ancestors," 31–32, 36

"The Origin of the Sixth Month
Sacrifice," 34–35
Origin tales, 21, 43
"The Origins of Raosanling," 47
"The Origins of the Seven-Star
Shawl," 47
Oukunbo. See Xu Kun

Painting, primitive, 289, 292
"The Palm Tree and the Cassia Tree,"
50
Pan Gu, 67, 73
Pan Zhifa, 112
Paper cutting, 291
Parry, Milman, 14, 32
Pastoral life, 283, 284, 286
Pawku, 281
Payatian, 44
Peacock Dance, 274
Peasant uprisings, 46
Pestalozzi, Johann, 11
Plains, ethnic groups of, 10
Plants, 49
Plekhanov, Georgy, 45
Poetry, 14, 274, 275, 279, 288, 289, 291
Polo, Marco, 284
Population, minority, 8
Polytheism, 201, 272, 277, 287
Poyana, 201
Poyayi, 201
"Precious Lantern," 48
"The Precious Shoulder Pole." See
"The Magic Shoulder Pole"
Preliterate culture. See Oral culture
Primi people, 286
Proverbs, 32–33
Pu people, 272, 275, 288
Pu Song, 66
Pumi people. See Primi people
Punu language, 289
Pure Brightness Festival, 106
Pusa, 115

Pyu kingdom, 5

Qiang people, 7, 9, 286, 290; language of, 286, 288
Qilu Hu (Lake), 165
Qing Ming Festival, 106
Qiu people. See Drung people
Qiuzi people. See Drung people
Qu Minzhou, 136
Qu people. See Drung people

Railroads, 4
"The Rainbow," 27, 29, 32, 51
Realistic tales, 50–51
Rebellions, 282
Red River, 121. See also Yuan River
Redaction, 22–23, 38, 54–55
Reed Pipe Dance, 282–83
Religion, 268–91 passim. See also Ancestor worship; Animism; Buddhism; Christianity; Daoism; Gods; Islam; Lamaism; Polytheism; Shamanism
Repetition, 33
"The Rhinoceros Hornbill," 27, 28, 30, 31, 32, 34, 35
Romantic tales, 50–51
Rousseau, Jean-Jacques, 11

Sailiangmu, 213
Salween River, 3, 285
Sayings, 32–33
Scarification, 276
Schizoid behavior, 30
Sequences, repetitious, 33
Sha Che, 73
Shamanism, 48, 270, 278, 281, 284, 287
Shan people. See Dai people
Shangguan, 47
Sheep Guide rite, 286
Shen Congwen, 11, 18, 23
Singing, 278–79, 281. See also Songs

Sino-Finnish folklore project, 20–21, 22
Sipsong Panna, 4, 103
Slavery, 222, 290–91
Social organization, 222, 279, 280, 284, 285–86, 290–92
Song Hong River, 3
Songs, 273, 277, 292. See also Singing
Sound in oral culture, 30–32
South China, migration into, 9
Space in oral literature, 27
Speech in oral culture, 30–32
Spirits, 48, 66, 280
Spring City. See Kunming
Stalin, Joseph, 6
Stars, 94
"Stories about Bubo," 29, 34
Story telling. See Oral literature
Structure, literary, 33–34
"Suffocating the Living King of Hell," 50
Sui people, 287
Sun, 44
Sunbird, 87
Swords, Husa, 266

Tai people, 291; language of, 289
Talk-story, ix, xi
Tang, 247
Tangut people, 7
Tao Yonghua, 87
Taoism. See Daoism
Tea: buttered, 284; Pu'er, 272, 277, 279
Tests in folk literature, 33
Third Month Fair, 270
Three Lakes District, 165
Thunder God, 29, 150
Tian Zheng, 46
Tibetan people, 7, 280, 284, 287–88; language of, 288, 292; literature of 288
Time in oral literature, 27

Tongba, 247
Torch Festival, 46, 283, 291
"The Torch Festival," 47
Totemism, 282, 285–86
Translation, x-xi, 15, 16, 23–26, 53–54
Trees, 50; sha, 150
"Two Sisters and the Boa," 29, 30, 31

Uighur people, 277; language of, 292

Vernacular literature movement, 12
Villages, stockaded, 113, 288–89
Vitale, Guido Amedeo, 13

Wa Lancang Cliff Paintings, 289
Wa people, 288–89; tales of, 44; lan-
    guage of, 289
Wang Na, 169
Wang Renbo, 281
War in literature, 285
Water Drum Dance, 275
Water-Splashing Festival, 4, 37, 274,
    275
"The Water-Splashing Festival," 34,
    37, 47
"Why Sui People Live in Two-Story
    Wooden Loft-Houses," 31, 32, 34,
    36, 37
"Wine-Flavored Spring," 32, 34
Wei Yurong, 112
West River. See Xi River
Wiens, Harold J., 10
Witches, 48
Woni people. See Hani people;
    Kucong people
Wordsworth, William, 14
Written literature, 26, 27, 28, 38, 283,
    288, 291
Wudi, Emperor, 268

Xi River, 3
Xiaguan, 47
Xingyun Hu (Lake), 165
Xishuangbanna. See Sipsong Panna

Xu Jiarui, 243
Xu Kun, x-xi, 9, 15, 16, 22, 23–25, 177,
    243, 265

Yaks, 284
Yama, 50
Yang Yuke, 22
Yangtze River, 3
Yao people, 289–90
Ye Shengdao, 11
Yi people, 279, 280, 284, 290–91; tales
    of, 48, 50, 51; language of, 279, 283,
    285, 288; Black, 285–86, 290–91;
    White, 291
Yongning, 284
You River, 3
Youle, 279
Yuan River, 3, 121
Yuefu, 12
Yun Mountain, 3
Yunnan: geography, 3–6; mean-
    ing of name, 3; establishment of
    province, 268
Yunnan-Guizhou Plateau, 3–4

Zang people. See Tibetan people
Zhage, 157
Zhalai, 157
Zhang Shijie, 20
Zhang Tianyi, 11
Zhang, 121
"Zhanuzhabie," 45
Zhao Jingxiu, 222
Zhao Qiguang, x
Zhayue, 189
Zheng He, 46
Zheng Xinshun, 213
"Zhepoma and Zhemima," 43
Zhou Xingbo, 177
Zhou Zuoren, 11, 13
"Zhuang Brocade," 48
Zhuang people, 150, 291–92; tales of,
    48; language of, 292